West European Politics Series

*Edited by **Klaus H. Goetz**, University of Potsdam, Germany, **Peter Mair** -European University Institute, Italy and **Gordon Smith** - London School of Economics and Political Science, UK*

West European Politics has established itself as the foremost journal for the comparative analysis of European political institutions, politics and public policy. Its comprehensive scope, which includes the European Union, makes it essential reading for both academics and political practitioners. The books in this series have originated from special issues published by West European Politics.

Immigration Policy in Europe
The politics of control
Edited by Virgine Guiradon and Gallya Lahav

Norway in Transition
Transforming a stable democracy
Edited by Oyvind Osterud

Policy Change and Discourse in Europe
Edited by Claudio M. Radaelli and Vivien Schmidt

Politics and Policy in Greece
The challenge of 'modernisation'
Edited by Kevin Featherstone

France's Political Institutions at 50
Edited by Emiliano Grossman and Nicolas Sauger

Interest Group Politics in Europe
Lessons from EU Studies and Comparative Politics
Edited by Jan Beyers, Rainer Eising and William A. Maloney

Italy – A Contested Polity
Edited by Martin Bull and Martin Rhodes

European Politics
Pasts, presents, futures
Edited by Klaus H. Goetz, Peter Mair and Gordon Smith

The Politics of Belgium
Institutions and policy under bipolar and centrifugal federalism
Edited by Marleen Brans, Lieven De Winter and Wilfried Swenden

Towards a New Executive Order in Europe?
Edited by Deirdre Curtin and Morten Egeberg

Towards a New Executive Order in Europe?

Edited by Deirdre Curtin and Morten Egeberg

LONDON AND NEW YORK

First published 2009 by Routledge
2 Park Square, Milton Park, Abingdon, Oxfordshire OX14 4RN

Simultaneously published in the USA and Canada
by Routledge
711 Third Avenue, New York, NY 10017

First issued in paperback 2015

Routledge is an imprint of the Taylor & Francis Group, an informa business

© 2009 Edited by Deirdre Curtin and Morten Egeberg

All rights reserved. No part of this book may be reprinted or reproduced or utilised in any form or by any electronic, mechanical, or other means, now known or hereafter invented, including photocopying and recording, or in any information storage or retrieval system, without permission in writing from the publishers.

British Library Cataloguing in Publication Data
A catalogue record for this book is available from the British Library

Typeset in Times by Value Chain, India

ISBN13: 978-0-415-85170-1 (pbk)
ISBN13: 978-0-415-48313-1 (hbk)

Contents

	Notes on Contributors		vii
1.	Tradition and Innovation: Europe's Accumulated Executive Order	**Deirdre Curtin and Morten Egeberg**	1
2.	Mapping the European Administrative Space	**Herwig C. H. Hofmann**	24
3.	Bureaucratic Change in the European Administrative Space: The Case of the European Commission	**Tim Balint, Michael W. Bauer and Christoph Knill**	39
4.	Beyond the Myth of Nationality: Analysing Networks within the European Commission	**Semin Suvarierol**	63
5.	Who Consults? The Configuration of Expert Groups in the European Union	**Åse Gornitzka and Ulf Sverdrup**	87
6.	At a Critical Juncture? Change and Continuity in the Institutional Development of the Council Secretariat	**Thomas Christiansen and Sophie Vanhoonacker**	113
7.	European Administration: Centralisation and Fragmentation as Means of Polity-building?	**Johannes Pollak and Sonja Puntscher Riekmann**	133
8.	Delegation of Powers in the European Union: The Need for a Multi-principals Model	**Renaud Dehousse**	151

9. Reshaping European Regulatory   **Mark Thatcher and**
   Space: An Evolutionary Analysis   **David Coen**   168

10. Halfway House: The 2006
    Comitology Reforms and the
    European Parliament   **Kieran St Clair Bradley**   199

    Index   217

Notes on Contributors

Tim Balint is Research Assistant at the Chair of Comparative Public Policy and Administration at the University of Konstanz. He studied Public Administration at the Universities of Konstanz and Granada (2000–2006) and holds a Master's in Politics and Administration. Since 2007, Tim Balint has been investigating administrative reforms and cultures in international organisations in the context of a research project supported by the University of Konstanz's Centre of Excellence 'Cultural Foundations of Social Integration'.

Michael W. Bauer is Assistant Professor of Comparative Public Policy and Public Administration in the Department of Politics and Management at the University of Konstanz. He received his doctoral degree from the European University Institute, Florence. His research interests are comparative policy analysis, public sector reform and subnational governance. He is co-editor of Management Reforms in International Organizations (Nomos, 2007) and has recently worked on issues of reforming international executive institutions.

Kieran St Clair Bradley is Head of the Unit for Justice and Civil Liberties in the European Parliament's Legal Service. He has represented Parliament in a number of cases before the Court of Justice concerning comitology questions, and was legal advisor to Parliament's team in the negotiations leading to the 2006 decision and associated agreements. He has written extensively on the institutional law of the European Union, including on comitology, and has lectured on European law in a number of universities and institutes, including Harvard Law School, the University of Melbourne and the College of Europe (Natolin).

Thomas Christiansen is Professor in European Institutional Politics at Maastricht University and also holds positions at the European Institute of Public Administration in Maastricht and at the College of Europe in Bruges. He is Executive Editor of the Journal of European Integration co-editor of the 'Europe in Change' series at Manchester University Press and member of the steering committee of the Standing Group of the European Union of the European Consortium of Political Research. His publications include Informal Governance of the European Union (Edward Elgar, 2004), edited with Simona Piattoni, and The Social Construction of Europe (Sage, 2001), edited with Knud Erik Jørgensen and Antje Wiener.

David Coen is Deputy Head of Department and Reader in Public Policy in the School of Public Policy at University College London. Prior to joining UCL, he held appointments at the London Business School and the Max Planck Institute in Cologne. His research interests are EU business–government relations and EU regulatory reform. His recent publications include EU Lobbying: Theoretical and Empirical Developments (Routledge, 2007), and Refining Regulatory Regimes: Utilities in Europe (Edward Elgar, 2005) (ed. with A. Héritier).

Deirdre Curtin is Professor of European Law at the University of Amsterdam as well as (part-time) Professor of International and European Governance at the multi-disciplinary Utrecht School of Governance. Previously she was Professor of International Organisations at the Law Faculty of the University of Utrecht (1992–2002). She has published widely on issues relating to the constitutional and institutional development of the European Union as well as on issues relating to public accountability and democracy.

Renaud Dehousse is Jean Monnet Professor of EU Law and Politics at the Institut d'études politiques in Paris. He directs Sciences Po's Centre for European Studies. His recent work has focused on the transformation of European governance and EU constitutional politics.

Morten Egeberg is Professor of Public Policy and Administration at the Department of Political Science and at ARENA – Centre for European Studies, University of Oslo. He has published several books and chapters and articles in international journals on governance and public administration at national and EU levels, within an organisation theory framework. His latest book is Multilevel Union Administration. The Transformation of Executive Politics in Europe (Palgrave Macmillan, 2006).

Åse Gornitzka is senior researcher at ARENA – Centre for European Studies at the University of Oslo. Her main research interests are in the analysis of European research and education policies and the role of expertise in European policy-making. She has published extensively on reformand governance of knowledge systems. Her most recent publications include contributions to Peter Maassen and Johan P. Olsen (eds.) University Dynamics and European Integration (Springer, 2007).

Herwig C. H. Hofmann is Professor of Law and Director of the Centre of European Law in the Faculty of Law, Economics and Finance at the University of Luxembourg. He teaches and publishes in the fields of European constitutional law, regulatory and administrative law as well as WTO law.

Christoph Knill is Professor of Political Science and Public Administration at the University of Konstanz. His publications include The Europeanisation of National Administrations (Cambridge University Press 2001); Environmental Politics in the European Union (Manchester University Press, 2007, with Duncan Liefferink); Environmental Policy Convergence in Europe? The Impact of International

Institutions and Trade (Cambridge University Press, 2008, with Katharina Holzinger and Bas Arts).

Johannes Pollak is Senior Research Fellow at the Institute for European Integration Research of the Austrian Academy of Sciences, Vienna. His research on democratic theory, representation and integration has been published in the European Law Journal, Journal of Common Market Studies, Journal of European Integration and Journal of Comparative Politics, as well as numerous book contributions. Recent book publications include: Repräsentation ohne Demokratie (2007); and Einführung in die EU (with P. Slominski) (2006).

Sonja Puntscher Riekmann is Professor of Political Theory and European Integration at the Paris Lodron University Salzburg, Vice-Chancellor at the University of Salzburg and head of the Institute of European Integration Research at the Austrian Academy of Sciences, Vienna. Her recent publications include: The Constitutionalisation of the EU (co-ed. with W. Wessels) (2006); and Europäisierung durch Recht? (co-ed. with B. Bapuly and P. Slominski) (2005).

Semin Suvarierol completed her Ph.D. thesis entitled, Beyond the Myth of Nationality: A Study on the Networks of European Commission Officials analyses the effect of nationality on the networking behaviour of European Commission officials at the Utrecht School of Governance in 2007. Her research interests include EU institutions, international organisations and the role of culture within multinational organisations. She currently works as a policy adviser at Andersson Elfers Felix.

Ulf Sverdrup is a Senior Researcher at ARENA – Centre for European Studies at the University of Oslo. Sverdrup holds a Ph.D. in political science. He has a research interest in the emerging European administrative space, and has published articles on issues related to Europeanisation of national administrations and the implementation of EU legislation.

Mark Thatcher is Reader in Public Administration and Public Policy, Department of Government, LSE. His research centres on comparative public policy and regulation. His recent publications include Internationalisation and Economic Institutions (OUP, 2007), Beyond Varieties of Capitalism (OUP, 2007) (co-ed. with B. Hancké and M. Rhodes).

Sophie Vanhoonacker is Professor in Administrative Governance in the EU in the Department of Politics at the Faculty of Arts and Social Sciences, University Maastricht. She has a background in history and political science and holds a Ph.D. from Leiden University (1999). Her research focuses on the Common Foreign and Security Policy. Her recent work examines the role and influence of nonelected administrative actors in the European foreign policy process.

Tradition and Innovation: Europe's Accumulated Executive Order

DEIRDRE CURTIN and MORTEN EGEBERG

In our view the question is not whether a common European executive order is emerging or not.[1] We use the term 'executive order' to convey our focus on the changing nature of executive power in Europe and to capture both the political level (ministers and other political office holders) and the administrative level (bureaucracy) of the order in our analysis. Europe has in fact had an executive order for centuries. After the peace of Westphalia this order became increasingly sophisticated as regards its institutional characteristics. However, it was not until the advent of the European Union and its predecessors that Europe's executive order started to transcend its basically intergovernmental pattern inherited from the past. We ascribe this phenomenon in particular to the consolidation of the European Commission (Commission) as a new and distinctive executive centre at the European level, outside of the intergovernmental locus, the Council of Ministers (Council). This institutional innovation triggers significant centrifugal forces within national governments due to the Commission's strategy of establishing direct partnerships with national (regulatory) authorities (agencies and others) that might be crucial for the implementation and formulation of EU policies.

The agencification that has taken place in most western European countries during the last couple of decades has been conducive to the development of this new administrative configuration across levels of governance. Precisely because agencies are kept at arm's length from ministerial departments they have been able to establish their own autonomous and close contacts with executive bodies at the EU level. Such new arrangements imply that although the implementation of EU legislation is still mainly in the hands of national governments, it can be questioned whose agents the semi-autonomous national agencies really are. Such an order also raises sensitive questions about which actors should be held to account: holding governments to account may no longer be enough and may need to be complemented with mechanisms and forums that focus both on the accountability of supranational executive bodies as well as national agencies with dual loyalties.

In the next section we briefly outline the executive order that prevailed in Europe from the Peace of Westphalia (1648) until the advent of the EU and its predecessors. Arguably, in comparison with bilateral diplomacy and international governmental organisations (IGOs), the emergence and consolidation of the position of the Commission as a central executive actor placed the development of the European executive order on a radically different trajectory. The following section therefore deals with the conditions under which the Commission is able to act relatively independently of national governments and thus constitutes an executive force in its own right. We then turn to how these distinctive institutional conditions at the European level seem to trigger administrative constellations across levels of governance and across national borders that challenge the coherence of national governments in an unprecedented way. We also ask how a new order and new patterns of executive politics might affect implementation practices. The subsequent sections focus on the issue of accountability as it is raised and dealt with within the shifting executive orders. Finally, as part of the conclusion, we touch briefly on the factors behind the changing orders. The new order does not seem to replace the former order; instead it tends to be layered around already existing orders so that the result is an increasingly compound and accumulated executive order at the European level. Needless to say, such a layered and cumulative order complicates the discussion on accountability of the various actors for their varied tasks.

Pre-existing Executive Orders

Our point of departure is the Treaty of Westphalia (1648), which in a sense semi-institutionalised a system of territorially defined states in Europe. A system of formally sovereign states presupposes information about the ideas and activities of system participants. Bilateral diplomacy was seen as the means of ensuring that the requisite information was made available. From the second half of the seventeenth century resident ambassadors became the rule even among the smaller countries (Cross 2007). Within the time frame we cover (from 1648 onwards), we consider bilateral diplomacy on a regular basis as the first executive order in Europe. It constitutes an order because it is organised and because common norms and codes of conduct gradually developed so that diplomats came to perceive themselves as being grounded in two distinct worlds: their respective home state, on the one hand, and the diplomatic community, on the other (Batora 2005; Jönsson and Hall 2005). At the Congress of Vienna in 1815, the diplomatic institution became more formalised: for example, the senior ambassador, i.e. the ambassador who had been longest at the post in a particular capital became the doyen or dean of the diplomatic body, or corps, in that particular country (Nicolson 1969). The fact that this person represents the other ambassadors in any disputes affecting their corporate rights and interests reflects very well the existence of a community. 'Even as scientists, philatelists and other experts find, when they meet together, that the interests of their calling transcend all differences of nationality or language, so also do the diplomatic services of the several countries evolve a form of solidarity and establish certain tacit standards which they all respect' (Nicolson 1969: 40). In her study of key international congresses from 1648 onwards Cross (2007) found that diplomats tended to share opinions more often that their respective political masters.

We date the start of the second executive order to the Vienna Congress (1815). The congress semi-institutionalised multilateral diplomacy in the form of conferences at the ministerial and ambassadorial levels among Europe's great powers (the Concert of Europe) although they did not meet on a regular basis and there was no permanent location or secretariat attached to it (Schroeder 1994). It was the highly specialised sectoral or functional IGOs established from the second half of the nineteenth century (e.g. the International Telegraph Union and the Universal Postal Union) that gave rise to new initiatives such as a permanent secretariat with a fixed location, the division of labour between a general conference and an executive council, and regular meetings. According to Claude (1964: 175), 'nothing essentially new has been added by the multi-lateralization and regularization of diplomacy until the secretariat is introduced; this is the innovation that transforms the series of conferences into an organization'.

One consequence of IGOs having been established in pretty much all imaginable sectoral and functional policy areas is that a huge number of non-diplomatic civil servants coming from sectoral or functional ministries and agencies have become involved in their work. In addition, national scientific experts may also be included in their work with the result that the European administrative space became much denser than before. The Organization for Economic Cooperation and Development (OECD) alone today runs 42 'committees' and 98 'working parties' composed of national officials (Marcussen 2004). Studies have shown that the power distribution and conflict pattern within IGOs seem to reflect very much the power distribution and territorial pattern of conflict found in the wider system (Cox and Jacobson 1973). This is hardly surprising given that they are basically structured according to geography, organisationally expressed in the pivotal role of the respective councils of ministers. However, IGOs are institutions that provide a context for the collection, elaboration and diffusion of data, analyses, visions and ideas, for agenda-setting and collective problem-solving (Barnett and Finnemore 2004; Marcussen 2004). Expert-based permanent secretariats contribute significantly to task expansion at the international level and they also may be able to forge transnational coalitions by linking previously disconnected actors (Cox and Jacobson 1973; Barnett and Finnemore 2004; Trondal *et al.* 2005). Thus, although IGOs have been created by states, once established they do not necessarily operate as straightforward tools or agents of those states.

Because modern states are highly specialised both in sectoral and functional terms, and since problems to be dealt with generally presuppose the availability of rather specialised expertise, specialised institutions tend to interact directly with their counterparts in other countries or in the secretariats of IGOs rather than going through their respective foreign ministries or other central state authorities. This is what Keohane and Nye (1977) term 'complex interdependence'. Slaughter's (2004) portrayal of a 'new world order', consisting of disaggregated states that interact in a compound manner within and alongside IGOs, builds heavily on the complex interdependence perspective. Although such information, harmonisation and enforcement networks may encourage the formation of coalitions along functional lines, she claims that national governments retain primary power and that officials participating in those networks represent national interests (pp. 7, 262).

Executive Centre Formation at the European Level

We attribute the birth of what may be termed the third executive order first and foremost to the consolidation of the Commission as an executive centre (Bartolini 2005). The High Authority of the European Coal and Steel Community (ECSC) and its successors were indeed an institutional innovation at the European level: for the first time an executive body with its own leadership had been established outside the national ministers' 'council'. The Commission over time increased its actual autonomy in relation to national governments. As regards the services of the Commission, the move from an administration that had to rely heavily on seconded personnel from the member states to an administration in which a large majority are employed on a permanent basis is significant. The growing 'internalisation' (into the services) of recruitment and appointment processes is also indicative of such a development. The process of appointing top officials has been described as having become 'objectivised', meaning that a transparent procedure and clearly specified requirements have been adopted. Staff resources have been allocated to the process, and the committee, which presents the shortlist of candidates to the commissioners, is dominated by career officials. Normally, the recruiting commissioner seems to accept the candidates recommended by this committee (Egeberg 2006b). Thus, the internalisation of appointment processes means that the highly contentious practice of attaching national flags to particular posts in the various directorates general (DGs) has been considerably reduced (see also Wille 2007a).[2] Consistent with this, Balint et al. (2008) show that the Commission administration, as regards the degree of politicisation of the higher management and the degree of openness of the career system, over time has moved away from its Continental origin and instead moved closer to a British or Scandinavian model, i.e. in crucial respects a more independent service.

As regards the political leadership of the Commission it, too, has gained autonomy vis-à-vis national governments over time. Concerning the college, the Amsterdam Treaty assigned more leeway to the Commission president-elect as regards the selection of commissioners. The president also acquired the final say in how portfolios are allocated and even the right to reshuffle the team during the five-year term of office by redistributing dossiers, thus making it difficult for governments to attach particular national flags to particular portfolios. Also, the president is authorised to dismiss individual commissioners. Concerning the cabinets, there must now be three nationalities in any cabinet, gender balance and three posts reserved for Commission officials rather than outsiders brought in by the commissioners or foreign ministries. 'The resulting changes produced *cabinet* constellations which would be unrecognisable to old Commission hands' (Spence 2006: 72). Given that the average size of an 'ordinary' (not vice-president/president) commissioner's cabinet seems to be seven members, such a composition has changed the role of entities previously portrayed as national enclaves (Michelmann 1978) and as being sensitive to national interests (Cini 1996: 111–115). We are, however, short of empirical evidence on how cabinet members actually behave.

We are somewhat better equipped as regards studies on the role conceptions and behaviour of Commission officials. From an organisational theory point of view, the most important independent variables are, under most circumstances, features of the organisational structure within which decision-makers are embedded. For example, it matters whether this structure is the actor's primary or only secondary affiliation, and according to which principle (function, geography, etc.) the structure is specialised (Egeberg 2004). The approximately 900 national experts who are seconded by national administrations to the Commission for a maximum of four years represent an interesting category since they work full-time within the Commission's administrative hierarchy, while being paid by their home government with a return to former positions in domestic ministries or agencies usually foreseen. However, even under these conditions, their primary structure – i.e. Commission affiliation – seems to be most important. A survey study of 71 national experts showed that they overwhelmingly identify with their respective DGs/Units or an independent expert role rather than with their respective national governments. Accordingly, in their daily work, they pay most attention to signals from their directors in the Commission and little attention to signals from their home governments (Trondal 2006).

Concerning Commission officials in general, Michelmann (1978), in a study based on interviews and a survey originally administered by the Commission among its personnel, analysed the flows of information across hierarchical levels within DGs. He found no statistically significant effects of nationality on these flows. Contact patterns reflected rather neatly the formal hierarchy of posts. The qualitative interview data revealed, however, that officials might be approached by their compatriots and used as 'access points' to the inner circles of the services. In her study of 82 officials three decades later, combining quantitative and qualitative data, Suvarierol (2008) provided support for Michelmann's conclusions. She focused on 'task-related informal networks' (for information and advice) as distinguishable from 'task-related formal networks', 'career networks' and 'leisure networks' and found that nationality is not even a factor shaping these informal (information and advice) networks which are not hierarchically predefined. Egeberg (1996) used 35 Commission trainees with at least two years' experience from national administration as informants on decision-making within 15 different DGs. Only in a clear minority of units was nationality seen to matter for officials' policy choices, and the concerns of the respective DGs constituted the dominating frame of reference for decision-making. And a questionnaire study of 218 national officials from 14 member states showed that an overwhelming majority considered the Commission's representatives in Commission expert committees, Council working parties and comitology committees as mainly independent of particular national interests (Egeberg *et al.* 2003).

The interview and questionnaire study of Commission top officials by Hooghe (2001) seems at first glance to contradict the results reported above. She found that officials' preferences as regards supranationalism vs. intergovernmentalism and regulated capitalism vs. market liberalism were related to their experiences before they entered the Commission and that their stay at the Commission had no significant impact on these attitudes. For example, those originating from federal states were more in favour of supranationalism than those from unitary states. But this conclusion did not hold for all Commission officials. The effect of Commission socialisation was considerably stronger for the officials who joined the institution before their thirtieth birthday. 'The relative weight of international and national socialization is reversed' (Hooghe 2005: 876). Hooghe's dependent variables tapped attitudes at a very general level. Arguably, therefore, her observations might be quite compatible with studies showing that the organisational setting is important as regards explaining more 'operationalised' preferences in actual decision situations. For example, several studies have portrayed decision-making at the Commission very much as politics between various DGs (Coombes 1970: 203; Cram 1994; Cini 2000; Hooghe 2000; Mörth 2000). Had the Commission been structured according to geography so that each member state had been served by a particular DG, and if these DGs had in addition been staffed by people from their respective 'client countries', we would expect the various national interests to be at the forefront of Commission decision-making. However, in a sectorally and functionally specialised Commission which is also multi-nationally staffed, even at the unit level, it is hard to see how different DG interests can be meaningfully linked to socialisation experiences at the national level.

Like national experts in the Commission services, commissioners have the Commission as their primary organisational affiliation, are on short-term 'contracts' and might return to posts in their home government. These features could make them more susceptible to the wishes of their respective home governments compared to those on long-term contracts. Döring (2007) and Wonka (2007) suggest that the careful selection process at the national level of candidates for a commissioner post results in a close relationship between a commissioner and his or her home government, but they do not present any data substantiating this conclusion. By examining 70 controversial legislative proposals from the Commission, Thomson (2008) tried to establish the level of agreement between a Commission proposal and the position of the home government of the commissioner in charge of the relevant portfolio. On a 100-point scale, the average distance between the Commission's position and the position of the responsible commissioner's home government was 35.92 scale points under qualified majority voting (QMV) in the Council. The distance for countries not having the prime commissioner was on average 41.17 scale points. The difference (5.25 scale points) falls short of statistical significance. For issues requiring unanimity in the Council the difference is in the opposite direction: those member states nominating the lead commissioner are further away from the Commission's position than the other member states, although this difference is not statistically significant either. According to Thomson, the Commission has no 'favourite' among the member states; however, its positions are on average slightly closer to those of smaller and medium-sized countries than to those of large states.

Literature emphasising the importance of extra-institutional socialisation and incentives might underestimate the role of decision-makers' primary organisational affiliation, i.e. the structure within which they are embedded on a daily basis. Egeberg (2006c) tried to map commissioners' role behaviour in college meetings by using those top officials who take the minutes as informants. The study showed that the role most frequently evoked is the 'portfolio role', i.e. the role in which commissioners represent their respective sectoral or functional areas of responsibility, in practice the relevant DG. They may also, although less frequently, act on behalf of the Commission as such (the 'Commission role'), their country of origin (the 'country role') or their political party ('party role'), thus not that much different from national ministers adhering to the concerns of their respective departments, local constituencies, parties and the cabinet as such.

Features of the organisational structure most probably explain why politics at the Commission tends to become to such a large degree sectoral politics, while politics in the Council remains mainly territorial (international) in character (Egeberg 2006a). The sectoral and functional specialisation of the Commission at all levels, from the level of the expert committees (Gornitzka and Sverdrup 2008) up to the very top makes it qualitatively different from the (basically) geographically specialised Council in which all member states are represented at all levels and within all sectoral portfolios. Thus, even if a government might succeed in making 'its' commissioner into its spokesperson, the primary influence will, most probably, be exercised only within his or her particular remit. However, we need studies on the extent to which commissioners and their respective cabinets are able to intervene in other commissioners' portfolios. Due to the limited size of cabinets (approximately seven members for an ordinary commissioner) and the considerable increase in the number of commissioners, it could be expected that such interference only takes place to a modest degree.[3]

The original conception of the Commission as an EC institution was of a technocratic and impartial body with the specific constitutional obligation to act in the 'Community interest'. It was meant to provide the impetus for integration and to be the guardian of the common European interest. Such integration and mediating functions would be guided by the judgement of a technocratic elite rather than by political considerations. Politics was organised out of the Commission in the original conception. As Wille has pointed out, in the contemporary EU we can however discern an evolving politics–administration dichotomy in the Commission, with Commissioners increasingly considered in terms of executive politicians (Wille 2007b). The college of commissioners functions much like a ministerial cabinet (government) in that each commissioner is responsible for a particular policy area and for overseeing one or more directorates-general, which, in turn, are the functional equivalent of national government departments.

At the same time, the Commission has become more connected to the European Parliament (EP). For example, the EP has more to say on the appointment of commissioners and the outcome of the elections to the EP does seem to matter for the selection of the Commission president. European-level political parties may well play a role in this selection process. The fact that those nominated to commissioner posts are increasingly political heavyweights may add to this party politicisation (MacMullen 2000; Döring 2007). In sum, the Commission has in several respects become 'normalised' as a political executive with a clearer demarcation between the political and the administrative levels, in terms of both recruitment and decision-making (Egeberg 2006a; Wille 2007b).

Executive Satellite Formation in the EU

The European Commission is not however the only political executive under the auspices of the EU, even if it still is the most fully fledged executive actor at that level. Another instance of political administration is the growing powers and role of the General Secretariat of the Council of Ministers. When it was originally created it was designed to fulfil the functions of conference organisation and committee servicing; in recent decades a considerable expansion in its tasks and responsibilities has taken place (Hayes-Renshaw and Wallace 2006: 101). Little empirical work has been carried out on the nature of its influence on decision-making processes over and above purely secretariat-like functions. Beach (2004: 429) studied the role of the Council Secretariat General in two intergovernmental conferences (the 1996–97 and 2000 IGC) and concluded that it shifted outcomes in many issues, albeit often unseen. More recently, research into the management of EU foreign policy has demonstrated the contribution that this body has made to EU decision-making more generally (Christiansen 2006; Duke and Vanhoonacker 2006).

The Council Secretariat plays a particularly important role when it comes to the Common Foreign and Security Policy (CFSP) and the European Security and Defence Policy (ESDP). Because the member states were afraid of losing sovereignty to the supranational European Commission, they have instead delegated authority to the Council Secretariat in this policy area. Those tasks include agenda setting, policy formulation and implementation, especially in the fields of internal and external security. At the same time the General Secretariat is rather hybrid in its composition with certain policy divisions (especially those relating to defence) being almost entirely composed by national civil servants and seconded national military officers (the European Union Military Staff). Since January 2007 the Council Secretariat even has its own independent Operation Centre. It seems as if parts of the Council Secretariat in this field have very incrementally – and on the whole quietly – developed features that are more similar to those found in executive offices than in classical secretariats (Christiansen and Vanhoonacker 2008). The endowment of the Council Secretariat with executive tasks has been particularly striking since the establishment of ESDP and the appointment of Javier Solana as High Representative of CFSP and Secretary General of the Council Secretariat. The work of the executive management of foreign and security policy requires 'more rapid reactions to changing circumstances, direct actions by Council Secretariat staff and thus a public profile to the role of the institution that is totally alien to the "old" Secretariat' (Christiansen and Vanhoonacker 2008: 764).

There are other satellite 'political administrations' around the main executive actors, the Commission and the Council. Among the most important of these are 'comitology committees' composed of national civil servants (and independent scientific experts) who come together at the Union level in order to contribute directly to rule-making at the Union level (Bradley 2008). They are conferred with specific EU-level tasks on rule-making (largely implementation of more general legislative rules) that operate under both the auspices of the Commission and the Council of Ministers. Both lawyers and political scientists have studied empirically such committees over the years (Joerges and Neyer 1997; Joerges and Vos 1999; Vos 1999; Egeberg et al. 2003; Schaefer and Türk 2007). In addition, both the Commission and the Council have had established under their auspices – in one form or another – a whole series of EC/EU-level agencies, some of which have executive, regulatory and management tasks (Curtin 2006; Dehousse 2008; Pollak and Puntscher Riekmann 2008) and are composed of both European civil servants – and some nationals on secondment. Little empirical study has been undertaken to date on the dynamics of EU-level agencies (but see Trondal and Jeppesen 2008).

From a comparative perspective, it is not surprising that the Commission and also the Council have come to share executive functions with an increasing number of EU-level agencies, since agencification has taken place all over the western world during recent decades (Christensen and Lægreid 2006). Agencies at the European level can be viewed as a compromise between the Commission's wish to gain more powers at the EU level and expectations by the member states that they would be able to control their policies better by delegation to agencies and not the Commission (Keleman 2002). Yet their considerable growth in recent years also points to the fact that the core executives (primarily the Commission but also in certain respects the Council) are engaged in a process of either delegating executive-type powers to lower level actors ('agents') in the EU political and administrative system, or of creating new executive and operational tasks at the EU level and tasking newly created actors in that regard (Curtin 2007). It is not so unusual that these agencies may have multiple principals (e.g. the Commission and the Council) since in the EU one finds more power distribution among key institutions than in most parliamentary systems (Dehousse 2008). Although established as separate bodies, empirical study indicates that the Commission (and also the Council) is actually very influential vis-à-vis agencies (Busuioc 2007).

Multi-level Executive Governance

Implementation at the national level of rules and standards adopted by IGOs usually takes place in an indirect way. By this is meant that it is left up to the member governments to transpose and apply the rules. Implementation in the context of the EU has most commonly been perceived as indirect: transposition and application of EU legislation have on the whole been seen as part of the 'administrative sovereignty' that the member states enjoy. The fact that the Commission has a monitoring role in this respect does not in itself change this division of labour between levels of governance. Indirect implementation portrays the Union as a system in which the constituent states are integrated into a larger whole as coherent entities.

Even though EU legislation is mainly adopted by the 'community method', indirect implementation is also compatible with an intergovernmental order in which national governments constitute the basic building blocks and in which lines of conflict and cooperation strongly coincide with national borders. Such a mode of governance also has clear policy implications, making community policies highly vulnerable to distortion. Studies have revealed how indirect implementation exposes common policies to considerable influence from national politics and administrative traditions (Goetz 2000; Héritier et al. 2001; Knill 2001; Olsen 2003). In addition, it has been shown that member states' administrative capabilities are positively related to their compliance with EU rules (Sverdrup 2006).

Arguably, however, a new pattern of executive politics across levels of governance might emerge due to two features of institutional development: first the 'emancipation' and consolidation of the Commission as a new executive centre outside the ministers' council, and, second, the fragmentation of national governments, vertically as well as horizontally. These two developments have triggered centrifugal forces within national governments, forces that could probably not have occurred if there was simply a combination of a classical IGO and internally integrated governments (Egeberg 2006a). Since the Commission does not possess its own agencies at the member state level, it (and EU-level agencies) seems to establish a kind of partnership with those national bodies responsible for the application of EU legislation as well as some involvement in the development of EU policies. Such bodies may be found among national agencies that are already somewhat detached from their respective ministerial departments.

The term 'Europe's integrated administration' (Hofmann and Türk 2006; Hofmann 2008) takes on board the situation where in contemporary European integration processes the traditional distinction of direct and indirect administration has become blurred, with the levels being interwoven to form a more unitary pattern of 'integrated administration'. The EU level is also involved in implementing activities undertaken by member state authorities, while member states' administrations are involved in creating EU legislation and implementing acts. Case studies within five different policy fields have shown that national agencies in fact seem to act in a 'double-hatted' manner, constituting parts of national administrations while at the same time becoming parts of a multi-level Union administration in which the Commission in particular forms the new executive centre. As parts of national administrations, serving their respective ministerial departments, agency officials play a crucial role in transposition of EU legislation as well as in Council working parties and comitology committees. However, when it comes to the application of EU legislation in particular, agencies also cooperate rather closely with their respective directorates in the Commission, often by-passing their ministerial departments (Egeberg 2006a).

Not surprisingly, in this situation agencies may face competing policy expectations from their two 'masters' that may be hard to reconcile. A questionnaire study showed that the importance of the 'parent ministry' partly depends on its organisational capacity in the field and the extent to which the legislative area is politically contested (Egeberg and Trondal forthcoming). Obviously, the role of the Commission will tend to vary as well depending on, for example, the relative strength of the DG involved (Barbieri 2006). Also, lack of knowledge and novelty make national agencies in new member states more receptive to inputs from the Commission (Martens 2007). 'Double-hattedness' entails new patterns of cooperation and conflict in executive politics, evoking conflicts that cut across national boundaries as well. It could also be expected to lead to more even implementation across countries compared to indirect implementation, although not as even as if the Commission had its own agencies or if the application of EU law was in the hands of EU-level bodies. We need empirical studies on how 'double-hattedness' impacts on implementation practices.

A third possibility is that implementation of EU legislation and other measures are networked. In the policy analysis literature of the past decade, networks is one of the most frequently used terms. Its emphasis is on informal, loose structures that extend across and beyond hierarchies and are composed of bureaucrats and other policy experts, on the one hand, and interest representatives, NGOs and purely private actors, on the other. Elected politicians are not frequently at the core of networks (Papadopoulos 2007). Social complexity often requires decision-making to be devolved to experts and the informal policy networks and epistemic communities by which they pool their existence. In other words, policy networks are a prime example of administration unbounded in the sense of eroding boundaries between government and non-government (Shapiro 2001).

Networked implementation means that vertical relationships between, on the one hand, national agencies and, on the other hand, ministerial departments, Commission directorates or EU-level agencies are complemented by horizontal relationships among 'sister agencies' in various countries. A national agency may see itself as part of a transnational network of institutions pursuing similar objectives and facing analogous problems (Majone 1996; Slaughter 2004). Thus, the actual amount of discretion that national agencies exercise when implementing EU legislation might be circumscribed in practice through information exchange and consultation among 'sister agencies' rather than through 'steering dialogues' with 'superior' bodies. In this sense, strong agency networks could challenge the authority of national governments as well as that of EU-level bodies.

It follows that such networks might enhance implementation uniformity across member states, though not necessarily in accordance with the intentions of the politically superior institutions. In order to enhance its control, the Commission may itself have initiated the creation of such a network, as in the telecom sector (Nørgård 2006) or in the education area (Gornitzka 2008). However, the EU executive has also successfully linked into already existing networks that have been relatively independent in the past (Eberlein and Grande 2005: 101–102), but for which it has gradually taken over the coordinating functions, as seems to be the case for the implementation network of pollution authorities (Martens 2006). Thatcher and Coen (2008) have observed that, over time, networks have become gradually more institutionalised and centralised around EU-level bodies. This finding is underpinned by Egeberg and Trondal's (forthcoming) questionnaire study: national officials applying EU legislation find inputs from 'sister agencies' in other countries much less important than inputs from their respective ministries or from the Commission.

Accumulating (Democratic) Accountability Across Orders?

Accountability is a broad term that reflects a range of understandings rather than a single paradigm. Until recently, accountability was not a term in common use, nor did it figure as a term of art outside the financial contexts of accountancy and audit (Harlow 2002). Today as Richard Mulgan (2000: 555) has aptly noted, the word 'crops up everywhere performing all manner of analytical and rhetorical tasks and carrying most of the burdens of democratic "governance"'. What can be designated the original or 'core' sense of accountability is that associated with the process of being called 'to account' to some authority for one's actions. Such accountability has a number of features: it is external, it involves social interaction and exchange and it implies rights of authority in that those calling for an account are asserting rights of superior authority over those who are accountable, including the rights to demand answers and to draw consequences, possibly including the imposition of sanctions.

In the context of a democratic state, the key accountability relationships in this core sense are those between citizens and the holders of public office, and within the ranks of office holders, between elected politicians and bureaucrats. In a delegation model of accountability, relationships are established as a means of carrying out the delegation of tasks and the communication of expectations. The very effort of establishing such a relationship implies that there is no intention of completely surrendering authority over the exercise of the task but rather that some control will attempt to be maintained by the principal. At the same time, the need for accountability and the introduction of accountability mechanisms are relevant precisely because the principal has delegated powers to an agent and, thus, renounced direct control. Accountability is needed in order to compensate for the absence of direct control through oversight once the principal is no longer steering directly (Busuioc 2007).

One core understanding of the politics of delegation to the EU is that there was a strong element of deliberate construction by national executives in order to escape the constraints of representative democracy that applied at the national levels (Mair 2005). In terms of the core institutions of the EU today, the Commission and the Council, they still reflect the way that they were originally conceived and constructed. In transferring or delegating authority to the Commission, an executive and technocratic institution (political administration), the primary bases for legitimacy were a combination of seemingly 'depoliticised' expertise, ministerial oversight, as well as a (judicially enforced) respect for the tenets of administrative legality (Lindseth 2003). What has changed is the role that the European Parliament gradually acquired in being able to hold the Commission to account, both *ex ante* and *ex post*, for its actions and inactions. This role had nothing to do with it being conceived as the political 'principal' of the Commission (unlike national parliaments vis-à-vis national governments) but rather with it being an available and logical accountability forum at the same power level as the Commission itself, with some 'political clout' to bring in to a developing relationship. The coupling that has taken place between the European Parliament and the European Commission has attempted to deal with the reality that the Commission has developed in some salient respects as an autonomous actor at the level of the EU political system itself.

The central role of the Commission in the EC system was since the beginning balanced by the intergovernmental role of the Council of Ministers. Here there were no supranational technocrats and experts, but rather national government ministers, permanent representatives, national civil servants that, in theory at any rate, act under constant instruction from national executives, just as they would at home. They can be recalled or re-instructed by the national level and the ministers are subject to the general supervisory role of the national parliaments. National civil servants are subject to the chains of national administrative or hierarchical account-ability, to their superiors in the civil service, ultimately to the minister and via the doctrine of ministerial responsibility back to the parliament.

Little indeed has changed in this original understanding vis-à-vis the Council of Ministers. The role that national parliaments actually play in holding their ministers (and through them their civil servants) to account *ex post* varies substantially from country to country and is dependent on national constitutional traditions and cultures (Auel 2007). The problem has been sharpened by the advent of and increase in qualified majority voting in the sense that government ministers can be outvoted (or until recently could claim to have been, because of secretive meetings) and *ex post* accountability can only be for the input of that one government minister or prime minister (in the case of the European Council). What has not changed at all in terms of the original understanding is that the Council of Ministers, as a body or institution, is not subject to any other, non-principal-based, accountability forum of a political nature. The European Parliament has no role to play of any significance in holding the Council of Ministers to account for its actions or inactions (Harlow 2002).

What has changed with regard to the Council of Ministers compared to the original understanding is the manner in which the Council of Ministers has evolved as an institution at the EU level. This is as a result of the evolution of the rules applying and the manner in which it is organised as an institution. In addition, the fact that its administrative apparatus has undergone considerable institutional change has had an effect in terms of how we must understand the institution overall. The fact, for example, that the General Secretariat of the Council has acquired tasks of an executive and even operational nature in certain policy fields (defence and security issues) and exercises this in a fashion that is autonomous of a veto by individual ministers makes it difficult to understand the Council of Ministers as a complex institution in purely intergovernmental terms in the contemporary EU. Even with regard to the Council of Ministers, therefore, the notion that the only control (other than a legal one) is via the national representative circuit (leaving to one side for present the question whether it is an effective one) does not suffice.

The concept of 'holding to account' not only obliges actors to disclose information and justify their behaviour, but also requires a social relationship between the actor and what can be loosely termed an accountability forum of one type or another, and moreover may require the establishment of a mechanism. Bovens (2007) has defined accountability as a social relationship between an actor and a forum, in which the actor explains his conduct and gives information to the forum, in which the forum can reach a judgement or render an assessment of that conduct, and on which it may be possible for some form of sanction (formal or informal) to be imposed on the actor. The attractiveness of this rather limited definition for many of those working on accountability related issues is that it provides a clear procedural and organisational framework with a focus on the relationship between the actor, potentially any actor (including for example actors that can never be understood as agents, such as networks), and an accountability forum, potentially any kind of accountability forum (it can be legal, administrative, financial as well as the more obviously political). In addition, it limits the focus of accountability to the *ex post* and to those mechanisms that provide in some manner for the imposition of sanctions or consequences in a looser, not strictly legal, sense. Quite a number of those working on accountability in the EU context take the Bovens definition as their point of departure precisely because it enables them to take account of actors and forums that are not necessarily in any delegation relationship (Harlow and Rawlings 2007; Papadopoulous 2007).

The advantage of the Bovens definition is that it seems to offer many possibilities for analysis of empirical practices that are evolving in the context of the contemporary EU political system. Thus non-majoritarian agencies may not be subject to a single easily definable political principal, but they are being constructed in such a fashion, at least in recent years, that one can discern a structural coupling with a number of emerging accountability forums. Moreover, those accountability forums are themselves engaged in a process of self-construction and adaptation to ensure that they can consolidate such serial structural coupling in specific circumstances. To give one example, the powers of the European Parliament to act as a public accountability forum with regard to a number of these agencies are being given flesh and blood in the manner in which the Committee on Budgets very actively engages in processes of requiring information and insisting on mutual processes of deliberation on their actions and inactions, subject to sanctions such as withholding 10 per cent of their reserves or – in the final analysis – refusing to authorise their budget (Curtin 2006; Busuioc 2007).

Another more complicated example is provided from the annals of comitology and especially the evolving role of the European Parliament in that context. The recent (inter-institutional) agreement from July 2006 squarely recognises the role of the EP as the political accountability forum *par excellence* in the EU political system, despite the fact that the EP can in no sense be qualified as a principal (Bradley 2008). This is a very clear example of inter-institutional politics producing change in the political system of the EU itself, over and above and in between the 'grand' moments of treaty revision. Indeed, the Lisbon Treaty will go even further, conferring the EP alongside its co-legislature the Council of Ministers with a right of legislative 'call-back' for executive rule-making delegated in specific legislative acts.

There are many other couplings taking place between various actors in the EU firmament and accountability forums. When it comes to networks of actors, be they policy networks, enforcement networks or others, the coupling with accountability forums on the democratic or legal circuit is much more problematic. One idea has begun to be developed to couple networks of actors with networks of accountability forums and to institutionalise in some ways a developing relationship. Harlow and Rawlings (2007) have done pioneering work in mapping various emergent practices from this perspective. Examples range from networks of parliaments to networks of courts and Ombudsmen.

At the same time, it is important to recall that the rather technical and precise definition of accountability in the manner in which empirical work is now being carried out will not, in and of itself, solve the crisis of legitimacy that the EU continues to suffer. Rather, accountability is not, in and of itself, 'the solution to the legitimacy problems of the European Union' (Puntscher Riekmann 2007). While accountability practices and procedures are important, even essential, they do not satisfy the citizens in an institutional set-up that is fundamentally contested (Benz *et al.* 2007). The EU political system is arguably 'special' by the degree of its de-politicisation, the fact that non-majoritarianism is so rife within the EU. Instead of politicians taking decisions embedded in a democratic principal–agent relationship with a transmission model of administration and accountability in the final analysis to the citizens who can throw them out, we have civil servants of all levels, experts and stakeholders with discrete powers and tasks who are not embedded in clear lines of political accountability (as in the national system).

There is at the level of the EU political system a lack of structural transparency in the system as a whole, a lack of visibility in who is acting, in what regard and where. This has to do with the manner in which the EU political system has evolved over the years, bit by bit, by virtue of treaty change and lower level institutional practice (Curtin and Dekker 1999). That lack of visibility also has to do with the fact that for a significant part the political system is multi-level and dependent on an elaborate interaction of various actors across various territorial levels. It is very difficult to get a sense that polity, policy and politics are 'joined up' and that there is a holistic coupling with what can be called the (representative) democratic circuit.

Europe's Executive Order – Old and New

One way of gauging whether a common European executive order is emerging or not is to observe the extent to which national administrations converge on a common European model (Olsen 2003). In this article, however, the focus has been on organised relationships among states and the advent of executive bodies at the European level. We have characterised the regularisation of bilateral diplomacy subsequent to the Peace of Westphalia as the first executive order. The gradual institutionalisation of multilateral diplomacy following the Vienna Congress and, not least, the growth of sectoral and functional IGOs from the second half of the nineteenth century on, constitute in our view a second order. However, although increasingly more subtle and sophisticated in organisational terms, and with more potential for collective problem solving, this second order did not transcend or replace the basically intergovernmental order inherited from the past.

We have argued that the EU and its predecessors have placed the development of the European executive order on a radically different trajectory. This is primarily related to the consolidation of the Commission as an executive centre with considerable integrity in its relations to governments and the Council, but also to the development of comparable executive units within the Council as regards security and defence policy and in the form of EU-level agencies as regards several other policy areas. Simultaneously, over the last couple of decades, fragmentation of national governments both vertically and horizontally has made national agencies that are responsible for policy implementation (and to some extent preparation) susceptible to 'agency capture' by EU-level bodies charged with similar tasks. Thus, unprecedented centrifugal forces within national executives have emerged, forces that were not likely to occur from the combination of IGOs and nationally integrated governments. The resulting 'double-hatted' national agencies and 'integrated administration' across levels of governance entail new patterns of executive politics in which conflict and cooperation may cut across national boundaries. Compared to indirect administration, we might also expect somewhat more even implementation practices across countries.

All the three executive orders dealt with in this article represent innovations as regards the ways Europe has been politically and administratively organised. Drawing on ideas from historical institutionalism on shocks as catalysts for radical institutional change (e.g. Steinmo *et al.* 1992; Thelen 2003), it is not that surprising that the innovations happened subsequent to major crises, namely the Thirty Years War, the Napoleonic Wars and the Second World War. Shocks provide windows of opportunity that entrepreneurs may exploit in convincing actors to accept things they would not accept under normal circumstances. In between 'critical junctures' institutions are changing less profoundly and incrementally, through processes of learning, design, diffusion and inter-institutional dynamics (Olsen 2007; Héritier, 2007), as we have seen as regards the Commission–EP relationship. However, path dependence and the 'stickiness' of pre-existing orders are also striking (see March and Olsen 1989): bilateral diplomacy among EU countries has not been declining over the last couple of decades, it has been strengthened in relation to new member states, and member states' staff at the permanent missions in Brussels has been steadily growing as well (Bratberg 2008). One could have expected that the growth of common institutions, integrated administration across levels of governance and transfer of policy tasks to the EU level would have reduced the need for embassies in member states. And, in general, IGOs seem to flourish more than ever (Schiavone 2005).

Thus, orders are co-existing in Europe (Olsen 2007). The accumulated executive order consists of qualitatively new elements that transcend the inherited intergovernmental order. The persistence of diplomacy and IGOs represents recognition and reproduction of a system of states (Jönsson and Hall 2005). Due to its complexity such an order may be rather robust and sustainable; 'a vehicle for highly variable terrain' (see Landau 1969). However, it raises sensitive questions about which actors should be held to account, at what level of order and to whom. It is obviously easier to establish a chain of control in relation to councils of ministers based on unanimity than to the EU Council based heavily on qualified majority voting. The consolidation of a full-fledged political executive as the Commission is particularly intricate and the advent of EU-level agencies with multiple principals challenges standard templates on how accountability should be dealt with. The same holds for the role of 'double-hatted' national agencies in an integrated administration across levels of governance.

Acknowledgements

We want to express our gratitude to the CONNEX Network of Excellence on 'Efficient and Democratic Governance in a Multi-level Europe', funded by the EU's Sixth Framework Programme. CONNEX made possible the thematic conference 'Towards a European Administrative Space' held at the University of London 16–18 November 2006 on which this Special Issue is based. We also appreciate very much the support of *WEP*'s co-editor Klaus Goetz in preparing this publication and the comments by Johan P. Olsen on our introductory article.

Notes

1. The articles that form the basis of this Special Issue were prepared in the context of the 'Connex Network of Excellence on efficient and democratic governance in the EU', funded by the European Commission as part of its Sixth Framework Programme of Research. The publication has been made possible with its support. Most of the authors presented first versions of their articles at the 'thematic conference' on 'The European Administrative Space' held at the University of London in November 2006.
2. The Commission services' self-control of appointment processes is neatly illustrated by Commissioner Verheugen's suggestion that commissioners should have more power to pick their directors-general to ensure their loyalty to their political masters. According to *European Voice*, Verheugen's comments echoed criticism by Chancellor Merkel, who had said 'commissioners' lack of control of their directors-general was unthinkable for a German minister' (12–18 October 2006).
3. According to a former cabinet member, the present size of the college implies that the president usually decides in consultation with the responsible commissioner, thus making it difficult for other commissioners to make themselves heard (Eppink 2007). Consistent with this, the Secretariat General of the Commission, serving the president in particular, has, from 2000, reinforced its central coordinating and monitoring role (Kassim 2006: 84).

References

Auel, K. (2007). 'Democratic Accountability and National Parliaments: Redefining the Impact of Parliamentary Scrutiny in EU Affairs', *European Law Journal*, 13, 487–504.

Balint, T., Bauer, M. W. and Knill, C. (2008). 'Bureaucratic Change in the European Administrative Space: The Case of the European Commission', *West European Politics*, 31:4, 677–700.

Barbieri, D. (2006). 'Transnational Networks meet National Hierarchies: The Cases of the Italian Competition and Environment Administrations', in M. Egeberg (ed.), *Multilevel Union Administration. The Transformation of Executive Politics in Europe*. Basingstoke: Palgrave Macmillan.

Barnett, M., and M. Finnemore (2004). *Rules for the World. International Organizations in Global Politics*. Ithaca, NY and London: Cornell University Press.

Bartolini, S. (2005). *Restructuring Europe: Centre Formation, System Building, and Political Structuring between the Nation State and the European Union*. Oxford: Oxford University Press.

Batora, J. (2005). 'Does the European Union Transform the Institution of Diplomacy?', *Journal of European Public Policy*, 12, 44–66.

Beach, D. (2004). 'The Unseen Hand in Treaty Reform Negotiations: The Role and Influence of the Council Secretariat', *Journal of European Public Policy*, 11, 408–39.

Benz, A., C. Harlow and I. Papadopoulos (2007). 'Introduction', *European Law Journal*, 13, 441–6.

Bovens, M. (2007). 'Analysing and Assessing Public Accountability. A Conceptual Framework', *European Law Journal*, 13, 447–68.

Bradley, K. (2008). 'Halfway House: The 2006 Comitology Reforms and the European Parliament', *West European Politics*, 31:4, 837–54.

Bratberg, Ø. (2008). 'Bilateral Embassies in an Integrated Europe: A Case of Institutional Robustness?', *Journal of European Integration*, 30, 235–53.

Busuioc M. (2007). 'Autonomy, Accountability and Control. The Case of European Agencies.' Paper presented at the 4th ECPR General Conference, Pisa, Italy, 5–8 September.

Christiansen, T. (2006). 'Out of the Shadows: The General Secretariat of the Council of Ministers', *Journal of Legislative Studies*, 8, 80–97.

Christiansen, T., and S. Vanhoonacker (2008). 'At a Critical Juncture? Change and Continuity in the Council Secretariat', *West European Politics*, 31:4, 751–70.

Christensen, T., and P. Lægreid, eds. (2006). *Autonomy and Regulation. Coping with Agencies in the Modern State*. Cheltenham: Edward Elgar.

Cini, M. (1996). *The European Commission. Leadership, Organisation and Culture in the EU Administration*. Manchester: Manchester University Press.

Cini, M. (2000). 'Administrative Culture in the European Commission: The Case of Competition and Environment', in N. Nugent (ed.), *At the Heart of the Union. Studies of the European Commission*. Houndmills: Macmillan Press.

Claude, I.L. (1964). *Swords into Plowshares. The Problems and Progress of International Organization*. New York: Random House.

Coombes, D. (1970). *Politics and Bureaucracy in the European Community*. London: George Allen and Unwin.

Cox, R.W., and H.K. Jacobson, eds. (1973). *The Anatomy of Influence. Decision Making in International Organization*. New Haven: Yale University Press.

Cram, L. (1994). 'The European Commission as a Multi-organization: Social Policy and IT Policy in the EU', *Journal of European Public Policy*, 1, 195–217.

Cross, M.K.D. (2007). *The European Diplomatic Corps. Diplomats and International Cooperation from Westphalia to Maastricht*. Basingstoke: Palgrave Macmillan.

Curtin, D. (2006). 'Delegation to EU Non-Majoritarian Agencies and Emerging Practices of Public Accountability', in D. Geradin, R. Munoz and N. Petit (eds.), *Regulation through Agencies in the EU. A New Paradigm of European Governance*. Cheltenham: Edward Elgar.

Curtin, D. (2007). 'Holding (Quasi-)Autonomous EU Administrative Actors to Public Account', *European Law Journal*, 13, 523–41.

Curtin, D., and I. Dekker (1999). 'The EU as a "Layered" International Organization: Institutional Unity in Disguise', in P. Craig and G. De Burca (eds.), *The Evolution of EU Law*. Oxford: Oxford University Press.

Dehousse, R. (2008). 'Delegation of Powers in the European Union: The Need for a Multi-principals Model', *West European Politics*, 31:4, 789–805.

Döring, H. (2007). 'The Composition of the College of Commissioners: Patterns of Delegation', *European Union Politics*, 8, 207–28.

Duke, S., and S., Vanhoonacker (2008). Administrative Governance in the CFSP', *European Foreign Affairs Review*, 11, 163–82.

Eberlein, B., and G. Grande (2005). 'Beyond Delegation: Transnational Regulatory Regimes and the EU Regulatory State', *Journal of European Public Policy*, 12, 89–112.

Egeberg, M. (1996). 'Organization and Nationality in the European Commission Services', *Public Administration*, 74, 721–35.

Egeberg, M. (2004). 'An Organisational Approach to European Integration: Outline of a Complementary Perspective', *European Journal of Political Research*, 43, 199–219.

Egeberg, M., ed. (2006a). *Multilevel Union Administration. The Transformation of Executive Politics in Europe*. Basingstoke: Palgrave Macmillan.

Egeberg, M. (2006b). 'Balancing Autonomy and Accountability: Enduring Tensions in the European Commission's Development', in M. Egeberg (ed.), *Multilevel Union Administration. The Transformation of Executive Politics in Europe*. Basingstoke: Palgrave Macmillan.

Egeberg, M. (2006c). 'Executive Politics as Usual: Role Behaviour and Conflict Dimensions in the College of European Commissioners', *Journal of European Public Policy*, 13, 1–15.

Egeberg, M., G.F. Schaefer and J. Trondal (2003). 'The Many Faces of EU Committee Governance', *West European Politics*, 26, 19–40.

Egeberg, M. and J. Trondal (forthcoming). 'National Agencies in the European Administrative Space: Government Driven, Commission Driven or Networked?', *Public Administration*, forthcoming.

Eppink, D.-J. (2007). *Life of a European Mandarin. Inside the Commission*. Tielt: Lannoo Publishers.

Goetz, K.H. (2000). 'European Integration and National Executives: A Cause in Search of an Effect', *West European Politics*, 23, 211–31.

Gornitzka, Å. (2008). 'Networking Administration in Areas of National Sensitivity. The Commission and European Higher Education', in A. Amaral, P. Maassen, C. Musselin and G. Neave (eds.), *European Integration and the Governance of Higher Education and Research*. Dordrecht: Springer.

Gornitzka, Å., and U. Sverdrup (2008). 'Who Consults? The Configuration of Expert Groups in the European Union', *West European Politics*, 31:4, 725–50.

Harlow, C. (2002). *Accountability in the European Union*. Oxford: Oxford University Press.

Harlow, C., and R. Rawlings (2007). 'Promoting Accountability in Multi-Level Governance: A Network Approach', *European Law Journal*, 13, 542–62.

Hayes-Renshaw, F., and H. Wallace (2006). *The Council of Ministers*. Basingstoke: Palgrave Macmillan.

Héritier, A., D. Kerwer, C. Knill, D. Lehmkuhl, M. Teutsch and A.C. Douillet (2001). *Differential Europe. The European Union Impact on National Policymaking*. Lanham, MD: Rowman & Littlefield.

Héritier, A. (2007). *Explaining Institutional Change in Europe*. Oxford: Oxford University Press.

Hofmann, H.C.H. (2008). 'Mapping the European Administrative Space', *West European Politics*, 31:4, 662–76.

Hofmann, H.C.H., and A.H. Türk, eds. (2006). *EU Administrative Governance*. Cheltenham: Edward Elgar.

Hooghe, L. (2000). 'A House With Differing Views: The European Commission and Cohesion Policy', in N. Nugent (ed.), *At the Heart of the Union. Studies of the European Commission*. Houndmills: Macmillan Press.

Hooghe, L. (2001). *The European Commission and the Integration of Europe. Images of Governance*. Cambridge: Cambridge University Press.

Hooghe, L. (2005). 'Several Roads Lead to International Norms, but Few via International Socialization: A Case Study of the European Commission', *International Organization*, 59, 861–98.

Joerges, C., and J. Neyer (1997). 'Transforming Strategic Interactions into Deliberative Problem-Solving: European Comitology in the Foodstuffs Sector', *Journal of European Public Policy*, 4, 609–25.

Joerges, C., and E. Vos (1999). *EU Committees: Social Regulation, Law and Politics*. Oxford: Hart Publishing.

Jönsson, C., and M. Hall (2005). *Essence of Diplomacy*. Basingstoke: Palgrave Macmillan.

Kassim, H. (2006). 'The Secretariat General of the European Commission', in D. Spence and G. Edwards (eds.), *The European Commission*. London: John Harper Publishing.

Keleman, D. (2002). 'The Politics of Eurocratic Structure and new European Agencies', *West European Politics*, 25, 93–118.

Keohane, R.O., and J.S. Nye (1977). *Power and Interdependence. World Politics in Transition*. Boston: Little, Brown and Company.

Knill, C. (2001). *The Europeanisation of National Administrations. Patterns of Institutional Change and Persistence*. Cambridge: Cambridge University Press.

Landau, M. (1969). 'Redundancy, Rationality, and the Problem of Duplication and Overlap', *Public Administration Review*, 29, 346–58.

Lindseth, P. (2003). 'The Contradictions of Supranationalism: Administrative Governance and Constitutionalization in European Integration since the 1950's', *Loyola-Los Angeles Review*, 37, 363.

MacMullen, A. (2000). 'European Commissioners: National Routes to a European Elite', in N. Nugent (ed.), *At the Heart of the Union. Studies of the European Commission*. Houndmills: Macmillan Press.

Mair, P. (2005). 'Popular Democracy and the European Union Polity', *Eurogov Working Papers* No. C-05-03, 18 May 2005 (available at http://www.connex-network.org/eurogov/).

Majone, G. (1996). *Regulating Europe*. London: Routledge.

March, J.G., and J.P. Olsen (1989). *Rediscovering Institutions. The Organizational Basis of Politics*. New York: The Free Press.

Marcussen, M. (2004). 'The Organization for Economic Cooperation and Development as Ideational Artist and Arbitrator: Reality or Dream?', in B. Reinalda and B. Verbeek (eds.), *Decision Making Within International Organizations*. Abingdon, Oxon: Routledge.

Martens, M. (2006). 'National Regulators between Union and Governments: A Study of the EU's Environmental Policy Network IMPEL', in M. Egeberg (ed.), *Multilevel Union Administration. The Transformation of Executive Politics in Europe*. Basingstoke: Palgrave Macmillan.

Martens, M. (2007). 'Linking the Commission and National Regulatory Agencies: A Study of the Role of the European Commission in Trans-governmental Networks', in M. Egeberg (ed.), *Institutional Dynamics and the Transformation of Executive Politics in Europe*. Mannheim: CONNEX Report Series No. 03.

Michelmann, H.J. (1978). 'Multinational Staffing and Organizational Functioning in the Commission of the European Communities', *International Organization*, 32, 477–96.

Mörth, U. (2000). 'Competing Frames in the European Commission – The Case of the Defence Industry and Equipment Issue', *Journal of European Public Policy*, 7, 173–89.

Mulgan, R. (2000). '"Accountability": An Ever-Expanding Concept?', *Public Administration*, 78, 555–73.

Nicolson, H. (1969). *Diplomacy*. London: Oxford University Press.

Nørgård, G.H. (2006). 'National Limits to Transnational Networking? The Case of the Danish IT and Telecom Agency', in M. Egeberg (ed.), *Multilevel Union Administration. The Transformation of Executive Politics in Europe*. Basingstoke: Palgrave Macmillan.

Olsen, J.P. (2003). 'Towards a European Administrative Space?', *Journal of European Public Policy*, 10, 506–31.

Olsen, J.P. (2007). *Europe in Search of Political Order. An Institutional Perspective on Unity/Diversity, Citizens/Their Helpers, Democratic Design/Historical Drift and the Co-existence of Orders*. Oxford: Oxford University Press.

Papadopoulos, I. (2007). 'Problems of Democratic Accountability in Network and Multi-Level Governance', *European Law Journal*, 13, 469–86.

Pollak, J., and Puntscher Riekmann, J. (2008). 'European Administration: Centralisation and Fragmentation as Means of Polity-Building?', *West European Politics*, 31:4, 771–88.

Puntscher Riekmann, S. (2007). 'In Search of Lost Norms: Is Accountability the Solution to the Legitimacy Problems of the European Union?', *Comparative European Politics*, 5, 121–37.

Schaefer, G.F., and A. Türk (2007). 'The Role of Implementing Committees', in T. Christiansen and T. Larsson (eds.), *The Role of Committees in the Policy Process of the European Union. Legislation, Implementation and Deliberation.* Cheltenham: Edward Elgar.

Schiavone, G. (2005). *International Organizations. A Dictionary and Directory.* Basingstoke: Palgrave Macmillan.

Schroeder, P.W. (1994). *The Transformation of European Politics 1763–1848.* Oxford: Oxford University Press.

Shapiro, M. (2001). 'Administrative Law Unbounded: Reflections on Government and Governance', *Indiana Journal of Global Legal Studies,* 8, 369–77.

Slaughter, A.-M. (2004). *A New World Order.* Princeton: Princeton University Press.

Spence, D. (2006). 'The President, the College and the *Cabinets*', in D. Spence and G. Edwards (eds.), *The European Commission.* London: John Harper Publishing.

Steinmo, S., K. Thelen and F. Longstreth, eds. (1992). *Structuring Politics. Historical Institutionalism in Comparative Analysis.* Cambridge: Cambridge University Press.

Suvarierol, S. (2008). 'Beyond the Myth of Nationality: Analysing Networks within the European Commission', *West European Politics,* 31:4, 701–24.

Sverdrup, U. (2006). 'Policy Implementation', in P. Graziano and M. Vink (eds.), *Europeanization: New Research Agendas.* Basingstoke: Palgrave Macmillan.

Thatcher, M., and D. Coen (2008). 'Reshaping European Regulatory Space: An Evolutionary Analysis', *West European Politics,* 31:4, 806–36.

Thelen, K. (2003). 'How Institutions Evolve. Insights from Comparative Historical Analysis', in J. Mahoney and D. Rueschemeyer (eds.), *Comparative Historical Analysis in the Social Sciences.* Cambridge: Cambridge University Press.

Thomson, R. (2008). 'National Actors in International Organizations: The Case of the European Commission', *Comparative Political Studies,* 41, 169–92.

Trondal, J. (2006). 'Governing at the Frontier of the European Commission. The Case of Seconded National Experts', *West European Politics,* 29, 147–60.

Trondal, J., and L. Jeppesen (2008). 'Images of Agency Governance in the European Union', *West European Politics,* 31:3, 417–41.

Trondal, J., M. Marcussen and F. Veggeland (2005). 'Re-discovering International Executive Institutions', *Comparative European Politics,* 3, 232–58.

Vos, E. (1999). *Institutional Frameworks of Community Health and Safety Regulation. Committees, Agencies and Private Bodies.* Oxford: Hart Publishing.

Wille, A. (2007a). 'Senior Officials in a Reforming European Commission: Transforming the Top?', in M.W. Bauer and C. Knill (eds.), *Management Reforms in International Organizations.* Baden-Baden: Nomos.

Wille, A. (2007b). 'Bridging the Gap: Political and Administrative Leadership in a Reinvented European Commission', in M. Egeberg (ed.), *Institutional Dynamics and the Transformation of Executive Politics in Europe.* Mannheim: CONNEX Report Series No. 03.

Wonka, A. (2007). 'Technocratic and Independent? The Appointment of European Commissioners and its Policy Implications', *Journal of European Public Policy,* 14, 169–89.

Mapping the European Administrative Space

HERWIG C. H. HOFMANN

The term 'European administrative space' has been used to describe an increasing convergence of administrations and administrative practices at the EU level and various member states' administrations to a 'common European model' (Olsen 2003: 506) and the Europeanisation of the member states' administrative structures (Page and Wouters 1995). It has also been used to describe the phenomenon of the coordinated implementation of EU law and the Europeanisation of national administrative law (OECD-PUMA 1998; Kadelbach 2002). Whilst the former definition of the European administrative space as an object of research is so broad that it is difficult to define sufficiently precise parameters for analysis (Olsen 2003: 507), the latter definition of the European administrative space is too narrow. Cooperation amongst administrations in the EU/EC goes beyond forms of cooperation for implementation of EU law by Community institutions and member states' agencies. It is marked by a high degree of close administrative cooperation between all levels of member states' administrations with the European institutions and bodies in various policy phases. The existing rules and procedures governing administrative cooperation have not been constant and have developed over time. They affect the very nature of the EU's system of shared sovereignty as well as the conditions for its accountability and legitimacy. The supranational legal and political order, established by the EU/E(E)C member states, has grown accordingly. Thus far, the reality of the European administrative space is closely related to, and its importance has grown with, the expansion over time of the *aquis communautaire*. Mapping the European administrative space is therefore a fundamental task which will be attempted in this article by means of a brief reconstruction of the development of supranational law and its relation to the notion of the territorially bound exercise of public policies. The article will thus explore the European administrative space mainly in the context of legal and legal-historic developments. This will lay the foundation for analysing the roles of the main actors – national, European and mixed – in exercising public authority in the administrative space, their main forms of interaction and the joint structures they have created.

Development of the European Administrative Space

The starting point of the creation of a supranational system of shared sovereignty through European integration was the existence of territorially more or less sovereign states in Europe. Under the 'traditional' notion of territoriality, the *summa potestas* of a sovereign state was characterised by the dichotomy of the concentration of public power within the territory, on the one hand, and the external independence of the state,[1] on the other. In this context, national administrations developed as state-specific structures reflecting different identities, historic traditions of organisation and certain underlying values such as regionalisation or centralised unification within a state. Supranationality was innovative as it created an alternative to this differentiation between internal functions of a state that result in national public law and external relations of the state conducted within the framework of public international law. With increasing European integration, the distinction between the 'inner sphere' of a state and its 'outer sphere' has become less prominent since states also allowed public power to be exercised from outside their territorial organisations. This 'opening' towards a supranational system of pooling sovereignty led to a certain de-territorialisation of the joint exercise of public power insofar as formally fairly 'closed' systems of the territorial states opened up through the emergence and establishment of a supranational legal order. This, in turn, had a great influence on the administrative institutions, bodies and procedures required for an effective exercise of shared sovereignty.

I will here reconstruct this transformation towards a European administrative space, in which shared sovereignty is jointly exercised, by outlining several distinct yet overlapping phases of development. Reconstructing EU integration through phase-models is a tool commonly used to simplify the far more complex reality (e.g. Weiler 1991; Bignami 2004; Joerges 2006) and to illustrate the shift of parameters in the exercise of public power in Europe.[2]

The Vertical Relation

The initial approach to creating the supranational order was the delegation of sovereign powers from the member states to the European Coal and Steel Community (ECSC) and the E(E)C (Weiler 1991: 2413–23). Member states opened up their political and legal systems vertically to the exercise of this power at the European level. The consequences of this delegation of powers were explained in no uncertain terms by the European Court of Justice (ECJ) most notably in the cases of *Van Gend en Loos* and *Costa v ENEL*, which established the notions of primacy and direct effect of EU law. The vertical opening of the national legal systems of European law meant that EU/EC law became part of the member states' 'legal heritage'. It had the ability to override member states' law in case of conflict and had direct effect within their territory.[3] In this context, it is important to recall that pooling sovereignty on the European level was acceptable to member states inter alia because the product, Community law, was not completely alien to the national systems. Member states' executives had become key figures in agenda setting, the legislative procedures and the creation of common rules for implementation (Weiler 1991; Hofmann and Türk 2006: 11–112).

This form of 'vertical' opening of the member states towards EU/EC law with direct effect and supremacy, however, did not yet call into question the traditional model of territoriality or the national model of administration. The effects of the exercise of public power at the European level remained limited to the state in which the legal order was established and to the territorial reach of its sovereignty. The 'legal heritage', of which supranational law had become part, was still exercised exclusively within the territory of each individual member state. In administrative terms, this corresponded to the model of implementation and indirect administration of Community law in each and every member state (Joerges 2006: 791–793).

The Horizontal Relation

The second major development towards a European administrative space was the 'horizontal' opening of member states' legal and political systems. The requirements of growing a single market in the Community without internal frontiers necessitated an opening of the strictly territorially organised structures. Since the mid-1970s, the ECJ case law increasingly focused on the obligation of the member states to mutually recognise the administrative and legislative decisions of other member states, especially when this was necessary to allow for the exercise of fundamental freedoms within the EC. The reasons and political context of this so-called 'negative integration' have been discussed in the literature on the evolution of Community law (see especially Weiler 1991). But in the context of the development of the European administrative space, it is important to note that the requirement for mutual recognition arose parallel with the findings that the EC Treaty provisions, including fundamental freedoms, could have a direct horizontal effect on the member states. These provisions could in some cases be relied on between individuals without implementation through Community secondary legislation or member states' intervention. This being the case, individuals would necessarily be allowed to rely on fundamental freedoms of the EC Treaty vis-à-vis other member state administrations.[4]

This horizontal opening is most closely associated with the case of *Cassis de Dijon,* which required member states to mutually accept and enforce each others' regulatory decisions in the absence of harmonising legislation at the European level.[5] Member states' administrative and legislative decisions, through mutual recognition, could establish effects beyond the territorial reach of the issuing member state. They thus had 'trans-territorial' effect throughout the EC. By this means, EC law required member states' public law to penetrate the classical territorial reach of the legal system of the country of origin.[6] This was in effect a more serious challenge to the notion of territoriality induced by Community law than the vertical opening that the member states' legal systems had created through the establishment of direct effect and supremacy of Community law. In order to address the requirements of horizontal cooperation, an obligation to provide mutual administrative assistance was introduced.[7] From this, reporting duties[8] developed for more regular administrative cooperation.

Developing Integrated Administration

Such reporting duties often evolved into joint planning structures.[9] These resulted in composite administrative procedures, with input from several different administrative actors both from the member states and the European level, tied together by procedural provisions emanating from EU law. The development of vertical and horizontal relations was therefore a stage in the creation of an integrated network administration. Network structures were beginning to be created around the possibility of regulatory decisions with trans-territorial effect, i.e. where national administrations' decisions, due to Community law, have an effect beyond the territory of a member state.

The third major development changing the conditions of the modern European administrative space is therefore the move towards an integrated administration in Europe. With respect to implementing activity, this can be closely linked to the evolution of the principle of 'subsidiarity'. Subsidiarity had long featured in the legal-doctrinal debates over the vertical distribution of legislative powers between the European and national levels. But, in reality, the practical impact of subsidiarity was stronger in political terms than in purely legal terms.[10] The principle was a powerful *topos* not so much in the discussion on the distribution of legislative competencies between the European and national levels. Instead it developed in the political debate about the distinction of powers between the EU and the member state levels often as a *topos* with respect to the distribution of powers between legislation and implementation. In reality, the emergence of subsidiarity as a constitutional notion goes hand in hand with the development of a system of decentralised, yet cooperative, administrative structures. If legislation takes place at the European level and implementation at the level of the member states, uniform application of the provisions and the creation of an area without internal frontiers require cooperation and coordination. This can take place, for example, through information exchange, joint warning systems, coordinated remedies for arising problems and a wealth of other similar systems. Since the single market programme in the late 1980s and early 1990s, increasingly diverse forms of implementation of EU/EC law have been developed, mostly aimed at providing for joint administration of EU/EC policies. These forms of cooperation have often taken the form of administrative networks with participants from the member states, Community institutions and private parties (see Hofmann and Türk 2006; Egeberg 2006).

But in the EU, the range of administrative activity goes beyond implementation. It also expands the coordinating and structuring roles which administrations play in all phases of the 'policy cycle' – the phases of agenda setting, policy formulation and finally implementation. In fact, the extent of the European administrative space can only be fully appreciated by looking behind the veil of administrations' implementation activity and taking into account the administrations' roles in the other phases of the policy cycle. This also enables an appreciation of the more hidden, often preparatory functions of administrations in Europe. Structures of integrated administration for all three phases operate in large part beyond the institutions and procedures established by the founding treaties.[11] They have developed in an evolutionary way, differing in each stage of the policy cycle and in each policy area and creating a rich diversity of administrative actors on the European levels and their forms of interaction. In part, this was fuelled by the relation between the increasing integration of policies with the increasingly close interaction between the European and the member states' actors in all phases of the policy cycle.

In agenda setting, national administrations play a central role in shaping the Commission's policy initiatives. This takes place mainly through expert groups which are generally composed of national civil servants as well as independent experts. These groups are used to develop and test ideas, build coalitions of experts and pre-determine policy incentives to be formally presented later by the Commission as initiative. Expert groups are used as arenas for deliberation, brainstorming and intergovernmental conflict solving and coalition building amongst national experts (Larsson 2003; Trondal 2004; Larsson and Trondal 2006).

Similarly, supranational and national administrative actors exercise influence over the EU's decision-making process. The presence of the national administrations is felt mostly within the Council working parties that support the Committee of the Permanent Representatives (COREPER). Here, the national civil servants have to balance their national mandate against the need to reach a consensus in pursuance of EU tasks (Neuhold and Radulova 2006). Such interaction, albeit to a lesser extent, also exists through the 'Open Method of Coordination' (Hodson and Maher 2001; Linsenmann and Meyer 2002; de la Porte 2002; Regent 2003).

The most intensive administrative cooperation and interaction, however, takes place in the implementation phase. In this phase, institutions' activities range from single case decisions and preparatory acts thereof to acts of administrative rule-making and the amendment of specific provisions in legislation where so authorised. The current constitutional framework in the EU and EC treaties only partially reflects the evolutionary development of EU policy implementation,[12] which has been driven by practical necessity and political arrangements. The classical distinction between forms of either direct administration, which implies implementation of a policy through Community institutions, or indirect administration, which implies implementation of a policy at the member state level, has become less and less relevant. Instead, in many policy areas the development of the integration of EU and national administrative proceedings has led to 'composite proceedings' to which both national and EU administrations contribute (Cananea 2004; Cassese 2004; M.P. Chiti 2004; Sydow 2001, 2004; Schmidt-Aßmann 1996).

Diverse structures undertake implementation decisions and administrative rule-making in the various policy areas. Amongst these developments are 'comitology' committee procedures (see e.g. Bradley 1997; Joerges and Neyer 1997; Joerges and Falke 2000; Andenas and Türk 2000; Töller 2002; Bergström 2005), which were developed in the 1960s and which have subsequently been codified by the comitology decisions of 1987, 1999 and 2006.[13] In reality, in the framework of comitology procedures, the Commission often not only has to serve as decision-maker acting on delegated implementing powers, but also as manager of formal and informal networks in which member states' representatives, experts and private parties participate (Harlow 2002: 182).

This results from several factors: firstly, the increasing participation of the European Parliament;[14] secondly, the Commission's obligation, in certain cases, to secure the participation of affected third parties and the obligation to take their opinions into account,[15] as well as to consult scientific expertise in the adoption of implementing measures.[16] In certain policy areas this approach has been expanded to what is known as the 'Lamfalussy' procedures.[17] Further, agencies and their administrative networks play an ever-increasing role. European agencies are decentralised forms of administration that integrate national administrative bodies into their operations by providing structures for cooperation between the supranational and national levels and between the national authorities. They are separate, but auxiliary to the Commission's implementing tasks (E. Chiti 2004; Geradin and Petit 2004; Groß 2005). Despite the fact that their structure and scope of activities differ considerably, agencies often pursue their tasks within a wider administrative setting, which includes other patterns of EU implementation, such as comitology, while also providing a channel for the input of different public actors from the national and sub-national levels (Majone 2006). Networks may also include private parties acting as recipients of limited delegation.[18] Administrative networks, which have been created and adapted to the needs of each policy area, integrate the supranational and national administrative bodies within structures designed to conduct joint or coordinated action. The different forms of implementation structures are not mutually exclusive and are generally used in combination with each other in single policy areas.

Hence, the administrative networks embody various forms of cooperation. They are networks comprised of the European Commission and national as well as European agencies. They are also networks for direct contact between the different member states' agencies. In practice, these forms of cooperation consist of obligations of different intensity. They range from obligations to exchange information either on an ad hoc or a permanent basis to network structures which have been developed to include forms of implementation such as individually binding decisions.[19] Administrative networks can go so far as to use member states' administrations as types of EU agencies, in which the EU level decides on the type and scope of activities to be undertaken in individual cases at the national level.[20] The task of such network structures is to effectively enforce Community rules by integrating national regulators into a Community framework.[21] Further types of measures have been established, for example, with respect to the OMC (open method of cooperation). Here the Council decides on guidelines and establishes, where appropriate, quantitative and qualitative indicators and benchmarks. This system has been analysed as a network (Hodson and Maher 2001; de la Porte 2002; Olsen 2003: 518).[22]

As a consequence of these developments, no longer is there always a clear distinction between the European and national levels in the policy phases of agenda setting, policy-making and implementation. The originally more or less distinct vertical and horizontal relations between the European level and the member states as well as between member states' laws have been transformed into a network of complex relationships. Also, structures have been developed which link European networks with participants from non-EU member states.[23]

Regulating the European Administrative Space: Causes and Consequences

Based on these initial observations, it appears that European integration has led to an opening for the member states to exercise public power from outside their territories, be this at the European level or within other member states. At the same time, their branches of government are involved in the creation, implementation and adjudication of European law and other member states' Europeanised law. Member state and EU structures are not only subject to EU/EC law, they also jointly create and implement it. This network structure is the essence of the notion of shared sovereignty. In this respect the role of administrations is central to the creation and implementation of EU law. From this perspective, the European administrative space is a forum of interaction for the creation and the implementation of EU/EC policies. At the same time, there is mutual learning and a transfer of concepts. The European level adopts concepts developed in the individual member states, such as the principle of proportionality, hearing rights, public liability or freedom of information, to name just a few. It follows that these are often re-distributed to the member states' legal systems via European law by the transposition of EU law. Such concepts in turn often tend not only to influence the parts of member states' legal systems directly affected by requirements for transposition, but also lead to a certain cross-fertilisation into other member states' policy areas (Kadelbach 2002: 168).

One of the main reasons for this development of network administration, which at first sight seems to run counter to a well-established understanding of administration as being either direct or indirect within Europe's multi-level system, may lie in the relatively small administrative capacities of the EU in relation to its duties (Kassim 2003: 151). Further, the great differences in the member states' legal systems, their administrative traditions and socio-cultural conditions require the involvement of member state administrations from the first stages of planning a joint action to the last stage of its implementation. In a sense, therefore, the notion of subsidiarity in implementation is a victim of its own success. Member states' administrations are now so extensively involved not only in the implementation of decisions made at the EU level but also in the development and framing of policies that there has been a movement towards a truly integrated administration in all policy areas with EU competencies.

Europe's system of integrated administration has developed certain characteristics, however, which make it difficult to establish common rules and principles. EU administrative structures and administrative law are evolutionary by nature. They are fluid and in permanent development in the different policy areas. In addition, there is very little coordination between the policy areas. General EU administrative law exists mainly in the form of general principles of law. Few rules of general administrative law are applicable across several policy areas (Hofmann and Türk 2007). A further feature of integrated administration is its fragmented nature insofar as executive authority is spread within the EU across several institutions, most notably the Commission and the Council, which are increasingly supported by EU agencies. Additionally, executive functions are almost always undertaken in cooperation with administrative players and private parties from the member states and in some policy areas within networks with participants from outside the EU.

Understanding the full range of activities and functions for which Europe created its unique system of integrated administration requires avoiding the mistake of equating the role of administration with implementation of EU policies. Doing so would reflect a rather narrow functional understanding of administrative action. This leads to a view of the European administrative space not as two superimposed territorial structures, one being the European level with the territorial reach of the EU, as described in Article 299 EC, and the other being the member states each exercising public power only within their respective territories. Instead, the European administrative space has developed over time through a gradual de-territorialisation of the exercise of public power in the EU, on the one hand, and the establishment of a network of integrated administration for the creation and implementation of matters within the sphere of EU law, on the other. A more three-dimensional understanding of the European administrative space shows a space in which European, national and sub-national administrations and interested parties act together in agenda setting, rule-making and implementation. This system of integrated administration is not always visible to citizens because the final administrative or legislative decisions are generally taken by member state institutions and bodies.

Such conditions of integrated administration, however, pose real questions about the accountability of the actors involved in the network, which enjoys multiple ways of gathering, distributing and computing information. The latter is often far beyond the potential of national administrations acting in isolation beyond administrative networks. Such requirements for accountability become particularly urgent in cases where administrative networks have been created within the European administrative space which act on matters particularly sensitive to fundamental rights.[24] Because conditions for accountability differ at each policy phase, this requires the development of accountability structures that are adapted to integrated administration in the different policy phases (Hofmann and Türk 2007). Since administrative cooperation leading to an integrated administration in the European administrative space is mainly procedural in nature, a logical step would be to establish the utmost transparency in such procedures, accompanied by effective procedures for administrative, political and judicial review of integrated administrative structures and their composite procedures.

Shared Sovereignty through Integrated Administration

This article has attempted to show that the European administrative space cannot be reduced to a two-dimensional concept. EU/EC law does not simply create another distinct territorial layer over the pre-existing member states' territories. Also, it does not lead to a harmonisation of administrative structures and practices throughout the EU and its member states. Instead, the European administrative space is the area in which increasingly integrated administrations jointly exercise powers delegated to the EU in a system of shared sovereignty.[25] The integration is largely procedural, mostly maintaining a diversity of internal organisational forms. The notion of the European administrative space is linked to administrative action in the creation, administration and maintenance of EU/EC policies as well as the Europeanised national policies. The European administrative space is thus a three-dimensional concept with complex vertical, horizontal and diagonal relations among the actors (Joerges 2006). Its development has been evolutionary and fluid. Its structures have been developed on a case-by-case basis in different policy areas. Moreover, the various forms of administrative cooperation differ according to the policy phases. Since the different policy phases cannot always be clearly distinguished, the different forms of cooperation are designed and have developed to facilitate the development of EU policies by working hand in hand with each other.[26] Despite differentiation in different policy areas, the phenomenon of administrative cooperation has led to an 'integrated administration', i.e. an intensive and often seamless cooperation between national and supranational administrative actors and activities.

These observations illustrate the necessity of an analysis of the realities of European administration that departs from a familiar two-level model and moves towards an integrated approach. This has consequences not only for our understanding of the role of administration in Europe but also for the analysis of key aspects such as accountability. This article has shown that integrated administration lies at the core of the EU's legal and political system. It is the substance behind the theoretical notion of shared sovereignty and gives the European administrative space its shape.

Notes

1. As a general principle of public international law, territoriality limited the right of a state to exercise its sovereign powers outside its borders, thereby limiting government activity on foreign territory. As a principle of conflicts, territoriality became a connecting point for the applicability of public law to a real-life situation (Ress 1980).
2. However, the exact demarcation of the phases is relative to the goal to be achieved. Therefore, phase models in the literature, although generally following the same pattern, often differ considerably in detail and focus.
3. Case 26/62 *Van Gend en Loos* [1962] ECR 1, paras. 10, 12, 13; Case 6/64 *Costa* v *ENEL* [1964] ECR 585, para. 3. This was declared irrespective of the nature of the law which could be either primary treaty law, derived secondary law or individual decisions of administrative nature.
4. In Case 104/75 *de Peijper* [1976] ECR 613, for example, the ECJ limited the possibility of a member state to carry out an administrative procedure already undertaken in another member state. That would be a disproportionate limitation of the fundamental freedom. Where there were similar requirements for administrative procedures in two member states

but no harmonisation, the ECJ went a step further and requested national administrations to make contact to establish the necessary information, Case 251/78 *Denkavit* [1979] ECR 3369. Case 35/76 *Simmental I* [1976] ECR 1871 provided for the obligation of a member state to accept the veterinary certificates of another member state in the case of an investigation procedure harmonised by a directive.
5. Case 120/78 *Rewe Central AG (Cassis de Dijon)* [1979] ECR 649, paras. 8, 14.
6. The trans-territorial effect of administrative acts arises from obligations of mutual recognition of administrative acts. This is necessary, for instance, to coordinate the administration of the single market by different national authorities. Prominent examples of this type of activity are the supervision of banking and insurance companies through host and home country administrations and the effects of the European arrest warrant.
7. Mutual assistance obligations are based either on Article 10 EC or are individually provided for in secondary legislation. One early example for rules for mutual assistance and horizontal exchange of information was created for tax authorities in Council Directive 77/799/EEC of 19 December 1977 concerning mutual assistance by the competent authorities of the member states in the field of direct taxation (OJ 1977 L 336/15).
8. In reality, one of most important acts of secondary law creating standing reporting duties is the directive on information about technical standards and regulations. Member states and their standardisation bodies are under obligation to inform the Commission about any draft standardisation or technical regulation in areas which are not subject to harmonisation legislation. See Articles 1–2 and 8 of Directive 83/189/EEC of the European Parliament and the Council of 28 March 1983 laying down a procedure for the provision of information in the field of technical standards and regulations, OJ 1983 L 109/8 amended by Council Directive 88/182, OJ 1988 L 81/75. The directive was replaced by Directive 98/34/EC of the European Parliament and of the Council of 22 June 1998 laying down a procedure for the provision of information in the field of technical standards and regulations, OJ 1998 L 204/37 and amended by Directive 98/48/EC, OJ 1998 L 217/18 and others.
9. For example, Article 8 of the Directive 2002/3/EC relating to ozone in ambient air contains an information obligation both in the vertical and the horizontal direction for joint planning networks to avoid cases of trans-boundary ozone pollution. This contains information obligations by the member states' authorities vertically to the Commission and relevant agencies as well as horizontally to other member states' authorities which could be contributed to the causes or being affected by pollution. The information exchange leads to the creation and implementation of joint plans to reduce the production of ozone as well as emergency plans in case of an acute rise in ozone levels (Directive 2002/3/EC of the European Parliament and of the Council of 12 February 2002 relating to ozone in ambient air, OJ 2002 L 67/14).
10. The ECJ did not enter into an in-depth debate over the merits of subsidiarity related arguments – mainly due to respect for the legislative discretion of the Community legislator. See e.g. C-84/94 *Working Time Directive* [1996] ECR I-5755; C-233/94 *Deposit Guarantee Schemes* [1997] ECR I-2405; C- 376/98 *Germany v EP and Council (Tobacco Advertising)* [2000] ECR I-8419; C-377/98 *Biotechnological Inventions* [2001] ECR I-7079.
11. Instead, it is governed by general principles of law (De Bùrca 1999). General administrative legislation only exists in rudimentary beginnings, for example, in the form of the Comitology Decision (Council Decision 1999/468/EC laying down the procedures for the implementation of powers conferred on the Commission, [1999] OJ L 184/23 amended by Council Decision 2006/512/EC of 17 July 2006, [2006] OJ L 200/11, Council Regulation 58/2003 laying down the statute for executive agencies to be entrusted with certain tasks in the management of Community programmes, [2003] OJ L 11/1), or the famous Regulation 1/58 on the language regime in the EC of 6 November 1958.
12. References can be found in Articles 10, 202 and 211 EC.
13. Council Decision 87/373/EEC of 13 July 1987 laying down the procedures for the exercise of implementing powers conferred on the Commission, [1987] OJ L 197/33, Council

Decision 1999/468/EC laying down the procedures for the exercise of implementing powers conferred on the Commission, [1999] OJ L 184/23 amended by Council Decision 2006/512/EC of 17 July 2006, [2006] OJ L 200/11.
14. Especially with the new 2006 'regulatory procedure with scrutiny' where increasingly also the European Parliament is involved in recourses. See Article 2 and 5a of the 2006 Comitology decision. The regulatory procedure with scrutiny has been inspired by the distinctions between delegated acts and implementing acts by the Treaty establishing a Constitution for the European Union.
15. In competition cases, see e.g. Article 7(2) of Council Regulation 1/2003, [2003] OJ L 1/1.
16. This is a requirement under the case law of the ECJ and CFI, see e.g. C-212/91 *Angelopharm v Hamburg* [1994] ECR I-171 and T-70/99 *Alpharma v Council* [2002] ECR II-3495.
17. This approach to legislation and delegation consists of a four-tier system. On Level 1, legislative measures are adopted by the Council and the European Parliament, focusing on the core political principles including the nature and extent of the implementing measures (Directives, which have been issued as Level 1 measures deal with markets in financial instruments (Directive 2004/39/EC, [2004] OJ L 145/1–44), market abuse (Directive 2003/6/EC, [2003] OJ L 96/16–25), prospectus (Directive 2003/71/EC, [2003] OJ L 345/ 64–89), transparency (Directive 2004/109/EC, [2004] OJ L 390/38–57) and financial services (Directive 2005/1, [2005] OJ L79/9). At Level 2, the implementing details of Level 1 are adopted by the Commission in co-operation with the EU Securities Committee (ESC), the European Banking Committee (EBC) for the banking sector and the European Insurance and Occupational Pensions Committee (EIOPC) under the regulatory procedure provided in the 1999/2006 Comitology Decision plus several advisory committees. At Level 3, the EU Securities Regulators Committee (ESRC) ensures the consistent transposition and implementation of Level 1 and 2 acts. At Level 4, the Commission, as guardian of the Treaties, pursues the enforcement of the adopted measures (see e.g. Lastra 2004; Moloney 2003).
18. The 'new approach' Directives provide only the essential requirements that products must comply with in order to benefit from free movement within the EC. CEN (Comité Européen de Normalisation), CENELEC (Comité Européen de Normalisation Electrotechnique) and ETSI (European Telecommunications Standards Institute) are charged with providing specific standards on the basis of such requirements. Even though they are not binding on the producer of goods, these harmonised Community standards are given a presumption of conformity, where they have been published in the OJ and transposed into national standards. See e.g. Article 5(2) of Directive 98/37 of the European Parliament and of the Council (on machinery), [1998] OJ L 207/1.
19. A prominent example for the latter is enforcement networks in the area of competition law with the 'European Network of Competition Agencies'. See Council Regulation 1/2003, [2003] OJ L 1/1 and the Commission Notice on cooperation within the Network of Competition Authorities, [2004] OJ C 101/43.
20. Increasingly common are joint planning structures, in which EU law organises the Commission (and sometimes European agencies) together with national agencies into 'planning networks'. An example of such a network is 'Eionet' (Council Regulation 1210/90 of 7 May 1990, [1990] OJ L 120/1 and Council Regulation 933/99 of 29 April 1999, [1999] OJ L 117/1, amending Regulation 1210/90 on the establishment of the European Environment Agency and the European environment information and observation network) (see for further reference Sydow 2003).
21. See e.g. the 'European Regulators Group' in the telecommunications sector (Decision 2002/627), the 'Committee of European Securities Regulators' in the financial services sector (Decision 2001/527 [2001] OJ L191/43) and the 'European Competition Network' (Council Regulation 1/2003 [2003] OJ L1/1).
22. See No 37 of the Presidency Conclusions of the Lisbon European Council on 23 and 24 March 2000 (http://www.europarl.eu.int/summits/lis1_en.htm#c).

23. See e.g. the European environmental network Eionet based on Council Regulation 1210/90, OJ 1990 L 120/1 and Council Regulation 933/99 of 29 April 1999, OJ 1999 L 117/1, amending Regulation 1210/90 on the establishment of the European Environment Agency and the European environment information and observation network. This network contains also actors both private and public from non-EU member states.
24. See e.g. in the matters of customs administration (Convention on mutual assistance and cooperation between customs administrations (Naples II) – Council Act 98/C 24/01 of 18 December 1997 drawing up, on the basis of Article K3 of the Treaty on European Union, the Convention on mutual assistance and cooperation between customs administrations, OJ 1998 C 24/1), the Dublin Regulation replacing the Dublin agreement on asylum matters (Council Regulation (EC) No 343/2003 of 18 February 2003 establishing the criteria and mechanisms for determining the member state responsible for examining an asylum application lodged in one of the member states by a third-country national [2003] OJ L50/1 implemented by Council Directive 2003/9/EC of 27 January 2003 laying down minimum standards for the reception of asylum seekers [2003] OJ L31/18 and Council Directive 2004/83/EC of 29 April 2004 on minimum standards for the qualification and status of third country nationals or stateless persons as refugees or as persons who otherwise need international protection and the content of the protection granted [2004] OJ L 304/12) the joint visa information system (Council Decision 512/2004/EC establishing the Visa Information System (VIS) [2004] OJ L 213/5).
25. In the words of the ECJ, the EC thus 'created its own legal system which, on the entry into force of the Treaty, became an integral part of the legal systems of the member states'. Case 6/64 *Costa* v. *ENEL* [1964] ECR 585, para. 8.
26. Due to a lack of a clear positive hierarchy of norms in the EC, the legislative phase for example cannot be neatly distinguished from the implementing phase. Also, experience in the implementing phase often results in agenda setting activities for further reform.

References

Andenas, M., and A. Türk, eds. (2000). *Delegated Legislation and the Role of Committees in the EC*. The Hague: Kluwer.

Bergström, C.F. (2005). *Delegation of Powers in the European Union and the Committee System*. Oxford: Oxford University Press.

Bignami, F. (2004). 'Three Generations of participation Rights before the European Commission', *Law and Contemporary Problems*, 68, 61–84.

Bradley, K.St.C. (1997). 'The European Parliament and Comitology: On the Road to Nowhere?', *European Law Journal*, 3, 230–54.

Cassese, S. (2004). 'European Administrative Proceedings', *Law and Contemporary Problems*, 68, 21–36.

Chiti, E. (2004). 'Decentralisation and Integration into the Community Administrations: A New Perspective on European Agencies', *European Law Journal*, 10, 423–31.

Chiti, M.P. (2004). 'Forms of European Administrative Action', *Law and Contemporary Problems*, 68, 37–60.

De Búrca, G. (1999). 'The Institutional Development of the EU: A Constitutional Analysis', in P. Craig and G. De Búrca (eds.), *The Evolution of EU Law*. Oxford: Oxford University Press.

De la Porte, C. (2002). 'Is the Open Method of Coordination Appropriate for Organising Activities at European Level in Sensitive Policy Areas?', *European Law Journal*, 8, 38–58.

Della Cananea, G. (2004). 'The European Union's Mixed Administrative Proceedings', *Law and Contemporary Problems*, 68, 197–218.

Egeberg, M. (2006). 'Europe's Executive Branch of Governments in the Melting Pot: An Overview', in M. Egeberg (ed.), *Multilevel Union Administration*. London: Palgrave, 1–16.

Geradin, D., and N. Petit (2004). 'The Development of Agencies at EU and National Levels: Conceptual Analysis and Proposals for Reform', *Jean Monnet Working Paper* 01/04, 33 (http://www.jeanmonnetprogram.org/papers/04/040101.pdf).

Groß, T. (2005). 'Die Kooperation zwischen europäischen Agenturen und nationalen Behörden', *Europarecht*, 40, 54–68.
Harlow, C. (2002). *Accountability in the European Union*. Oxford: Oxford University Press.
Hodson, D., and Maher, I. (2001). 'The Open Method as a New Mode of Governance: The Case of Soft Economic Policy Co-ordination', *Journal of Common Market Studies*, 39, 719–46.
Hofmann, H.C.H., and A. Türk, eds. (2006). *EU Administrative Governance*. Cheltenham: Elgar Publishing.
Hofmann, H.C.H., and A. Türk (2007). 'The Development of Integrated Administration in the EU and its Consequences', *European Law Journal*, 13, 253–71.
Joerges, C. (2006). 'The Legitimacy of Supranational Decision-Making', *Journal of Common Market Studies*, 44, 779–802.
Joerges, C., and J. Falke, eds. (2000). *Das Ausschusswesen der Europäischen Union*. Baden-Baden: Nomos.
Joerges, C., and J. Neyer (1997). 'From Intergovernmental Bargaining to Deliberative Political Processes: The Constitutionalization of Comitology', *European Law Journal*, 3, 273–99.
Kadelbach, S. (2002). 'European Administrative Law and the Europeanised Administration', in Christian Joerges and Renaud Dehousse (eds.). *Good Governance in Europe's Integrated Market*. Oxford: Oxford University Press, 167–206.
Kassim, H. (2003). 'The European Administration: Between Europeanization and Domestication', in J. Hayward and A. Menon (eds.), *Governing Europe*. Oxford: Oxford University Press.
Larsson, T. (2003). 'Pre-Cooking – The World of Expert Groups'. Stockholm: ESO Report.
Larsson, T. and Trondal, J. (2006). 'Agenda Setting in the European Commission', in H.C.H. Hofmann and A. Türk (eds.), *EU Administrative Governance*. Cheltenham: Elgar Publishing, 11–43.
Lastra, R. (2004). 'The Governance Structure for Financial Regulation and Supervision in Europe', *Columbia Journal of European Law*, 10, 49–68.
Linsenmann, I., and Meyer, C. (2002). 'Dritter Weg, Übergang oder Teststrecke?', *Integration*, 25, 285–97.
Majone, G. (2006). 'Managing Europeanisation – The European Agencies', in John Peterson and Michael Shackleton (eds.), *The Institutions of the EU*. Oxford: Oxford University Press, 191–209.
Moloney, N. (2003). 'The Lamfalussy Legislative Model: A New Era for the EC Securities and Investment Services Regime', *International and Comparative Law Quarterly*, 52, 509–20.
Neuhold, C., and E., Radulova (2006). 'The Involvement of Administrative Players in the EU Decision Making Process', in H.C.H. Hofmann and A. Türk (eds.), *EU Administrative Governance*. Cheltenham: Elgar Publishing, 2006, 44–73.
Olsen, J.P. (2003). 'Towards a European Administrative Space?', *Journal of European Public Policy*, 10, 506–31.
OECD-PUMA, (1998). 'Preparing Public Administration for the European Administrative Space', *SIGMA Papers Paris*, No.23.
Page, E., and L. Wouters, eds. (1995). 'The Europeanization of the National Bureaucracies?', in Jon Pierre (ed.), *Bureaucracy in the Modern State*. Aldershot: Elgar Publishing, 185–204.
Regent, S. (2003). 'The Open Method of Coordination: A New Supranational Form of Governance?', *European Law Journal*, 9, 190–240.
Ress, G. (1980). 'Souveränitätsverständnis in den Europäischen Gemeinschaften als Rechtsproblem', in G. Ress (ed.), *Souveränitätsverständnis in den Europäischen Gemeinschaften*. Baden-Baden: Nomos.
Schmidt-Aßmann, E. (1996). 'Verwaltungskooperation und Verwaltungskooperationsrecht in der Europäischen Gemeinschaft', *Europarecht*, 31, 270–301.
Sydow, G. (2001). 'Die Vereinheitlichung des Mitgliedstaatlichen Vollzugs des Europarechts in Mehrstufigen Verwaltungsverfahren', *Die Verwaltung*. 517–42.

Sydow, G. (2003). 'Strukturen europäischer Planungsverfahren', *Die Öffentliche Verwaltung*, 56, 605–13.
Sydow, G. (2004). *Verwaltungskooperation in der Europäischen Union*. Tübingen: Mohr.
Töller, A.E. (2002). *Komitologie*. Opladen: Leske & Budrich.
Trondal, J. (2004). 'Re-Socialising Civil Servants: The Transformative Powers of EU Institutions', *Acta Politica International Journal of Political Science*, 39, 4–30.
Weiler, J.H.H. (1991). 'The Transformation of Europe', *Yale Law Journal*, 100, 2403–83.

Bureaucratic Change in the European Administrative Space: The Case of the European Commission

TIM BALINT, MICHAEL W. BAUER and CHRISTOPH KNILL

Compared to national bureaucracies, the supranational administration of the European Commission constitutes a rather young institution. As a result, the Commission has often been characterised as an 'adolescent bureaucracy', meaning that its structures, organisational practices and routines are still in an evolutionary stage and not yet completely institutionalised. Compared to national administrations, we should therefore expect a higher degree of malleability of the supranational bureaucracy and greater responsiveness to internal and external pressures for administrative reforms. This perspective, however, could easily be challenged by the fact that the Commission bureaucracy is rooted in institutional choices that date back to the foundation of the Community in the mid-1950s. Although the Commission in its current structure was only established in 1967, it is based on the merger of three organisations that were set up in the early days of the Community, namely the High Authority of the European Coal and Steel Community (established in 1952), the Commission of the European Economic Community and the Commission of the European Atomic Energy Community (both established in 1958). From this perspective, the Commission bureaucracy reflects an institution with a tradition of more than 50 years – a period of considerable length when compared to other institutions. Thus, the institutionalisation and consequent rigidity of supranational administrative structures and routines might be more pronounced than the picture of the 'adolescent bureaucracy' suggests. At the same time, we should expect more incremental patterns of administrative change along existing institutional paths rather than smooth responses to internal and external challenges or pressures such as performance crises, the global reform wave of the New Public Management, or respective demands from the member states.

Against the backdrop of these considerations, it is the central objective of this article to shed some light on patterns of administrative change within the European Commission. More specifically, we are interested in the following questions: (1) To what extent can we observe administrative change at the supranational level and to what extent are these changes characterised by a general trend or point in a specific direction? (2) How can the observed developments be understood? Are they simply the consequence of functional adaptation in light of internal challenges? Do they reflect immediate responses to administrative developments and respective preferences of the member states? Or can they be best interpreted as path-dependent adjustment?

To answer these questions, we do not limit our analysis to the investigation of persistence and change of administrative traditions at the Commission level. We pursue instead a more comprehensive approach, embedding and interpreting the Commission development in light of the administrative trends and reform developments that took place in what can be termed a European administrative space. This means that we do not exclusively focus on the Commission, but compare supranational administrative changes to respective developments in the public administrations of the member states of the European Union. This more encompassing comparative perspective provides an innovative scheme for the interpretation of the Commission's development in a broader context. In conducting our analysis, we concentrate on two central dimensions of administrative change. First, we analyse the nexus between the administrative and political spheres, i.e. the degree of politicisation of the supranational bureaucracy. Second, because a policy-oriented organisation such as the Commission depends largely on the quality of its personnel to realise its aims, we examine how issues of recruitment and career development are organised and have changed over time.

The paper is structured as follows. We first specify our research design and explain the selection of our indicators for measuring administrative change. In the next section, we present our empirical findings and compare the developments within the Commission to those within the broader European administrative space. The question of how these empirical developments might be interpreted in theoretical terms is addressed thereafter. We argue that none of the mechanisms commonly invoked to explain administrative change – functional adaptation, path dependency, isomorphism or policy windows – can convincingly account for the complete pattern and the magnitude of change that we observe in the case of the European Commission. While we see no convincing evidence for functional adaptation or path dependency at all, the concepts of isomorphism and policy windows appear to help explain at least parts of the empirical puzzle. In the concluding section, we discuss the general implications of our findings and outline promising approaches for future research.

Research Design and Method

To measure administrative change within the Commission and the broader administrative space, we compare the development of respective administrative arrangements in the EU member states over time. On this basis, we are not only able to identify if and to what extent administrative characteristics within the Commission have changed. It is also possible to assess whether these changes constitute moves towards institutionalised patterns and traditions in the member states (Dyson 1980; Knill 1998; Schnapp 2004). To measure such developments, we focus on two analytical dimensions that have been identified as important yardsticks for the distinction between different types of public administration systems (see Auer *et al.* 1996; Knill 1999, 2001; Peters and Pierre 2004; Schnapp 2004).

The first dimension draws on the distinction between open (position-based) systems and closed (career-based) civil service systems (Auer *et al.* 1996; OECD 2004). Patterns of an open system are typically found in countries associated with the Common Law or Scandinavian tradition of public administration; almost pure representatives of this model are the United Kingdom and Sweden (Bauer 2005; Schnapp 2004: 298). These countries adopted a career system that can be compared to the private sector (Bossaert *et al.* 2001: 87–96). It is based on the merit principle in order to find the best-suited candidate for each position. In the United Kingdom, for example, there exist no formal recruitment procedures for civil servants in the sense that 'departments and agencies are themselves responsible for organising staff recruitment with respect to timing, needs, requirements' (Bossaert *et al.* 2001: 92). Moreover, in an open career system salary depends upon duty and not merely on years of service and formal rank, as is the case in the closed system. If the United Kingdom and Sweden are usually referred to as ideal types of open systems, Germany and France represent civil services of the more closed Continental tradition (OECD 2004). Table 1 lists the indicators we use to measure the degree of openness of the recruitment and career system in the member states and the European Commission. The assignment of 'yes' and 'no' to the two different systems was done in accordance with previous studies (Auer *et al.* 1996; Bossaert *et al.* 2001; Schnapp 2004). To calculate an additive index, we coded an indicator of an open system with '1', while a value of '0' is assigned if the characteristics of a closed system are given.

The second dimension under study refers to the degree of politicisation of the higher management within a civil service. Following the pertinent literature, we define politicisation broadly as the level of 'substitution of political criteria for merit-based criteria in the selection, retention, promotion, rewards, and disciplining of members of the public service' (Peters and Pierre 2004: 2). In this regard, the appointment procedure for senior staff and the use of political-administrative structures created to provide government control over bureaucracy are crucial (Bekke and van der Meer 2003: 281–282). Again, we can distinguish between two major groups of countries that differ in this respect. In the Continental countries, such as France, Belgium and Greece, ministers have so-called cabinets at their disposal that ensure the political control of the bureaucracy and coordinate the ongoing work of the service (Page and Wright 1999; Peters and Pierre 2004). In Germany, the same functions are fulfilled by deputy ministers and personal advisors. By contrast, in the United Kingdom and the Scandinavian systems we find a stricter separation between politics and administration. The advisers of the ministers have no formal role in the bureaucracy, and ministers normally abstain from interfering in appointment processes according to inherited norms of appropriateness (Knill 1999, 2001; Page and Wouters 1995: 200).

TABLE 1
INDICATORS MEASURING THE OPENNESS OF RECRUITMENT AND CAREER SYSTEMS

Indicators	Open system	Closed system
Recruitment only to entry level	no (1)	yes (0)
Specific diplomas needed for specific career	no (1)	yes (0)
Probationary period for beginners	no (1)	yes (0)
Formal recruitment procedures	no (1)	yes (0)
Maximum age limits in recruitment	no (1)	yes (0)
Recognition of professional experience outside the public sector	yes (1)	no (0)
Public advertisement of jobs	no (1)	yes (0)
Life-long employment/tenure	no (1)	yes (0)
Statutory remuneration scheme	no (1)	yes (0)
Set progression in pay	no (1)	yes (0)
Performance-related pay	yes (1)	no (0)
Seniority system for promotion	no (1)	yes (0)
Specific regulations for labour negotiations	no (1)	yes (0)

Source: own specification on the basis of Auer *et al.* (1996) and Schnapp (2004: 145).

Table 2 shows the indicators for measuring the degree of politicisation in the European Commission and the EU member states. In this context, we take into account the fact that in the national systems, politicisation primarily emerges from party politics. In the Commission, by contrast, this pattern is substituted by nationality cleavages. Once again, we calculate an additive index assigning '0' to low or no politicisation and '1' to high politicisation.

To analyse administrative changes over time, we have compiled values for our indicators at the beginning of the 1980s and the beginning of the 2000s. The selection of the time period is based on the objective of covering the potential impact of different EU enlargements on administrative change at the Commission level. While there is general consensus in the literature that the Commission bureaucracy was strongly influenced by the Continental administrative traditions of the founding members of the EU (especially France and Germany), the 1973 enlargement led to a considerable increase in administrative heterogeneity in the EU administrative space. This can be traced to the fact that the then new members (United Kingdom, Ireland and Denmark) belong to 'administrative families' that are quite different from the Continental model (Peters 2003). Focusing on administrative arrangements of the Commission several years after this enlargement can thus reveal the extent to which the increasing administrative variety of the member states is reflected in the supranational bureaucracy. The analysis of the current status quo thus provides the opportunity to study the potential effects of further enlargement rounds during the 1980s and 1990s and hence the increasing heterogeneity within the EU administrative space.

TABLE 2
INDICATORS MEASURING THE LEVEL OF POLITICISATION

Indicators	Low	High
Senior staff is usually recruited from the administration itself	yes (0)	no (1)
Senior staff is recruited through formal procedures prior to the appointment	yes (0)	no (1)
Senior staff can be dismissed by the minister without cause	no (0)	yes (1)
Senior staff can be replaced when the government changes	no (0)	yes (1)
The incumbent minister can appoint senior staff	no (0)	yes (1)
A formalised cabinet system exists	no (0)	yes (1)
The appointment of cabinet staff is formalised	yes (0)	no (1)

Source: own specification based on Auer et al. (1996) and Schnapp (2004: 149).
Notes: Data on the member states are taken primarily from an index developed by Schnapp (2004) and were partially supplemented (Auer et al. 1996; Bossaert et al. 2001; Millar and McKevitt 1999; Nies-Berchem 1992; OECD 1996, 2004; Page and Wright 1999; Pollitt and Bouckaert 2004). For reasons of their rather recent accession, we excluded from our sample the member states that joined the EU in 2004 and 2007. Data on the European Commission is based on our own empirical investigations covering the administrative changes as triggered by the recent Kinnock reforms up to 2006 (Bauer 2006, 2007b; European Commission 2004a, 2004b; Knill and Balint 2008).

The Commission between De-politicisation and Aperture of Recruitment and Career

Based on the indexes introduced in the previous section, we are able to assess the characteristics of a public administration in two dimensions. Figure 1 is a 'snapshot' of the early 1980s showing the position of the public administrations of the then nine EU member states and the European Commission. Due to the additive logic of the indexes, a value of '13' on the horizontal axis corresponds to full openness of the recruitment and career system. In a similar vein, a value of '7' on the vertical axis corresponds to the maximum level of politicisation of an administrative system.

Figure 1 shows that the European Commission is almost perfectly aligned with its supposed public administration 'parent model' France. The only odd-man-out from the founding members is the Netherlands, which phased out its career-based system in 1982 (Demmke 2005: 105–107). The United Kingdom, Ireland and Denmark – all joined the EU in 1973 – enriched the European administrative space with a quite open recruitment and career system and an institutionalised separation of politics and administration. Nevertheless, the administrative features of the European Commission in the 1980s remained similar to patterns of the early Commission administration (see for an overview Heyen 1992). Since 1961, a set of staff regulations (the Statute) has determined the recruitment and career of the Commission's civil servants (Stevens and Stevens 2006: 455). These regulations define the rights and obligations of officials, underscoring the privileged position of civil servants as guardians of European interests. In

FIGURE 1
ADMINISTRATIVE PATTERNS IN THE EU-9 AND THE EUROPEAN COMMISSION
(IN THE EARLY 1980s)

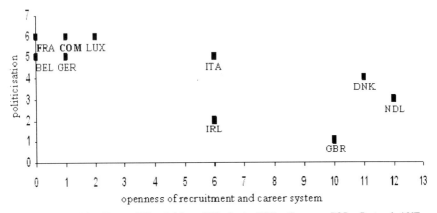

GRC = Greece, FRA = France, BEL = Belgium, ESP = Spain, GER = Germany, POR = Portugal, AUT = Austria, LUX = Luxemburg, COM = European Commission, IRL = Ireland, DNK = Denmark, ITA = Italy, NDL = the Netherlands, FIN = Finland, GBR = Great Britain, SWE = Sweden.
Source: own illustration.

the founding years, the formalisation of recruitment and career was understood as a crucial step towards safeguarding the independence of the emerging European civil service and as a commitment of the six founding members to the supranational nature of the 'European project' (Coombes 1970: 140).

Entry into the European civil service usually took place at the first grade, and the recruited civil servants received life tenure with set progression in payment (Coombes 1970; Getz and Jüttner 1972; Rogalla 1973; Scheinmann 1966; Scheinmann and Feld 1972; Stevens and Stevens 2001). Moreover, the French method of recruiting civil servants (also used in Belgium and Italy) – the concours system – was adopted. It is based on a competitive entry examination with prior public advertisement in order to choose the best-suited candidates. Furthermore, age limits (candidates had to be younger than 45) as well as a probationary period of six months for every civil servant (apart from the senior staff) were specified (Getz and Jüttner 1972: 130).

The career structure was based on strictly segregated functional categories (A, B, C, D), being nearly totally impermeable (Coombes 1970: 138–141; Stevens and Stevens 2001). Similar to the German and French custom, specific diplomas and educational achievements served as entry criteria for a particular career track and were valued more highly than professional experience or specific skills (Rogalla 1973: 333). To join category A, the candidate needed a university degree, and for category D at least several years of high school were required. The categories were divided into eight grades with two to eight seniority steps, respectively. Possible promotions were restricted to narrow ranges (Coombes 1970: 138–141). As a consequence, most officials reached the highest grade after 15 to 20 years of service, i.e. on average 15 years before their retirement (Stevens and Stevens 2001: 98). The deficiencies of the promotion and appraisal system had been emphasised already in the Spierenburg report of 1979, but until recently, seniority, good connections to senior managers and nationality continued to carry more weight than individual performance with regard to promotions (Davies 2002: 178; Spence 1997: 75). Finally, the statutory remuneration scheme was fixed by the budget of the European Communities and the 'method of annual salary adjustments' that linked the salaries of European civil servants automatically to the development of the respective salaries in the member states (Stevens and Stevens 2001: 48).

The closed patterns of recruitment and career coincided with a high degree of politicisation within the Commission bureaucracy. In the 1980s, the recruitment and selection of senior staff was poorly formalised and heavily influenced by individual Commissioners, cabinets and member states (Lequesne 1996: 405; Rogalla 1973: 338). The staff regulations even foresaw the possibility of initiating 'a procedure other than the competition procedure', thus giving the Commissioner a high degree of discretion when making appointments to his DG (Coombes 1970: 157; Stevens and Stevens 2001: 82–84). Directors-General could be replaced 'in the interests of service', i.e. they were forced into early retirement if they did not get along with the Commissioner. Furthermore, the member states intervened in the selection procedure by parcelling out the positions among each other in a process of 'horse trading' (Michelmann 1978: 23). Although an official quota system had not been introduced, member states typically tried to ensure a high representation of their compatriots by influencing the appointment procedure in their 'inherited' Directorates-General (Cini 1996). As a consequence of the high level of politicisation, the positions of Directors and Directors-General were not considered to be an achievable step in the career of European civil servants under normal circumstances (Coombes 1970: 146; Stevens and Stevens 2001: 74).

By contrast, the members of the Commissioners' cabinets had the best chances of getting quick promotion or circumventing ('parachuting') the standardised selection procedure for normal officials (Stevens and Stevens 2001). They had a formalised rank in the administration and became 'the centre of a complex web of policy pressures, negotiations and package deals and an indispensable part of the policy-making process in the European Community' (Ritchie 1992: 106). Early on, Walter Hallstein, the first President of the Commission of the EEC, saw the danger of a politicised European civil service because both the Commissioners and the member states used the cabinets as instruments to push through their interests (Cassese and della Cananea 1992: 94). A Commissioner could appoint more than six cabinet members, and only one cabinet member was required to come from a country different from that of the Commissioner (Donelly and Ritchie 1997: 43–45). 'Any dominance of single nations in the policy process is more possible in the College of Commissioners itself than in the civil service, since the *cabinets* are dominated by members from the commissioner's home state' (Page 1997: 136). In a nutshell, the nexus between politics and administration in the European Commission was quite firm, and the Commission thus scores high on the politicisation axis.

Twenty years later, we observe profound changes in the Commission administration. Figure 2 shows that the European Commission has departed considerably from its Franco-German parent models. While patterns of recruitment and career have remained rather stable in these countries, the Commission has made a clear move towards an open career system. The changes on the politicisation dimension are even more evident. The arrangements in the Commission are now much closer to the United Kingdom and the Scandinavian countries. This is even more significant since the French and German parent models are just as or even more politicised than in the early 1980s.

The composition of the administrative space in the EU-15 suggests that the EU is indeed characterised by two distinctive groups of public administration models, with one group clustered around the right end of the horizontal axis (including primarily Scandinavian and Anglo-Saxon models) and the other located at the left top of the vertical axis (comprising countries

FIGURE 2
ADMINISTRATIVE PATTERNS IN THE EU-15 AND THE EUROPEAN COMMISSION
(POST-KINNOCK AND BEFORE 2004 ENLARGEMENT)

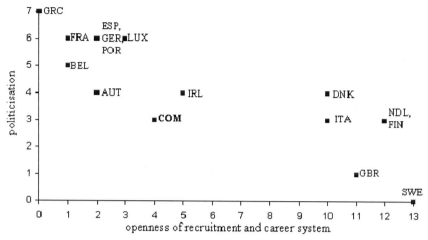

GRC = Greece, FRA = France, BEL = Belgium, ESP = Spain, GER = Germany, POR = Portugal, AUT = Austria, LUX = Luxemburg, COM = European Commission, IRL = Ireland, DNK = Denmark, ITA = Italy, NDL = the Netherlands, FIN = Finland, GBR = Great Britain, SWE = Sweden.
Source: own illustration.

with Napoleonic and German traditions). Exceptions hold for the Netherlands, Italy and Ireland. As mentioned above, the Netherlands had opened up its recruitment and career system in the 1980s. Italy, generally seen as a representative of the Napoleonic tradition, has moved considerably towards de-politicisation as well as openness of the career system of the civil service since the massive political crisis in the 1990s (Kickert 2007: 37–48). Ireland represents the third exception. The politicisation of the Irish civil service generally departs from the Common Law ideal type (see Millar and McKevitt 2003). Notwithstanding these exceptions, our two-dimensional classification still fits very well with the overall assignment of EU member states to specific administrative traditions. Although all EU member states have reformed their public administration in certain – and sometimes profound – ways (see OECD 2005; Pollitt and Bouckaert 2004), reforms did not imply a complete departure from the pre-existing administrative traditions, nor did the reform developments lead to an overall convergence of civil service systems (see Pollitt *et al.* 2007).

Against this backdrop, the patterns observed in the European Commission constitute a rather exceptional case. The Commission has clearly departed from its Continental roots and – for both administrative dimensions under study – has moved somewhere in between the positions of the Continental and Anglo-Saxon/Scandinavian models.

Regarding the recruitment and career system, the move towards a more open approach first becomes apparent with the ending of the maximum recruitment age. Initially, the reform advocates within the Commission as well as the President of the European Parliament sought to maintain this entry criterion for the European civil service (see European Ombudsman 2002). In the context of the Commission reform, however, a joint recruitment office was set up that is responsible for the selection of candidates for all European institutions, including the Council, Parliament, and the Committee of the Regions, as well as the office of the European Ombudsman. Here, the veteran ombudsman Jacob Söderman refused to sign the regulation that would make the European Personnel Selection Office (EPSO), the new common recruitment office, operational. His major critique was that age limits were discriminatory and contradicted the EU's own life-long learning and ageing policies. 'An own-initiative inquiry by the Ombudsman has shown that more modern bodies such as the European Central Bank, Europol and most of the executive agencies have never used age limits. Perhaps this is because they never formed part of the old-fashioned traditional administrative culture, which is proving so resistant to change' (European Ombudsman 2002). Eventually, Jacob Södermann got his way, and the age limit was abolished.

Two other important administrative changes concerned aspects of the career structure and the linkage of promotion to the individual performance of civil servants (Bauer 2006). With the new staff regulations, the European Commission abolished its rigid career structure by reducing the former four categories to two, namely Administrators (AD) and Assistants (AST). The new system contains 16 grades, each having five seniority steps (European Commission 2004b). The career system is now more permeable, with enhanced opportunities for horizontal differentiation (at the same grade) and many more merit-based promotions than before. Promotion itself occurs automatically if the individual has attained a certain number of merit points (annually distributed from a fixed pool by its Head of Unit and the Director-General). European civil servants are now unlikely to reach 'fin de carrière' long before reaching their retirement age (Knill and Balint 2008). The seniority principle is still important, but the salary increase now proceeds digressively and is even frozen after five consecutive seniority steps without prior promotion.

As is typically the case in closed recruitment and career systems, remuneration is statutory but in practice negotiated by the government, the public employers and the staff unions (Bossaert *et al.* 2001: 152). Whereas the 1980s were characterised by various pay disputes between member states, Commissioners and staff unions, the integration of the 'method of annual salary adjustments' into the staff regulations valid until 2013 avoids yearly negotiations and ensure social peace (Ahrens 2004: 447). Furthermore, the European Commission increased the probationary period from six to nine months and also extended it to the recruitment of senior staff (European Commission 2004b).

By contrast, the other features of the recruitment and career system have remained unchanged. Entry into the civil service still takes place at the first grade, and the category AD is only open to applicants possessing a university degree. The recruitment procedure in the European Commission is still based on a highly formalised approach; specific professional experience and skills are still of minor importance. All permanent Commission staff are recruited through open competitions that are publicly advertised and published in the *Official Journal* of the European Union. Finally, the officials are employed on a lifelong basis and receive no performance-related pay.

While the changes related to the openness of the recruitment and career system can still be characterised as relatively modest, the nexus between politics and administration has changed more profoundly. To be sure, the Commissioners still have the authority to appoint Directors-General and Directors, and informally there is the exit option for Directors-General in terms of 'voluntary' early retirement (Wille 2007: 44). However, Commissioners have lost discretionary power since the positions of higher management undergo a formalised selection procedure in which the Consultative Committees of Appointments (CCA) plays a crucial role in evaluating the quality of the candidates (European Commission 2004a). The CCA serves as the 'interviewing and evaluation board' and prepares a shortlist of candidates from which the Commissioner may choose. The CCA tries to avoid unbalanced representation of certain nationalities. In the case of appointment procedures for Directors-General, the CCA is now composed of the Secretary-General, the Director-General for Personnel and Administration, the Head of Cabinet of the President, the Head of Cabinet of the Commissioner for Personnel and Administration, the Permanent Rapporteur, the Rapporteur for the case and supporting actors. The Permanent Rapporteurs and the supporting actors are specialists in human resource management techniques and are responsible for making objective recommendations. At the same time, neither cabinets nor national governments seem to have much real influence over the selection procedure (Egeberg 2006: 39–41).

For senior staff coming from new member states or for external candidates, the European Commission has introduced an additional layer in the selection procedure which is quite commonly applied in the private sector: the 'assessment centre method'. Here, candidates are subject to one-day tests and examinations in order to assess through the use of sophisticated tools whether they have the generic competencies to become senior managers and whether they have the sense of leadership and communication (European Commission 2004a: 3). At the end of the selection procedure, the CCA sets up a shortlist of candidates (sometimes these are even ranked), which are recommended to the appointing Commissioner. The Commissioner is not obliged to choose a candidate from the shortlist, but, as shown by empirical studies, he/she generally accepts about 95 per cent of the proposed candidates (Egeberg 2006: 38).

A large majority of Directors-General are now appointed from within the European Commission (Wille 2007: 41). There is evidence that the positions of Directors and Directors-General increasingly constitute a potential step in an administrative career track. As a general rule, a Director-General should not have the same nationality as his/her Commissioner, nor should the distribution of nationalities in one Directorate constitute national clusters of senior officials (Peterson 2004: 26; Spence 2006: 143). National influence is also diminished by the new compulsory job rotation policy introduced in 1999 (European Commission 2004a). Directors and Directors-General have to move to another post after at least five to seven years.

While the formalised cabinet system and its influence on the establishment of informal policy networks still exist, potential channels for transmitting national interests were greatly restricted by formalising the appointment of cabinet members. As one of his first actions in office, the then Commission President Romano Prodi decided that at least three nationalities had to be represented in the six-headed cabinet (Nugent 2001: 121; Spence and Stevens 2006: 175). Furthermore, the positions of *Chef du Cabinet* and Director-General should be filled with nationalities different from that of the respective Commissioner.

Explaining Administrative Change inside the Commission

Based on our indicators, we find substantial administrative change inside the European Commission. In 2004, the relationships between higher management and Commissioners were considerably less politicised, and the career system had become more open than 20 years before. However, compared to the developments in the member states, administrative change at the supranational level can hardly be interpreted as the product of a general trend within the emerging European administrative space. When focusing on the EU-9 – apart from a few exceptions – national public administrations remain fairly stable; according to our indicators, member states have hardly changed their positions over time. By contrast, the European Commission is the public administration in the sample that changed most significantly. How can this development be explained? To answer these questions, we will examine theories developed in organisation sociology and public sector reform in more detail. We argue that the observed developments cannot be fully understood from perspectives that emphasise functional adaptation or institutional path-dependency. To understand both the direction and timing of the administrative changes, we must rely instead on a combination of theories of institutional isomorphism and Kingdon's (1984) policy windows.

Functional Adaptation

According to the perspective of functional efficiency, organisations adjust their structures and routines in light of new challenges and problems. From this perspective, administrative changes are primarily problem-driven; the emergence of new tasks, performance crises or the perception of functional inefficiencies should trigger respective organisational adjustments in order to cope with these challenges (March and Olsen 1989, 1995). The mechanism behind this explanation for change is functional adaptation. As needs and tasks change or new challenges emerge, organisations react in a deliberate and conscious way to fulfil their changing duties and live up to new expectations.

If the mechanism accounting for administrative change in the European Commission were functional adaptation, we would be able to link the observable reforms to new challenges. In the case of the Commission, two potential challenges can be identified. The first refers to the strong expansion of the Commission's tasks and duties caused by the intensifying and deepening of the European integration process over the years. The second – and related – challenge emerges from a vast and growing 'management gap' in the Commission, resulting from the lack of organisational adjustments needed to manage the increasing level of integration reached by the European Union (Metcalfe 1992).

These challenges and problems, however, did not result in respective administrative changes. It is thus highly unlikely that functional adaptation has been driving administrative change in the Commission. First, empirical findings show that there was a peak of activity towards the end of the 1980s and the beginning of the 1990s – usually related to the programme of completing the Single Market and the successful years of the Commission presidency under Jacques Delors (see Figure 3). Administrative changes, however, occurred more than ten years later rather than parallel to – or even prior to – the peak of the task expansion.

Second, a similar argument can be made with regard to the internal organisational needs of the Commission. It has been known since the end of the 1970s, i.e. roughly since the Spierenburg report, that the Commission's organisation is haunted by a number of grave organisational deficits, which

FIGURE 3
COUNCIL OUTPUT – REGULATIONS AND DIRECTIVES

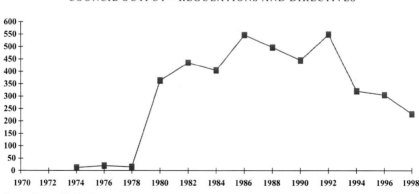

Source: Bauer (2001: 49).

resulted mainly from the unstructured merger of the three forerunner organisations in 1967 and the organisational expansion since that time.

There is no discernible connection between attempts at administrative reform and windows of opportunity in terms of grand constitutional bargains (see Figure 4). Reform attempts and organisational challenges are completely disconnected. For example, task expansion peaked under Jacques Delors while in terms of administrative change his presidency was very passive, almost consciously disengaged (Bauer 2007a). In sum, there is no evidence that supports an interpretation of administrative change in the Commission as functional adaptation to organisational challenges. Given the large time lag between the emergence of new demands and internal response, functional adaptation does not appear to explain much about the observed patterns of administrative change.

Institutional Path Dependency

The lack of an immediate and swift response to increasing problems points to the need for a more differentiated theoretical perspective that takes into account the role of institutional factors. According to the theories of the new institutionalism (Hall and Taylor 1996), institutions matter. Existing institutional arrangements influence not only the strategic opportunities of the actors involved, but also shape the preferences and ideas of these actors (March and Olsen 1989; Thelen and Steinmo 1992). As a result, institutions are generally expected to be rather autonomous with respect to responding to emerging challenges; respective adjustments should follow an incremental logic of change along trajectories or paths that are determined by earlier institutional choices.

FIGURE 4
ATTEMPTS AT ORGANISATIONAL REFORM AND TASK EXPANSION IN THE COMMISSION

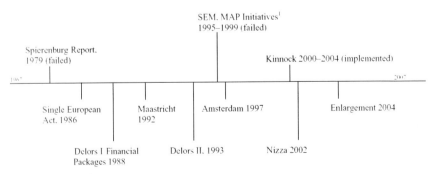

Source: own illustration.
Note: [1]The acronyms stand for Sound and Efficient Management and Modernisation of the Personnel and Administration Policy of the Commission, see Bauer (2001).

Accordingly, we would expect the Commission's administration to change alongside and in harmony with those traditions and models that gave rise to its very inception. There are two crucial empirical implications that would be discernible if organisational change within the Commission could be explained by the concept of path dependence. First, we would expect a rather low level of change. In addition, change would follow the original 'path' chosen when the Commission was created. Second, given that the initial administrative arrangements of the Commission were based on a melange of its French and German parent models, a path dependent logic would imply that administrative changes in the Commission occur within the same development corridor that could be observed for the parent models.

The comparison between Figures 1 and 2 suggests, however, that both expectations are not borne out by our data. First, compared to the 1980s, current administrative arrangements in the Commission clearly departed from the German or French developments. Moreover, the administrative changes in the Commission occurred on a scale that can hardly be classified as incremental.[1] The argument that path dependency does not solve our empirical puzzle is also supported by the fact that the Commission clearly moves in the direction of the Anglo-Scandinavian position, while the arrangements for its French and German parent models have remained stable over time. Although the Commission's position remains somewhere in the middle between the Continental and Anglo-Scandinavian poles, the magnitude and direction of change appear to be so substantial and obvious that it would be reasonable to reject a theoretical explanation based on institutional path dependency.

Institutional Isomorphism

In contrast to the theories analysed so far, the framework of institutional isomorphism places particular emphasis on the explanation of administrative changes as a result of developments in the organisational environment. This framework has been applied in order to account for phenomena of international spreading and diffusion of policy innovations and reform concepts, not least with regard to public sector reforms (DiMaggio and Powell 1991; Knill and Balint 2008; Levi-Faur 2002; Meyer and Rowan 1977; Meyer *et al.* 1997). The central argument advanced by DiMaggio and Powell is that legitimacy rather than functional efficiency is the major driving force of organisational change. To increase their legitimacy and ensure their persistence, organisations embrace rules, norms and routines that are widely valued in their organisational environment.

Hence, organisational change is essentially driven by external developments rather than by intra-organisational concerns about the organisation's efficiency. DiMaggio and Powell identify three mechanisms which drive isomorphic organisational change, namely coercive, mimetic and normative isomorphism. An important driving force of isomorphic organisational change emerges from coercion. Organisations adjust their structures and procedures in line with organisations on which they are financially or legally dependent (DiMaggio and Powell 1991: 74). However, organisational adjustment to the environment takes place not only as a result of coercive pressures but may also occur in constellations of high uncertainty, e.g. ambiguous goals, uncertain means–end relations or the confrontation of new problems. In such constellations, it is argued, organisations imitate the structures of other organisations which they perceive to be particularly successful. Instead of a time-consuming search for their own solutions to existing problems, organisations strive to ensure their legitimacy through emulation (DiMaggio and Powell 1991: 75; Guler *et al.* 2002: 213). Another mechanism driving isomorphic organisational change is based on similar dominant normative orientations and beliefs of staff members. In this context, the impact of similar professional backgrounds and the role of professional organisations and epistemic communities (Haas 1992) in spreading common understandings and perceptions of policy problems and solutions are emphasised in particular in the literature (Hasse and Krücken 2005: 26).

While our research design does not allow for a sound assessment of the relevance of the different mechanisms for the administrative changes in the Commission, it seems highly plausible to assume that isomorphic mechanisms might have played a role in this case. Coercive changes, for instance, could have emerged from respective pressures of the member states on which the Commission depends financially. According to this logic, the Commission is likely to adapt to the (anticipated) preferences and administrative practices of its member states. At the same time, the Commission might have incentives for emulating successful reforms in the member states, given the high uncertainty emerging from the unprecedented challenges of recent enlargements and deepening integration. Finally, there are good reasons to assume potential effects of normative isomorphism due to the emergence of a European administrative space which is characterised by intensified linkages and exchange among domestic and supranational administrations.

As already mentioned, institutional isomorphism predicts the adoption of such models that are highly valued or dominant in the organisational environment. This implies that isomorphic change requires a certain degree of homogeneity of the environment. In contrast, no clear predications are possible when a high degree of heterogeneity is present. The latter scenario of competing models, however, is given with regard to the administrative space in which the Commission is located. While this space in the early days of the Community was still characterised by the dominance of a Continental administrative tradition, the subsequent enlargement rounds contributed to considerably greater heterogeneity. It is thus hardly possible to identify dominant models of administrative arrangements and structures which might have served as a blueprint for the Commission reforms.

This conclusion, however, does not mean that institutional isomorphism does not constitute a promising framework for our case. Rather, the analysis of the Commission reforms against the background of a heterogeneous environment might serve as a starting point for refining this approach. The reason for this lies in the interesting way the Commission copes with the diversity of its organisational environment. A comparison of Figures 1 and 2 strikingly illustrates that the Commission has moved over time to a position between the two poles of the Continental and Anglo-Scandinavian administrative systems. In other words, the Commission may have increased its legitimacy by adopting a balanced position between these poles rather than simply adopting one of the two dominant approaches. The robustness of this pattern is underscored by the fact that the pattern holds for both dimensions of administrative change (career and recruitment as well as politicisation), although these dimensions encompass rather diverse characteristics. The argument is further supported by the fact that internal changes at the domestic level are unlikely to have had a major impact because, with respect to our indicators, most member states have remained fairly stable over time; hence there has been no dynamic for this source of change. The major discernible dynamic between Figures 1 and 2 emerges from enlargement, i.e. the proliferation of new member states from an administrative tradition distinct from that of the founding members and from the European Commission during the 1980s.

The Impact of Policy Windows

While institutional isomorphism provides a promising framework for understanding the observed patterns of administrative change in the Commission, its central weakness is the neglect of the process dimension. Institutional isomorphism helps us to understand the direction of administrative reforms, but tells us little about the factors that actually led to the adoption of the changes at a certain point of time. Why did the reforms of the Commission only take place very recently, while enlargements and the consequent increase in heterogeneity in the EU administrative space took place many years before?

We argue that the framework of policy windows as developed by Kingdon (1984) or the garbage can model (Cohen *et al.* 1972) constitute useful approaches to answering this question. As argued by Kingdon (1984), the chance to set reforms successfully on the political agenda depends on the specific constellation of problems, solutions and processes which are needed for opening the famous policy window. In the case of the Commission reforms, administrative problems had been identified and spelled out continuously from the late 1970s and onwards. As shown in Figure 4, until the Kinnock reform several reform attempts had been undertaken, all of which failed (Bauer 2007b). At the same time, there was no shortage of potential solutions. They were developed not only inside the Commission. Their numbers grew constantly through the enrichment of the EU administrative space in successive enlargement rounds. In addition, the global reform wave of New Public Management offered a large tool box for resolving administrative problems. This process of international diffusion was fuelled to a considerable extent by the communication activities of international organisations, such as the OECD or the World Bank in the early 1990s (Hood 1995; Lægreid 2002). Notwithstanding these developments, administrative reforms in the Commission only took place very recently.

This phenomenon can be explained through a closer look at the process dimension. The fundamental political crisis of the Commission, which was triggered by highly politicised problems of corruption and fraud, considerably increased the need for political action. The Commission was under enormous pressure to demonstrate its willingness to cope with these problems. Moreover, this fundamental challenge greatly reduced the possibility for reform opponents to veto respective changes. In calibrating these reforms, however, the Commission looked at solutions that had already been developed elsewhere (i.e. the garbage can) rather than going through an ideal-type rational process of problem analysis, search for solutions, evaluation of solutions and finally adoption of the best alternative (Committee of Independent Experts 1999; Schön-Quinlivan 2007). The political crisis thus provided the basis for linking problems and solutions that had been identified long before (Bauer 2001, 2002; Metcalfe 2000). Through this approach, we can understand the timing of administrative reforms whose eventual adoption was not based on a rationalist process, but required an accidental trigger in the form of the Santer resignation crisis (Peterson 1999; Ringe 2005).

Conclusion

In this article we presented data on two administrative dimensions characterising the European Commission, namely the degree of the politicisation of its higher management and the degree of openness of its career system. In a two-dimensional space comprised of these two features, we estimated the position of the Commission in the early 1980s and in the early 2000s. In addition, we compared the position of the Commission at these two points in time with the positions of the respective member states. The data shows that the Commission started from a position close to the Continental model of public administration and over time partially moved towards the Anglo-Saxon and Scandinavian models. The change of position by the Commission is striking insofar as the position of most member states in the two-dimensional space remained stable, i.e. they did not depart from well-established administrative arrangements (Pollitt and Bouckaert 2004).

As space and data availability did not allow for painting a complete picture of the Commission bureaucracy, our results have to be interpreted carefully. Although we applied established categories from the field of comparative public administration, we do not claim to depict the full range of possible changes the public administrations in our sample may have experienced. Our results should thus not be misread as claiming that national public administrations which appear 'stable' in our dimensions would not have changed at all. Indeed, the purpose of this article was not to find out why (or why not) national administrations do change but whether and why the European Commission does change in accordance with, or in contrast to, those member state administrations which taken together make up a European administrative space.

To settle this question we explored four explanatory mechanisms of organisational change. Taken individually, none of the four concepts – functional adaptation, institutional path dependency, isomorphism or policy windows – could convincingly account for the pattern of administrative change within the Commission as displayed by our data. However, while none of these concepts explains everything, some solve parts of the empirical puzzle better than others. While we find little evidence for functional adaptation or path dependency, isomorphism and policy windows appear more promising. More precisely, if one takes into account the fact that – due to various rounds of enlargements – there is no longer a single dominant administrative standard but a competition between the Continental, Anglo-Saxon and Scandinavian models, isomorphism is able to specify the direction of the change we would expect the Commission to engage in. Legitimacy pressure from two peer groups makes it plausible that the Commission seeks a central position in between without fully embracing either way of doing things. Moreover, the long-term stability – some would call it managerial stagnation – that is characteristic of the development of the Commission's administration, which is disrupted by a substantial change triggered by some chance event, accurately describes the logic of a policy window as developed by Kingdon (1984). In other words, the Commission's fixation on the Continental model despite the emergence of a new centre of gravity with the increasingly strengthened Anglo-Scandinavian camp is part of the 'normal' irrationality of inter-organisational change in the public sphere.

We do not claim that bureaucratic change in the European administrative space can always or exclusively be explained by isomorphism and policy windows. But on the basis of our empirical observations, we suggest that these two concepts appear to be the most promising theoretical approaches researchers should address if they want to understand administrative change at the supranational level. In other words, our conclusion should be seen to open rather than to settle the theoretical discussion on bureaucratic change in the European administrative space.

In keeping with our argument, we expect that the future patterns of bureaucratic change in the European Commission will depend on the direction in which the public administrations of the new member states develop. Unlike the EU-15, we see the public administrations of most of the newcomers – especially those with a background of transition from communism – as still in search of an orientation (Hajnal 2003; König 2002; Randma-Liiv and Connaughton 2005). It is still an open question as to whether the majority will move towards the Continental model (which due to historical reasons lies closest to most of the newcomers) or towards the Anglo-Scandinavian model. If either the Continental or the Anglo-Scandinavian tradition becomes dominant, we expect that future changes in the Commission will converge with the direction taken by the model dominating at the time. If the European administrative space continues to be shaped by two competing models as equal centres of gravity, bureaucratic change should bring the European Commission to a central position between those two models – just as our empirical data showed with respect to recent change in the area of the politicisation of higher management and the openness of the European civil servants career system. These predictions, of course, are subject to further research.

Acknowledgement

An earlier version of this article was presented at the CONNEX Conference on 'Institutional Dynamics and the Transformation of Executive Politics in Europe', Barcelona, 7 to 9 June 2007. We are grateful to the participants of this conference and the anonymous referees of WEP for their valuable comments.

Note

1. Although admittedly the definition of incremental change is ill-specified in the literature on institutional path dependency; it is obviously difficult to empirically falsify the concept.

References

Ahrens, Gerlind (2004). 'Die Reform des EU-Beamtenstatuts – eine unendliche Geschichte vor dem Abschluss?', *Neue Zeitschrift für Verwaltungsrecht*, 23:4, 445–47.
Auer, Astrid, Christoph Demmke and Robert Polet (1996). *Civil Services in the Europe of Fifteen: Current Situation and Prospects*. Maastricht: EIPA.
Bauer, Michael W. (2001). *A Creeping Transformation? The European Commission and the Management of EU Structural Funds in Germany*. Dordrecht: Kluwer Academic Publishers.
Bauer, Michael W. (2002). 'Reforming the European Commission – A (Missed?) Academic Opportunity', *European Integration online Papers (EIoP)*, 6:8, available at http://eiop.or.at/eiop/texte/2002-008a.htm.
Bauer, Michael W. (2005). 'Damit ist ein Staat zu machen: Verwaltungsstudium in Ostmitteleuropa', *Osteuropa. Zeitschrift für Gegenwartsfragen des Ostens*, 55:11, 55–66.
Bauer, Michael W. (2006). 'Die Reform der Europäischen Kommission: Eine Studie zur Managementmodernisierung internationaler Organisationen', *Verwaltungsarchiv*, 97:3, 270–92.
Bauer, Michael W. (2007a). 'Introduction: Management Reforms in International Organizations', in Michael W. Bauer and Christoph Knill (eds.), *Management Reforms in International Organizations*. Baden-Baden: Nomos, 11–23.

Bauer, Michael W. (2007b). 'The Politics of Reforming the European Commission Administration', in Michael W. Bauer and Christoph Knill (eds.), *Management Reforms in International Organizations*.. Baden-Baden: Nomos, 51–69.

Bekke, Hans A.G.M., and Frits M. van der Meer (2003). 'West European Civil Service Systems: Variations and Similarities', in Hans A.G.M. Bekke and Frits M. van der Meer (eds.), *Civil Service Systems in Western Europe*. Cheltenham/Northampton: Edward Elgar, 275–90.

Bossaert, Danielle, Christoph Demmke, Koen Nomden and Robert Polet (2001). *Civil Services in the Europe of Fifteen. Trends and New Developments*. Maastricht: European Institute of Public Administration.

Cassese, Sabino, and Giacinto della Cananea (1992). 'The Commission of the European Economic Community: The Administrative Ramifications of its Political Development (1957–1967)', in Erk V. Heyen (ed.), *Early European Community Administration. Yearbook of European Administrative History 4*. Baden-Baden: Nomos, 75–94.

Cini, Michelle (1996). *The European Commission. Leadership, Organisation and Culture in the EU Administration*. Manchester: Manchester University Press.

Cohen, Michael D., James G. March and Johan P. Olsen (1972). 'A Garbage Can Model of Organizational Choice', *Administrative Science Quarterly*, 17:1, 1–25.

Committee of Independent Experts (1999). Second report on reform of the Commission: Analysis of current practice and proposals for tackling mismanagement, irregularities and fraud: 10 September 1999, available at http://www.europarl.europa.eu/experts/default_en.htm.

Coombes, David (1970). *Politics and Bureaucracy in the European Community. A Portrait of the Commission of the EEC*. London: Allen & Unwin.

Davies, Michael D.V. (2002). *The Administration of International Organizations: Top Down and Bottom Up*. Aldershot: Ashgate.

Demmke, Christoph (2005). *Die europäischen öffentlichen Dienste zwischen Tradition und Reform*. Maastricht: European Institute of Public Administration.

DiMaggio, Paul J., and Walter W. Powell (1991). 'The Iron Cage Revisited: Institutional Isomorphism and Collective Rationality in Organizational Fields', in Walter W. Powell, and Paul J. DiMaggio (eds.), *The New Institutionalism in Organizational Analysis*. Chicago: University of Chicago Press, 63–82.

Donelly, Martin, and Ella Ritchie (1997). 'The College of Commissioners and their Cabinets', in Geoffrey Edwards and David Spence (eds.), *The European Commission*. London: Cartermill, 33–67.

Dyson, Kenneth H.F. (1980). *The State Tradition in Western Europe. A Study of an Idea and Institution*. Oxford: Robertson.

Egeberg, Morten (2006). 'Balancing Autonomy and Accountability: Enduring Tensions in the European Commission's Development', in Morten Egeberg (ed.), *Multilevel Union Administration. The Transformation of Executive Politics in Europe*. Basingstoke: Palgrave, 31–50.

European Commission (2004a). *Document synoptique sur la politique concernant les fonctionnaires d'encadrement superieur. Communication de M. Kinnock*, available at http://ec.europa.eu/reform/pdf/SEC_2004_1352-2.pdf.

European Commission (2004b). *Reforming the Commission. An Administration at the Service of Half a Billion Europeans*, available at http://ec.europa.eu/reform/2002/index_en.htm.

European Ombudsman (2002). Press releases concerning the abolishment of maximum age limits, available at http://www.ombudsman.europa.eu/age/en/default.htm.

Getz, Heinrich, and Heinrich Jüttner (1972). *Personal in internationalen Organisationen*. Baden-Baden: Nomos Verlagsgesellschaft.

Guler, Isin, Mauro F. Guillén and John M. Macpherson (2002). 'Global Competition, Institutions and the Diffusion of Organizational Practices. The International Spread of ISO 9000 Quality Certificates', *Administrative Science Quarterly*, 47, 207–33.

Haas, Peter M. (1992). 'Introduction: Epistemic Communities and International Policy Coordination', *International Organization*, 46:1, 1–36.

Hajnal, György (2003). 'Diversity and Convergence: A Quantitative Analysis of European Public Administration Education Programs', *Journal of Public Affairs Education*, 9:4, 245–58.

Hall, Peter A., and Rosemary C.R. Taylor (1996). *Political Science and the Three New Institutionalisms*. Köln: MPIFG.

Hasse, Raimund, and Georg Krücken (2005). *Neo-Institutionalismus*. Bielefeld: Transcript-Verlag.

Heyen, Erk V., ed. (1992). *Early European Community Administration. Yearbook of European Administrative History 4*. Baden-Baden: Nomos.

Hood, Christopher (1995). 'The "New Public Management" in the 1980s: Variations on a theme', *Accounting, Organizations and Society*, 20:2/3, 93–109.

Kickert, Walter (2007). 'Public Management Reforms in Countries with a Napoleonic State Model: France, Italy and Spain', in Christopher Pollitt, Sandra van Thiel and Vincent Homburg (eds.), *New Public Management in Europe. Adaptation and Alternatives*. Basingstoke: Palgrave, 26–51.

Kingdon, John W. (1984). *Agendas, Alternatives and Public Policies*. Boston: Little, Brown and Company.

Knill, Christoph (1998). 'European Policies: The Impact of National Administrative Traditions', *Journal of Public Policy*, 18:1, 1–28.

Knill, Christoph (1999). 'Explaining Cross-National Variance in Administrative Reform: Autonomous versus Instrumental Bureaucracies', *Journal of Public Policy*, 19:2, 113–39.

Knill, Christoph (2001). *The Europeanisation of National Administrations. Patterns of Institutional Change and Persistence*. Cambridge: Cambridge University Press.

Knill, Christoph, and Tim Balint (2008). 'Explaining Variation in Organizational Change. The Reform of Human Resource Management in the European Commission and the OECD', *Journal of European Public Policy*, 15:2, forthcoming.

König, Klaus (2002). 'Zwei Paradigmen des Verwaltungsstudium – Vereinigte Staaten von Amerika und Kontinentaleuropa', in König, Klaus (ed.), *Deutsche Verwaltung an der Wende zum 21. Jahrhundert*. Baden-Baden: Nomos, 393–423.

Lægreid, Per (2002). 'Transforming Top Civil Servant Systems', in Tom Christensen and Per Lægreid (eds.), *New Public Management*. Burlington: Ashgate, 145–71.

Lequesne, Christian (1996). 'La Commission européenne entre autonomie et dependence', *Revue française de science politique*, 46:3, 389–408.

Levi-Faur, David (2002). 'The Politics of Liberalization. Privatisation and Regulation for Competition in Europe's and Latin America's Telecoms and Electricity Industries', *European Journal of Political Research*, 42:5, 705–40.

March, James G., and Johan P. Olsen (1989). *Rediscovering Institutions. The Organizational Basis of Politics*. New York: Free Press.

March, James G., and Johan P. Olsen (1995). *Democratic Governance*. New York: Free Press.

Metcalfe, Les (1992). 'After 1992: Can the Commission Manage Europe?', *Australian Journal of Public Administration*, 51:1, 117–30.

Metcalfe, Les (2000). 'Reforming the Commission: Will Organisational Efficiency Produce Effective Governance?', *Journal of Common Market Studies*, 38:5, 817–41.

Meyer, John W., and Brian Rowan (1977). 'Institutionalized Organizations. Formal Structure as Myth and Ceremony', *American Journal of Sociology* 83:2, 340–63.

Meyer, John W., David J. Frank, Ann Hironaka, Evan Schofer and Nancy Brandon-Tuma (1997). 'The Structuring of a World Environmental Regime, 1870–1990', *International Organization*, 51:4, 623–51.

Michelmann, Hans J. (1978). *Organisational Effectiveness in a Multi-national Bureaucracy*. Farnborough: Saxon House.

Millar, Michelle and David McKevitt (2003). 'The Irish Civil Service System', in Hans A.G.M. Bekke and Frits M. van der Meer (eds.), *Civil Service Systems in Western Europe*. Cheltenham/Northampton: Edward Elgar, 36–60.

Nies-Berchem, Martine (1992). 'L'administration luxembourgeoise et les débuts de l'administration européenne (1952–1967)', in Erk V. Heyen (ed.), *Early European Community Administration. Yearbook of European Administrative History 4*. Baden-Baden: Nomos, 255–68.
Nugent, Neill (2001). *The European Commission*. Basingstoke: Palgrave.
OECD (1996). *Putting Citizens First. Portuguese Experience in Public Management Reform*. OECD: Paris.
OECD (2004). *Trends in Human Resources Management Policies in OECD Countries. An Analysis of the Results of the OECD Survey on Strategic Human Resources*, available at http://appli1.oecd.org/olis/2004doc.nsf/43bb6130e5e86e5fc12569fa005d004c/9af0f2e9e8fb0304c125700b003b7a13/$FILE/JT00184766.PDF.
OECD (2005). *Modernising Government. The Way Forward*. Paris: OECD.
Page, Edward C. (1997). *People Who Run Europe*. Oxford: Clarendon Press.
Page, Edward C., and Linda Wouters (1995). 'The Europeanization of national bureaucracies?', in Jon Pierre (ed.), *Bureaucracy in the Modern State. An Introduction to Comparative Public Administration*. Aldershot: Edward Elgar, 185–204.
Page, Edward C., and Vincent Wright, eds. (1999). *Bureaucratic Élites in Western European States. A Comparative Analysis of Top Officials*. Oxford: Oxford University Press.
Peters, B. Guy (2003). 'Administrative Traditions and the Anglo-American Democracies', in John Halligan (ed.), *Civil Service Systems in Anglo-American Countries*. Cheltenham: Edward Elgar, 10–26.
Peters, B. Guy, and Jon Pierre (2004). 'Politicization of the Civil Service: Concepts, Causes Consequences', in B. Guy Peters and Jon Pierre (eds.), *Politicization of the Civil Service in Comparative Perspective. The Quest for Control*. London: Routledge, 1–13.
Peterson, John (1999). 'The Santer Era: The European Commission in Normative, Historical and Theoretical Perspective', *Journal of European Public Policy*, 6:1, 46–65.
Peterson, John (2004). 'The Prodi Commission: Fresh Start or Free Fall?', in Dionyssis G. Dimitrakopoulos (ed.), *The Changing European Commission*. Manchester: Manchester University Press, 15–32.
Pollitt, Christopher and Geert Bouckaert (2004). *Public Management Reform – A Comparative Analysis*. Oxford: Oxford University Press.
Pollitt, Christopher, Sandra van Thiel and Vincent Homburg, eds. (2007). *New Public Management in Europe. Adaptation and Alternatives*. Basingstoke: Palgrave.
Randma-Liiv, Tiina, and Bernadette Connaughton (2005). 'Public Administration as a Field of Study: Divergence or Convergence in the Light of "Europeanization"?', TRAMES, 9:4, 348–60, available at http://www.ceeol.com/aspx/getdocument.aspx?logid=5&id=844CA901-AD65-4857-8E89-C348C557CCD1.
Ringe, Nils (2005). 'Government–Opposition Dynamics in the European Union: The Santer Commission Resignation Crisis', *European Journal of Political Research*, 44:5, 671–96.
Ritchie, Ella (1992). 'The Model of French Ministerial Cabinets in the Early European Commission', in Erk V. Heyen (ed.), *Early European Community Administration. Yearbook of European Administrative History 4*. Baden-Baden: Nomos, 95–106.
Rogalla, Dieter (1973). 'Das Dienstrecht der Europäischen Gemeinschaften', in Joseph H. Kaiser, Franz Mayer and Carl H. Ule (eds.),*Recht und System des öffentlichen Dienstes. ILO, IAEA, OECD, Europarat, NATO und Europäische Gemeinschaften*. Baden-Baden: Nomos, 305–66.
Scheinmann, Lawrence (1966). 'Some Preliminary Notes on Bureaucratic Relationships in the European Economic Community', *International Organization*, 20:4, 750–73.
Scheinmann, Lawrence, and Werner Feld (1972). 'The European Economic Community and National Civil Servants of the Member States', *International Organization*, 26:1, 121–35.
Schnapp, Kai-Uwe (2004). *Ministerialbürokratien in westlichen Demokratien. Eine vergleichende Analyse*. Opladen: Leske + Budrich.

Schön-Quinlivan, Emmanuelle (2007). 'Administrative Reform in the European Commission: From Rhetoric to Relegitimization', in Michael W. Bauer and Christoph Knill (eds.), *Management Reforms in International Organizations*. Baden-Baden: Nomos, 25–36.

Spence, David (1997). 'Staff and Personnel Policy in the Commission', in Geoffrey Edwards and David Spence (eds.), *The European Commission*. London: Cartermill, 68–100.

Spence David (2006). 'The Directorates General and the Services. Structures, Functions and Procedures', in David Spence and Geoffrey Edwards (eds.), *The European Commission*. London: John Harper Publishing, 128–55.

Spence, David, and Anne Stevens (2006). 'Staff and Personnel Policy in the Commission', in David Spence and Geoffrey Edwards (eds.), *The European Commission*. London: John Harper, 173–208.

Stevens, Anne, and Handley Stevens (2001). *Brussels Bureaucrats? The Administration of the European Union*. Basingstoke: Palgrave.

Stevens, Handley, and Anne Stevens (2006). 'The Internal Reform of the Commission', in David Spence and Geoffrey Edwards (eds.), *The European Commission*. London: John Harper, 454–80.

Thelen, Kathleen, and Sven Steinmo (1992). 'Historical Institutionalism in Comparative Politics', in Sven Steinmo, Kathleen Thelen and Frank Longstreth (eds.), *Structuring Politics. Historical Institutionalism in Comparative Analysis*. Cambridge: Cambridge University Press, 1–32.

Wille, Anchrit (2007). 'Senior Officials in a Reforming European Commission: Transforming the Top?', in Michael W. Bauer and Christoph Knill (eds.), *Management Reforms in International Organizations*. Baden-Baden: Nomos, 37–50.

Beyond the Myth of Nationality: Analysing Networks within the European Commission

SEMIN SUVARIEROL

By the nature of their composition, nationality is a salient factor within international organisations. On the one hand, member states demand to be represented within these organisations through their citizens; on the other hand, the same organisations are expected to be independent, i.e. to have an international outlook free of national influences. The need for representation is linked both to the question of legitimacy and to making successful policies that take national circumstances into account. The need for independence in turn stems from the desirability of assuring an overarching interest for all member states. International organisations need to deal with this dilemma[1] by starting with the recruitment of their officials. The United Nations was the first to formally acknowledge this dilemma by embedding the principles of 'recruiting staff on as wide a geographical basis as possible' and 'not seeking or receiving instructions from any government or from any other authority' into its Charter (Claude 1971: 193). The European Commission followed suit by endorsing and applying both of these principles to its College of Commissioners (through the treaties) and to its officials (through its staff regulations).

Career aspects, however, are just one facet of the nationality issue within an international bureaucracy. Personnel management in a multinational context has challenges of its own, as the diverse cultural backgrounds of officials might be seen as a barrier to creating a common working culture (Claude 1971: 192; Mazey and Richardson 1996: 419; McLaren 1997: 57–59; Page 1997: 97) or because the working culture might be 'cross-cut and fractured by particularistic attachments and cultures' (Nugent 2000: 297), as has been argued in the case of the Commission.

The European Commission is not only the largest of the EU institutions; it is unique for its exclusive formal competence in initiating and drafting EU legislation (Hooghe 2005: 863). Additionally, the Commission is an interesting institution to study from an organisational perspective because its formal organisational structure makes it less likely that nationality and national attachments will play a role. Comparable to national ministries, the Commission is divided into Directorates-General (DGs) which reflect sectors or functions instead of territories or national components (Egeberg 2004).[2] Furthermore, the geographical balance principle is applied from the bottom up, starting with the multinational composition of units to avoid national enclaves (ibid.: 212).

Setting up a formal structure based on the multinationality ideal, however, is only one side of the story. Ethnographic studies have shown that most bureaucratic organisations tend to develop disorganised yet successful informal sectors that follow very different cultural codes and principles beneath the external appearance of order and formality (Shore 2000: 207). It is this informal culture of the Commission that has been at the origin of the reference to national influences, clubs and networks. It has been argued that these national networks provide instrumental functions such as the exchange of information, contacts with more influential compatriots within and outside the Commission, and political opinionating (Hooghe 1999: 415).

Indeed, the idea of compatriots seeking and supporting compatriots seems plausible. As organisational network theory asserts, people interact more with their own kind, that is, with people similar to themselves, and this basic human tendency structures network ties of every type, from marriage and friendship to work, advice, support and information transfer (McPherson *et al.* 2001). But what about the networks of Commission officials? Are national networks a myth or everyday reality?

This article assesses whether European Commission officials are homophilic in terms of their networks. Put differently, do Commission officials have national networks and how can this be explained? In answering this question, this study moves beyond the current literature which confines itself merely to stating that networks are key to the functioning of the Commission (Hooghe 1999; Shore 2000; Stevens and Stevens 2001) and that they are partly shaped by nationality (Egeberg 1996: 731; Hooghe 1999: 405; Laffan 2004: 90; Shore 2000: 199). The concept of networks is defined and deconstructed, and a differentiation is made between task-related (formal and informal), career, and leisure networks. The task-related, informal networks are, in turn, singled out in order to analyse whether and how nationality plays a role in shaping the networking behaviour of Commission officials. The research is based on original empirical data consisting of 82 interviews with Commission policy officials of four Commission DGs between April and June 2005. The analysis is derived from both the quantitative and qualitative survey data.

The Effect of Nationality in Perspective

The role of national origins and culture within the European Union is a popular theme in the European integration literature. Michelle Cini (1996: 125) has argued that national affiliation remains a fundamental characteristic of internal Commission affairs, in spite of the non-nationalistic vision of the EU set out by the founders of the European Commission. It has been observed that the convergence that results from a common professional experience does reduce national identification to a certain extent and brings distance to relations with the native state (Bellier 1995: 60), but that individuals are notably still conscious of their differences and sensitivities (Abélès and Bellier 1996: 435). The assumption is, 'However open-minded, flexible and adaptable an official may be, . . . background matters because he or she will bring into work at least some of the values, presuppositions and habits that have been acquired in early life' (Stevens and Stevens 2001: 116).

The core issue here is not that officials have different backgrounds, which is a given, but that the differences are perceived to influence the behaviour of officials from different backgrounds and that these perceptions 'can feel empirically true' (Abélès et al. 1993: 42; McDonald 2000: 66). To manage these differences, officials tend to make assumptions about each other that emphasise such diverging characteristics (Page 1997: 87). Such assumptions involve national stereotyping by a significant proportion of officials, which especially comes to the fore during times of stress (Michelmann 1978: 494). One blatant example of this was when the Jacques Santer Commission (1995–99) had to resign due to allegations of fraud and nepotism. In particular, Edith Cresson (then the French Commissioner responsible for Science, Research, and Development) was accused of favouritism involving the appointment of several associates to well-paid positions in the Commission.

> [M]any Commission officials agreed that Cresson had been victim of an 'Anglo-Saxon political crusade' and deplored the way the 'Germans had joined the [N]ortherners in a Protestant crusade against the [S]outhern culture of state administration'. As Cresson declared, much

to the embarrassment of her colleagues, she was 'guilty of no behaviour that is not standard in the French administrative culture'. (Shore 2000: 202)

As this example demonstrates, even though the EU bureaucracy is relatively culturally homogenous compared to, for instance, the UN Secretariat, the differences between the *North* and *South* have been often cited as a dividing line (Abélès *et al.* 1993; Beyers and Dierickx 1997, 1998; Egeberg 1996; Hofstede 1994; McDonald 2000), where Austria, Britain, Denmark, Finland, Germany, Ireland, Luxembourg, Netherlands, and Sweden constitute the Northern group and Belgium, France, Greece, Italy, Portugal, and Spain comprise the Southern group.[3]

Arguably, the North–South division influences how officials behave in the Commission. Culturally, Northerners are taken to be well adapted to the rational, impersonal Weberian forms of bureaucracy, whereas Southerners are assumed to link loyalties and virtues to personal or patron–client type obligations (Egeberg 1996: 727; McDonald 2000: 67–68). To take the example of the issue of information flow, the Northern officials have been observed to complain of the lack of readily shared information in the Commission, whereas Southerners are said to find it simple to obtain information by making friends (McDonald 2000: 67).

The foregoing examples are not insignificant observations about life in the multinational administration of the Commission. Yet, for these observations to become practically significant for scholars of public administration and policy studies, the question has to be answered as to how these differences influence the behaviour of administrators when it comes to their substantive work, so that it is possible to analyse whether this eventually has any consequences for policy-making. This is why nationality and national differences have to be put into perspective by looking into the organisational context of the Commission.

Such an organisational approach has been brought into the European integration literature primarily by Morten Egeberg (2001, 2004, 2006a, 2006b). While acknowledging the fact that Commission officials are pre-packed with national experiences, norms and values, he argues, 'Although these personal attitudes may be seen as some sort of paradigm, belief system or conceptual lens that might somehow make a difference in a given decision situation, they are, nevertheless, of a relatively general nature. To become relevant in a given decision context, they have to be operationalised and pass several potential organisational filters' (Egeberg 2004: 212).

As mentioned above, the organisational structure of the Commission closely reflects that of a national administration in which DGs are the ministries, each with its own policy area or function. The DG attachment is particularly important for understanding the actual decision-making behaviour of Commission officials (Cram 1994; Cini 1996, 2000; Egeberg 1996, 2004, 2006b). The fact that the officials' posts are organised according to purpose and function makes it less likely that officials will focus on territorial (national) concerns (Egeberg 2004: 212–213). Moreover, in order to avoid national clusters, units are multinationally composed and staff immediately above and below a given senior post are of a different nationality.

Still, 'Formal relations coordinate roles or specialised activities, not persons' (Selznick 1957: 8). This is why nationality can still be expected to play a role in contrast to or simultaneously with the formal role expectations, especially in areas where formal tasks and obligations leave leeway for individual fulfilment. It is when individuals use informal channels to conduct their formal tasks that the informal becomes relevant for the performance of an employee and in turn for the functioning of the organisation.

Networks in the Commission and Organisational Network Theory

Having access to the right information at the right time is vital, especially for conducting knowledge-intensive work such as professional services which require employees to solve complex problems within short time horizons (Cross and Borgatti 2004: 137). For the most part, such issue-specific and problem-centred information is in individuals' heads since 'specialisation (among other factors) ensures that each individual maintains different bundles of knowledge' (Cross et al. 2001: 216).

When interactions with people are the only way to get information that matters (Cross and Borgatti 2004: 137), connections to other colleagues become very valuable. This is the underlying idea behind networks as social capital (Borgatti and Foster 2003: 993). The social capital of individuals consists of their personal networks and their chances of accessing whatever is circulating there, e.g. information (Cross and Parker 2004: 11). Accordingly, 'whom you know has a significant impact on what you come to know, because relationships are critical for obtaining information, solving problems, and learning how to do your work' (ibid.). As such, personal networks are an important factor in an employee's performance within an organisation (ibid.). This is why it is of particular interest to look into the networking behaviour of individuals in organisations.

Stevens and Stevens (2001: 177) underscore the value of information within the policy-making processes of the Commission and argue that information is a key resource in daily relationships within this organisation. Information flow constitutes an important informal aspect of power relationships in the Commission (Abélès et al. 1993: 6). Consequently, it becomes a tool for both incorporating and excluding colleagues. 'The Commission is riven with internal divisions and inclined to habits which prevent the free flow of information and ideas' (Stevens and Stevens 2001: 243). In such a system, key personal contacts become vital for building support and alliances within the fixed deadlines (ibid.: 178).

Before continuing with the discussion, it is important to offer a clear definition of the concept of networks. Networks are taken here as the 'personal contacts within the context of organisational contacts' (Jönsson and Elgström 2005: 3). As such, they are complementary to formal hierarchical channels that are set by the hierarchical division of labour and formal rules and procedures in an organisation. Whereas hierarchical channels are used for task-oriented formal communication, networks come into play to fill in the gaps or to make up for the inefficiencies of the hierarchical channels. James March and Herbert Simon even argue that 'formal hierarchical channels tend to become general-purpose channels to be used whenever no special-purpose channel or informal channel exists or is known to the communicator' (March and Simon 1958: 167–168). Networks involve a relationship of mutual exchange and dependency and usually remain highly informal and to a degree invisible (Morgan 1986: 174). Networking may occur over the telephone, through old-boy networks and other friendship groups, through informal meetings, or through chance contacts (ibid.). 'The informality of networks rests on the personal relationships that develop as a result of frequent interaction' (Jönsson and Elgström 2005: 3).

Networks are central to understanding the way the Commission works in practice (Shore 2000: 200). Liesbet Hooghe (1999: 405) refers to some nationalities in the Commission as having a strong reputation of clubness, which she defines as 'a set of formal and informal networks within which members tend to act in concert'. Hooghe argues further that officials with weak national networks are at a disadvantage, as successful policy-making in the EU often depends on the quality of intelligence (ibid.: 415). 'Access to information can create a form of power parallel to the official hierarchies and sometimes much more efficient than them' (Abélès *et al.* 1993: 57–58).

In their study of the communication networks of national officials within European Council working groups, Jan Beyers and Guido Dierickx (1997: 436) found nationality to be a major factor when negotiators have to select partners to forge informal communication links with. Moreover, they tend to view their partners in terms of larger 'regions' (ibid.: 465). Their study showed that Northern negotiators communicated more with other Northern Europeans and Southern Europeans were more attached to each other than to Northern Europeans (ibid.: 437). The influence of nationality within the Council setting is perhaps not so puzzling since the officials are expected to represent their nation-states there. It is more intriguing to look into the networks of Commission officials, where nationality is not supposed to play a role due to the Commission's sectoral organisational structure. In turn, one would expect officials to have supranational intra-organisational[4] networks, maintaining contacts with all member state officials. Is this the case or do officials rely on their national intra-organisational networks, predominantly contacting officials of their own nationality?

In order to be able to answer this question, the concept 'network' needs to be specified further. Daniel Brass (1984: 519) refers to the existence of three types of social networks within organisational structures as the workflow, communication, and friendship networks. I apply this tripartite division to the Commission as follows:

1) *Task-related formal network:* formal contacts dictated by the official's task description and obligations.
2) *Task-related informal network*: informal contacts used to conduct one's tasks.
3) *Leisure network*: contacts during social activities and gatherings which fall outside working hours and obligations.

In the case of the Commission, the fieldwork leads me to propose adding a fourth type:

4) *Career network* – contacts maintained for one's own career advancement.

The theoretical expectations and the pilot interviews conducted with Commission officials to fine-tune the questionnaire utilised for this study led to making the task-related informal networks the primary focus for studying how nationality shapes the intra-organisational networks of Commission officials. The reasoning behind this is as follows. First, the task-related formal networks of Commission officials are hierarchically defined. There is no choice element involved here, so the organisational structure and formal responsibilities are the factors that determine these networks. Accordingly, nationality is by default not an explanatory factor here since these contact persons are pre-defined. Second, there is no direct link between the pure leisure and career networks and policy-making processes within the Commission. These networks are a case apart. This does not exclude the possibility of using these contacts for work purposes as well. Whether these contacts are activated for substantive work-related issues, however, depends on the relevance of these contact persons to the official's work. The task-related informal networks are where the formal and the informal merge. Moreover, the information and advice obtained through these networks have a direct effect on an official's performance and simultaneously on the functioning of the policy-making process in the Commission. I therefore argue that these are the most crucial networks for testing the effect of nationality.

I refer here to information that is not directly accessible through the formal channels, such as the intranet and official mailing lists. This is the kind of information one can usually only obtain through personal contacts, with the aim of receiving complementary information such as background information on an issue, analysis/interpretation of a problem, and advice on how to proceed with a given situation. When the issue at hand involves another DG or unit, this information might also merely be figuring out what is going on in the other DG since this information is not readily available until a draft proposal reaches a certain stage of maturity. These are mainly the types of information and advice which enable an official to build on what is formally available.

On the whole, informal practices require a measure of trust and a faith in commonality (Middlemas 1995: 680). 'Similarity breeds connection' (McPherson *et al.* 2001: 415). This principle, formulated by Aristotle simply as '[people] love those who are like themselves' (quoted in ibid.: 416), is called 'homophily' in social network research. Homophily is a simple principle which asserts that contact between similar people occurs at a higher rate than among dissimilar people (ibid.: 416). This principle rests on experimental literature in social psychology which establishes that similarities in attitudes, beliefs, and values lead to attraction and interaction (ibid.: 428). Interacting with similar others is efficient as it facilitates transmission of tacit knowledge, simplifies coordination and avoids potential conflicts (Borgatti and Foster 2003: 999). Crude as it may be, network research has shown that the homophily principle structures network ties of every type (McPherson *et al.* 2001: 415).

An interesting result of homophily research is that the strongest effect of homophily occurs with regard to race and ethnicity on a wide range of relationships from the most intimate bonds of marriage to work relations, networks of discussion about a particular topic, and 'knowing about' someone else (ibid.: 420). Furthermore, many facets of ethnicity (e.g., mother tongue, national origins, ethnic group, and region of birth) also display this characteristic (ibid.). Research on multi-national companies is a case in point: 'People in different countries preferred to interact with others of the same nationality' (Cross and Parker 2004: 16). Moreover, nationality is an easy characteristic to assess in comparison to personality and abilities (Pratt 2001: 25).

In this sense, the homophily theory forms a basic rationale to test the argument that Commission officials will generally try to deal, at least in the first instance, with people from the same country or from the same general geographic area (Page 1997: 136; Stevens and Stevens 2001: 180). The first step in finding out whether Commission officials rely on similar others for information or advice is to answer the question, 'Who do Commission officials contact?'

> **Hypothesis 1:** *Officials rely relatively more on officials with the same nationality for information or advice.*
> **Hypothesis 2:**
> a) *North European officials have relatively more contacts from the North and South European officials have more contacts from the South.*
> b) *South European officials have relatively more same region contacts than North European officials.*

c) *South European officials have relatively more same nationality contacts than North European officials.*

Hypothesis 3: Officials have more contacts who speak their native language for obtaining information or advice.

To test these hypotheses, the contacts with similar others in terms of nationality-related variables have been counted to see what their sheer numbers reveal in terms of the networking patterns of Commission officials (see the Appendix for details of research design and methodology). This analysis is followed by an explanation of these results.

National Networks in a Multinational Organisation?

When openly asked whether nationality or culture has an effect on the networks of Commission officials, 57.3 per cent of the interviewed officials said nationality mattered and 61 per cent of them said culture mattered. Commission officials acknowledge that it is easier to establish contacts with officials from their own nationality (Officials #2, #22). The contacts with compatriots are more spontaneous (Official #76) and smooth (Official #82). This is mainly due to the simple fact that they 'speak to each other in their own language and share the same cultural references' (Official #69). The communication is therefore faster and easier since they understand each other more quickly (Officials #75, #76, #119). You know how to approach someone from your own country (Official #87) and you are more open to helping a compatriot when approached (Official #17). You also have higher expectations of obtaining an answer or a favour when approaching a compatriot (Official #22). These aspects of same nationality contacts do indeed point to the advantages of speaking with someone of your own kind. Consequently, Commission officials might well have been homophilic if cultural commonalities had determined their communication patterns.

The quantitative network evidence, however, strongly refutes this argument: Only 17.8 per cent of the contact persons are of the same nationality. The average of same nationality contacts is 0.53 out of the maximum possibility of three. At the opposite end, 49 of the 81 officials have no same nationality contacts, i.e. 60.5 per cent of the officials have a purely multinational network which does not include any official of their own nationality. Officials with none or only one same nationality contact add up to 87.7 per cent of the sample. These indicators strongly suggest that task-related informal contacts are overwhelmingly supranational in the Commission and that national networks are a myth when it comes to asking for information and advice on task-related issues in the Commission.

Still, it is often argued that some nationalities have a stronger reputation of national clubness (Hooghe 1999, 2001) or, in the officials' words, a much higher tendency to stick to each other even within this multinational environment (Officials #3, #7, #17, #26, #29, #69, #72, #116, #117, #120).

The next question that has to be answered is: Are there really differences[5] among nationalities when it comes to contacting one's own nationals? Table 1 presents the network patterns per nationality. The results should be looked at with caution, however, due to the small size of officials per nationality in the sample.

Table 1 indicates that contacts between compatriots, if any, are a large member state phenomenon, with officials from Italy, France, United Kingdom, Belgium,[6] and Germany having the most same nationality contacts. Officials see this, however, as a mere effect and automatic consequence of size of these member state contingents (Officials #30, #31, #76). This observation is also reflected in the quantitative analysis. While the mode is '0' for both small and large member states,[7] the median is '0' for small member states and '1' for large member states. Even though large member state officials have relatively more same nationality contacts, their networks are still predominantly supranational.

The accounts of officials are supportive of these results: 'There is not more contact with one nationality more than others ... Normally, the most part of colleagues who are here don't think in national terms' (Official #10). 'Nationality is not a dominating factor in networks. Work-related networks are multinational' (Official #52). Nationality does not matter for work (Official #117). A lot of it is perception (Official #105).

Yet five of the six nationalities which have no same nationality contacts are North European. Is the difference between the individualistic Northerners and the collectivistic Southerners reflected in the data? Do the Southern officials stick more than the Northern officials to their own region

TABLE 1
AGGREGATED DISTRIBUTION OF SAME NATIONALITY CONTACTS PER NATIONALITY

Nationality	Ratio contacts with same nationality: total contacts	Percentage of same nationality contacts
Italy	7/20	35
France	10/30	33.3
United Kingdom	3/9	33.3
Belgium	6/20	30
Germany	10/39	25.6
Greece	4/21	19
Czech Republic	1/6	16.7
Ireland	1/9	11.1
Spain	1/15	6.7
Finland	0/15	0
Austria	0/12	0
Denmark	0/12	0
Sweden	0/9	0
Netherlands	0/6	0
Portugal	0/3	0
Other	0/15	0
Total	43/241	17.8

and nationality? Or are both groups homophilic (contacting more people from their own region) such as the Council of Ministers working group participants of Beyers and Dierickx (1997, 1998)?

The North–South Division: Another Myth?

The successive enlargements of the EU have resulted in an increasing number of different nationalities. Arguably, as nationalities increased and spread throughout the Commission, regional identities have become more relevant reference points for officials. In terms of cultural differences, the reference point 'North–South' which had already been present at the time of the study of Abélès *et al.* (1993) became even more established with the Northern enlargement in 1995.

The relevance of the regional affiliation categories of North and South was demonstrated in the interviews. Namely, 52.4 per cent of the officials referred to the existence of a North–South division, the so-called 'wine-belt vs. beer-belt division' (Official #50), especially when asked whether culture has any influence on the shape of networks within the Commission. Officials from the North and the South say they understand and communicate better with people from their own cultural region because they have the same mentality (Officials #9, #75, #78, #108). Northerners acknowledge that they would call other Northerners if they wanted to get to the heart of the matter and receive a direct answer to the question they had in mind (Officials #9, #13, #42, #114). Southerners, on the other hand, feel that they can count on Northerners, obtain direct and reliable information from them (Official #53, #76) and they appreciate the fact that Northerners are easy-going, open, and not hierarchical (Officials #53, #55, #59, #95).

The perception of cultural differences with regard to the networking behaviour of North and South European officials is clearly present. Northerners have the impression that the Southerners are better at networking than Northerners due to the negative connation of networking/lobbying in the North, but that they are catching up (Officials #38, #67, #111, #113, #114). In contrast, Southerners have the impression that the concept of networking is itself Northern, but that Southerners, if by chance they find themselves in a network, maintain it better (Officials #22, #39, #58). The differences are also related to attitudes, i.e. introverted Northerners vs. extraverted Southerners (Official #35), and to preferences with regard to working methods, i.e. Northerners opting for autonomous work, written communication (e-mail) vs. Southerners' willingness to set up meetings and coffee breaks to enable face-to-face talking (Officials #13, #55). Given the ease of contact due to these cultural common denominators (Official #52), some Northerners or Southerners admit that they subconsciously have respectively more Northerners or Southerners in their network as a result (Officials #12, #47, #52, #92, #106). Some even go so far as to argue that the Northern and Southern networks tend to be separate

(Officials #75, #92). Are these perceptions reflected in the task-related informal networks of Commission officials or is this just another myth? Table 2 displays the distribution of contacts within and across Northern and Southern officials.

Comparing North and South Europeans, the difference[8] is very small between the two groups in terms of contacting other Northerners and Southerners. The results are contradictory to all expectations: There is neither an overall regional homophily (North with the North, South with the South), nor is homophily a tendency of the 'collectivistic' Southerners. The contacts are almost evenly distributed between same and different region contacts, and if there is a group that prefers people of their own region to those of the others, it is the Northerners. The difference between the proportion of same region contacts of Northerners and Southerners, though, is a mere 4.4 per cent.

In terms of contacting officials of the same nationality, however, the patterns of Northerners and Southerners are slightly different, as Table 3 shows. This time it is the Southern officials who contact their own nationality more than the Northerners. The Southerners have a relatively stronger tendency to rely on compatriots: Southerners have twice the number of same nationality contacts as Northerners (28 vs. 14). In sum, the results of the bivariate analysis of the difference between North and South are mixed and call for a recheck in a multivariate analysis.

Some officials also tend to dismiss this North–South division, calling it a prejudice (Official #82) that is often exaggerated (Official #73). It is a misconception, and the differences are rather in modality (the way Northerners and Southerners are perceived to network) and not in approaches (Official #105). As another official emphasises, 'Of course,

TABLE 2
DISTRIBUTION OF REGIONAL CONTACTS PER REGION (NORTH–SOUTH)[1]

Region	North	South	TOTAL
Same region contacts	53.2%	48.8%	118
Different region contacts	46.8%	51.2%	114
Total	111	121	232

[1]The East European officials (only two of them in the sample) and the officials with double nationality (a combination of North-South European) were excluded from the calculations.

TABLE 3
DISTRIBUTION OF SAME NATIONALITY CONTACTS PER REGION (NORTH–SOUTH)

Region	North	South	TOTAL
Same nationality contacts	12.6%	23.1%	42
Different nationality contacts	87.4%	76.9%	190
Total	111	121	232

people may be different if they come from the North or from the South ...,
but I don't think that influences our work. No, I don't see anything of that'
(Official #71).

The Language Issue in a Multilingual Environment

When asked whether nationality matters in terms of shaping networks, 46.3 per cent of the officials claimed that it was language that mattered more. As the explanations of officials in the previous two sections also suggest, speaking the same native language is seen as an important door-opener (Officials #9, #80). After all, one can only express and understand the nuances in one's native language (Officials #80, #81). This ease in communication also creates trust (Official #69), which at times becomes vital: 'Sometimes if you need sensitive background information, then it's easier if you speak the same language' (Official #81).

It comes as no surprise in a union with 23 official languages that officials tell anecdotes on misunderstandings due to language (Officials #46, #90, #95, #97) and emphasise the extent to which it is important to make yourself understood in such a multilingual environment (Official #97). Yet, at the same time, Commission officials are champions of speaking foreign languages. The interviewed officials speak on average 3.63 languages, the maximum being six.

The real question is to what extent the multiplicity of languages comes to life in the daily work of Commission officials. The Commission has three official working languages: English, French, and German. In practice, however, English and French are the languages used on a daily basis. The dominant language, however, has clearly shifted from French to English, a trend which has become even stronger with the Eastern enlargement of the EU. Most written documents are also increasingly produced first in English (Official #2). The diversity of languages is thus not reflected in daily practice. As one official explained, as the EU has become larger and more official languages have been added, the number of languages actually being used has decreased (Official #82).

The predominance of English and the decline in the use of French is also echoed in the empirical data. Respondents were asked to indicate in which language they communicate with the three officials they chose as their most important contacts. The aggregated responses showed that 52.3 per cent of the exchanges were in English, 25.7 per cent in French, 6.6 per cent in German, and 5.4 per cent in a mixture of English and French.[9] Only in 32.8 per cent of the cases do officials speak in their native language with contacts in their network.

Another issue that has been identified by the officials is whether one has English or French speaking networks (Officials #29, #73, #74, #90, #113, #117). However, this is not a significant divide either since Commission officials are very much accustomed to constantly shifting from English to

French in their daily work (Official #92). More importantly, as one official also explained, when people are working on the same specific issue, there is no language barrier (Official #48).

Explaining Networks in the Commission

The foregoing empirical evidence demonstrates that the homophily variables of nationality, region, and language do not shape the task-related informal networks of Commission officials. How can this be explained? Plausibly, the effect of homophily may be weakened or annulled by other factors. Being forced to interact with people different from oneself may be one such factor (Cross and Parker 2004: 83–84). In the specific case of the Commission, officials might contact officials of different nationalities due to their socialisation (prior to or during their time in the Commission), or they might be constrained in their willingness to contact their own nationals by organisational structures that counteract territorial clustering.

These socialisation and organisational variables that come to the fore in the EU literature have been tested in the following model to explain the choice of contact persons:

- *Control variable*: Size of member state to account for the lower/higher probability of contacts from small/large-member states due to the number of officials they have in the Commission.
- *Independent variables*: Testing for the homophily, socialisation, and organisational variables.
  North–South dummy – Retesting Hypothesis 2c in a multivariate equation.
  Experience in national administration – Testing prior national socialisation: officials who have previously worked at their home administration (who are socialised into defending national interests) are more likely to contact compatriots than officials who have no previous experience in national administration.
  Number of languages spoken – Testing prior transnational socialisation: the more languages an official speaks (the more affiliated an official is with other cultures), the less likely the official is to have same nationality contacts.
  Tenure – Testing Commission socialisation: the longer officials work for the Commission (the more an official is used to working in a multinational environment), the less likely they will have same nationality contacts.
  Number of contacts within the DG – Testing organisational structure: contacts within a DG are shaped primarily by functional requirements and are thus less likely to be shaped by nationality.
- *Dependent variable*: Explaining the occurrence of same nationality contacts.

The dependent variable 'same nationality contacts' was dichotomised into the values 0 and 1[10] in order to run logistic regression. The choice for logistic regression results from the distribution of the responses: there is no normal distribution, and as mentioned above, 49 of the officials have zero same nationality contacts. The combination of these factors makes a linear regression analysis an unsuitable choice. Logistic regression, however, accounts for a high number of zero responses when the dependent variable is dichotomous with the values 0 and 1. As such, logistic regression predicts the likelihood of the occurrence or non-occurrence of events in terms of odds (Pampel 2000: 11): 'Odds express the likelihood of an occurrence relative to the likelihood of a non-occurrence.'

The dependent variable 'number of same nationality contacts' has not been measured as a dichotomous variable, which means that dichotomising it leads to some loss of information. However, there were 9 and 1 respondents with 2 and 3 same nationality contacts, respectively, which meant that there was already not enough variance to be detected for a variable with four categories. Even though individuals with 1 and 3 nationality contacts may differ, this trade-off had to be made in order to be able to conduct a methodologically sound test. The SPSS output of the logistic regression including these variables is presented in Table 4.[11]

The model performs quite well with correctly predicted cells at 73.3 per cent and with a Nagelkerke Rô of .389.[12] Only two variables pass the significance test, namely those of size of member state and the number of

TABLE 4
EXPLAINING NETWORKS WITH LOGISTIC REGRESSION

Independent variables[1]	B	S.E.	Sig.	Exp(B)
Size of member state**	2.205	.741	.003	9.069
North–South dummy	.366	.613	.550	1.442
Tenure	.031	.040	.439	1.031
Experience in national administration	.343	.609	.574	1.409
Number of languages spoken	−.473	.321	.140	.623
Number of contacts within DG*	−.677	.307	.027	.508
Constant	.581	1.717	.735	1.788
Constant	.581	1.717	.735	1.788
**$p<0.01$, *$p<0.05$		Overall percentage correct: 73.3%		
N=75		Nagelkerke R Square: .389		

[1]The variables have been coded as follows:
- *Size of member state*: Small member state=0 (Austria, Denmark, Finland, Greece, Ireland, Netherlands, Portugal, Sweden), Large member state=1 (Belgium, France, Germany, Italy, Spain, UK);
- *North–South dummy*: North=0 (Austria, Denmark, Finland, Germany, Ireland, Netherlands, Sweden, UK), South=1 (Belgium, France, Greece, Italy, Portugal, Spain);
- *Tenure*: Number of years working for the Commission;
- *Experience in national administration*: No=1, Yes=1;
- *Number of languages spoken*: minimum 2, maximum 6;
- *Number of contacts within DG*: minimum 0, maximum 3;

same DG contacts. In logistic regression, an odds ratio, i.e. exponentiated coefficient – Exp(B), higher than 1 increases the odds of an event occurring and a coefficient smaller than 1 decreases the odds (Pampel 2000: 22). The control variable size of member state has the highest coefficient, and it is positive. This means that an official belonging to a large nationality group is far more likely to contact an official of the same nationality group. The coefficient of DG is relatively smaller, but it is smaller than 1 (negative) and significant: an official who has more contacts within a DG is less likely to turn to compatriots. This implies that contacts within a DG are less influenced by nationality compared to contacts outside the DG, which are more influenced by nationality.

These results find support in the accounts of the interviewed officials. Size of a national group is indeed an important factor that determines whether an official can build a network with compatriots at all. The underlying reason for this is that Commission officials are specialised in specific files which in some cases require very specific technical or scientific expertise. Especially when you are an official from a small member state, the chances are low that there is someone else from your nationality who is working in the same field of expertise (Officials #25, #100, #110, #116). Therefore, in practice nationality has limited effect because your nationality is not represented everywhere (Official #119). Furthermore, it would not be sufficient to have a solely national network as a small member state official (Official #67). In this sense, nationality potentially matters more for large member state officials. It is not as if there is a choice between various persons in your field who all have the answer to a particular question. If that were the case, some officials admitted, they might choose the person from their own nationality over someone who is not (Official #95). But the chances of this hypothetical case are very low, and the exceptions are large member states which have their officials in almost every unit (Official #106).

The fact that the DG is significant for the task-related informal networks of Commission officials is a reflection of the centrality of one's field of expertise. When it comes to performing one's tasks, the official's specific file (*dossier*) is the most important consideration. As one official put it, '[P]eople have their area of work that's specified, so you really have to talk to them. Sometimes you can talk to one of their colleagues, but normally in the Commission people have quite specific responsibilities' (Official #13). Within this organisational context, expertise determines a contact person's competence and utility. As a result, the policy issue one is working on 'creates things that are in common' and 'transcends the differences that might exist because of the main cultural differences' (Official #24). In the words of a French official:

> I don't see nationality playing a role because what comes first is the function, the technical aspect. I am not going to ask a French

colleague, simply because he is French, for information on a file managed by a Swedish colleague who knows the subject ... It is the technical knowledge, the function, the fact of being responsible for a subject that comes first. (Official #91) [Author's translation]

The identification with one's file (*dossier*) and expertise is so strong that there is little room left for general questions (Abélès and Bellier 1996: 437). The only kind of useful general information one can get from a fellow national tends to be on 'how things work in another DG' (Officials #81, #113). Seeking out a compatriot also comes in handy for finding out who is responsible (Officials #80, #81): 'It's just a point of first contact, but they can tell you to whom you have to turn. And then nationality doesn't play a role anymore' (Official #81). Especially in such circumstances, it is easier to contact people in other DGs in your own language (Official #3). However, there are also officials who do not appreciate this 'door-opener' function since it is not related to their expertise: 'I don't like someone who's phoning, "I was just checking someone who's Spanish on the list and wanted to ask you." To be Spanish, this is not a professional mark' (Official #46).

The North–South division had given mixed results in the bivariate analysis, but in the multivariate analysis this variable fails to pass the significance test. The socialisation variables also fail, which is in line with previous quantitative research on socialisation in the Commission (Hooghe 1999, 2001, 2005). Amongst the socialisation variables, however, the prior transnational socialisation variable 'number of spoken languages' performs the best.

Discussion and Conclusion

The foregoing analysis of the empirical data on the networks of Commission officials demonstrates that national networks are indeed a myth when it comes to the substance of their work. This is not only supported by the sheer numbers which demonstrate that same nationality contacts are the exception rather than the rule, but also through the accounts of Commission officials who stress that 'nationality is not a category that counts' in the Commission (Official #25) and that there is actually no need for advanced national networks (Official #31). Clearly, officials do not contact fellow nationals just because they come from the same country. By virtue of their supranational networks, they fulfil their role of independent international civil servants as designated in the treaties.

The analysis has also shown once more the significance of working with clearer concepts and the relevance of borrowing definitions and insights from other bodies of literature, in this case from organisational and network theory for investigating 'networks'. In particular, the deconstruction of the different types of networks has proven essential for analysing networks in the Commission. This study was only the first step in mapping out and explaining the networking behaviour of Commission officials in a systematic manner. The career and leisure networks still require a systematic study.

These results are in line with the results of a Commission survey in 1974, cited in Hans Michelmann's article (1978). Michelmann reports that the survey found no statistically significant relationship between nationality and interaction (ibid.: 492), and furthermore that the quality of interaction was also independent of nationality (ibid.: 493). This led Michelmann to conclude that 'under normal circumstances officials react to fellow civil servants as individuals and not as members of national contingents' (ibid.). These conclusions hold for Commission officials interviewed three decades later.

The results also provide support for the organisational/institutional perspective on the study of EU institutions on a more generic level (Egeberg 2001, 2004, 2006a, 2006b; Trondal 2006a, 2006b). The extent to which the networking patterns of Commission officials are shaped (or constrained) by the organisational structure of the Commission demonstrated that the organisational affiliation of officials influences their behaviour. The contrast between the networking behaviour of Council working group participants and Commission officials is a case in point: the Council fora remain 'after all a negotiation process among nations' (Beyers and Dierickx 1998: 313), whereas the Commission is where the European/supranational element visibly comes to life.

There are also interesting parallels to be drawn between the results presented and previous research conducted on the College of Commissioners and their Cabinets. Egeberg's research (2006a) had shown that the portfolio role was the most important factor in shaping decision-making behaviour in the College. As for the effect of size of member states, Joana and Smith (2004: 39) have previously argued that 'Commissioners from large countries are most often in a position of comparative advantage because they and their cabinets are able to call upon networks of national actors when preparing arguments and objections on *non-portfolio* issues' (emphasis added).

As for the Commissioners and their Cabinets, the portfolio/*dossier* is the most important factor shaping the daily work of Commission officials. The extra information and advice they need to obtain sometimes falls on the periphery or outside this portfolio, in which case they might turn to a compatriot. In such cases, coming from a large member state might become advantageous since there are by default more contact points for these officials to turn to.

The lessons to be drawn with regard to the effect of socialisation are more ambiguous. Even though the results confirm those of Hooghe (1999, 2001, 2005) in terms of dismissing the role of socialisation, the accounts of the Commission officials interviewed for this study, as well as earlier research focusing on the identities of EU officials (Risse 2004), point in a different direction: Commission officials have internalised the values of the institution, which is reflected in their daily behaviour at work. The failure of socialisation variables in quantitative analyses might therefore be related to the fact that the indicators used for tapping into socialisation are not powerful enough to capture this concept. In fact, the Commission attracts individuals with a cosmopolitan background, as the number of languages they speak also demonstrates. In this sense, I argue that self-selection plays a larger role than previously argued (Hooghe 2005). The Commission now recruits younger officials who have grown up in a globalised world, whereas Hooghe's research only focused on the earlier generation of senior Commission officials.

This study has shown the extent to which the Commission's organisational structure shapes the networks of officials. Even though the empirical data covered four social regulation DGs, the organisational structure is valid for the whole organisation. In sum, national networks in the Commission are a myth when it comes to officials performing their tasks. The ideal of civil servants 'whose nationality [is] supranationality' (quoted in Spence and Stevens 2006: 151) seems to be manifested in the everyday reality of the Commission.

Acknowledgements

I would like to thank Mark Bovens, Deirdre Curtin, Morten Egeberg, Martijn Groenleer, Frank Häge, Liesbet Hooghe, Michael Kaeding, Sebastian Princen, the participants of the CONNEX Research Group 1 Workshop in Vienna (May 2006) and the ECPR Conference in Istanbul (September 2006), and the anonymous reviewer for their comments and suggestions on earlier versions of this article.

Notes

1. This dilemma has previously been termed 'consociationalism vs. Weberianism' by Liesbet Hooghe (1999) and 'territorialisation vs. autonomisation' by Morten Egeberg (2006b).
2. Territorial subdivisions do, however, exist in some units of a few DGs.
3. It remains to be seen how the Eastern enlargement has added an 'East' category to this classification (Cyprus and Malta being the two exceptions which plausibly belong to the Southern group) or whether the new countries will be included and/or integrated in the Northern or Southern groups in the long term.
4. The networks of Commission officials with external actors on the EU or member state level fall outside the scope of this study.
5. Unfortunately, the differences cannot be tested for statistical significance since the data violates the basic assumptions of ANOVA due to the skewed distribution of the sample, the unequal distribution of the cells, and the violation of the assumption of independence of observations in the aggregated data (see among others Field 2005: 324).
6. Due to the location of the European Commission in Brussels, Belgium is also a large member state in terms of the number of officials.
7. Belgium, France, Germany, Spain, and United Kingdom were coded as large member states based on the number of their A-level officials in the Commission.

8. Similar to the case of the nationalities, the differences cannot be tested for statistical significance since the data violates the basic assumptions of ANOVA due to the skewed distribution of the sample and the violation of the assumption of independence of observations in the aggregated data (see among others Field 2005: 324).
9. The results should not suffer from a language bias since the respondents were given a choice between English and French for the language of the interview.
10. Responses 1, 2, and 3 have been aggregated and recoded as 1.
11. Collinearity diagnostics have shown that the variables do not suffer from a multicollinearity problem. Residual analyses resulted in only two cases with standardised residual values around 3.
12. It should be noted that the Nagelkerke Rô tends to be lower than the corresponding linear regression Rô. See, for example, http://www2.chass.ncsu.edu/garson/PA765/logistic.htm.
13. The new EU staff regulation adopted in 2004 has changed the names of these officials to Administrator (AD). Yet, since Commission officials themselves still refer to the term 'A-level', this term will be employed in the rest of the paper. Note that the sample also includes permanent and temporary officials (seconded national experts and temporary agents) with policy-making functions.
14. I rely on the classification Hooghe (2001) uses to group the DGs of the Commission into six policy areas: Administration, External Affairs, Market-Oriented, Social Regulation, Supply Side and Provision.
15. Two out of the 120 sampled officials were later excluded and not re-contacted after the first letter asking for an interview when it became clear that they were not A-level officials.
16. Social network scholars conducting research on ego-centred networks have asked their respondents to name three respondents (Cross *et al.* 2001; Cross and Borgatti 2004). This is based on the finding that an average adult has 20 regular interlocutors, only three of which are confidants (Degenne and Forse 1999: 20–21).

References

Abélès, Marc, and Irène Bellier (1996). 'La Commission Européenne: Du Compromis Culturel à la Culture Politique du Compromis', *Revue Française de Science Politique*, 46:3, 431–56.

Abélès, Marc, Irène Bellier and Maryon McDonald (1993) 'An Anthropological Approach to the European Commission'. Brussels: Report for the European Commission (unpublished).

Babbie, Earl (1992). *The Practice of Social Research*. Belmont: Wadsworth Publishing Company.

Bellier, Irène (1995). 'Une Culture de la Commission Européenne? De la Rencontre des Cultures et de Multilingualisme des Fonctionnaires', in Yves Mény, Pierre Muller and Jean-Louis Quermonne (eds.), *Politiques Publiques en Europe*. Paris: L'Harmattan, 49–60.

Beyers, Jan, and Guido Dierickx (1997). 'Nationality and European Negotiations: The Working Groups of the Council of Ministers', *European Journal of International Relations*, 3:4, 435–71.

Beyers, Jan, and Guido Dierickx (1998). 'The Working Groups of the Council of the European Union: Supranational or Intergovernmental Negotiations?', *Journal of Common Market Studies*, 36:3, 289–317.

Borgatti, Stephen P., and Pacey C. Foster (2003). 'The Network Paradigm in Organizational Research: A Review and Typology', *Journal of Management*, 29:6, 991–1013.

Brass, Daniel J. (1984). 'Being in the Right Place: A Structural Analysis of Individual Influence in an Organization', *Administrative Science Quarterly*, 29, 518–39.

Cini, Michelle (1996). *The European Commission. Leadership, Organization, and Culture in the EU Administration*. Manchester: Manchester University Press.

Cini, Michelle (2004). 'The Reform of the European Commission: An Ethical Perspective', *Public Policy and Administration*, 19:3, 42–54.

Claude, Inis R. Jr. (1971). *Swords into Plowshares: The Problems and Progress of International Organization*. New York: Random House.
Cram, Laura (1994). 'The European Commission as a Multi-organization: Social Policy and IT Policy in the EU', *Journal of European Public Policy*, 1:2, 195–217.
Cross, Rob, and Stephen P. Borgatti (2004). 'The Ties that Share: Relational Characteristics that Facilitate Information Seeking', in Marleen H. Huysman and Volker Wulf (eds.), *Social Capital and Information Technology*. Cambridge: MIT Press, 137–62.
Cross, Rob, Stephen P. Borgatti and Andrew Parker (2001). 'Beyond Answers: Dimensions of the Advice Network', *Social Networks*, 23, 215–35.
Cross, Rob, and Andrew Parker (2004). *The Hidden Power of Social Networks: Understanding How Work Really Gets Done in Organisations*. Harvard, MA: Harvard Business School Press.
Degenne, Alain, and Michel Forsé (1999). *Introducing Social Networks*. London: Sage Publications.
Edwards, Jack E., Marie D. Thomas, Paul Rosenfeld and Stephanie Booth-Kewley (1997). *How to Conduct Organizational Surveys: A Step-by-Step Guide*. Thousand Oaks, CA: Sage Publications.
Egeberg Morten (1996). 'Organization and Nationality in the European Commission Services', *Public Administration*, 74:4, 721–35.
Egeberg, Morten (2001). 'An Organizational Approach to European Integration: Outline of a Complementary Perspective', *ARENA Working Papers* No. 01/18.
Egeberg. Morten (2004). 'An Organizational Approach to European Integration: Outline of a Complementary Perspective', *European Journal of Political Research*, 43, 199–219.
Egeberg, Morten (2006a). 'Executive Politics as Usual: Role Behaviour and Conflict Dimensions in the College of European Commissioners', *Journal of European Public Policy*, 13:1, 1–15.
Egeberg, Morten, ed. (2006b). *Multi-Level Union Administration: The Transformation of Executive Politics in Europe*. Basingstoke: Palgrave Macmillan.
Field, Andy (2005). *Discovering Statistics Using SPSS*. London: Sage Publications.
Hofstede, Geert (1994). 'Images of Europe', *Netherlands Journal of Social Sciences*, 30, 63–82.
Hooghe, Liesbet (1999). 'Consociationalists or Weberians? Top Commission Officials on Nationality', *Governance*, 12:4, 397–424.
Hooghe, Liesbet (2001). *The European Commission and the Integration of Europe*. Cambridge: Cambridge University Press.
Hooghe, Liesbet (2005). 'Several Roads Lead to International Norms, but Few via International Socialization: A Case Study of the European Commission', *International Organization*, 59:4, 861–98.
Joana, Jean, and Andy Smith (2004). 'The Politics of Collegiality: The Non-portfolio Dimension', in Andy Smith (ed.), *Politics and the European Commission: Actors, Interdependence, Legitimacy*. London: Routledge, 30–46.
Jönsson, Christer, and Ole Elgström (2005). 'Introduction', in Ole Elgström and Christer Jönsson (eds.), *European Union Negotiations: Processes, Networks and Institutions*. London: Routledge, 1–11.
Laffan, Brigid (2004). 'The European Union and its Institutions as "Identity Builders"', in Richard K. Hermann, Thomas Risse and Marilynn B. Brewer (eds.), *Transnational Identities: Becoming European in the EU*. Lanham, MD: Rowman & Littlefield Publishers, Inc., 75–96.
Lohr, Sharon L. (1999). *Sampling: Design and Analysis*. Pacific Grove: Brooks/Cole Publishing Company.
Majone, Giandomenico (1996). 'The European Commission as Regulator', in Giandomenico Majone (ed.), *Regulating Europe*. London: Routledge, 61–79.
March, James G., and Herbert A. Simon (1958). *Organizations*. New York: John Wiley & Sons, Inc.
Mazey, Sonia, and Jeremy J. Richardson (1996). 'La Commission Européenne Une Bourse pour les Idées et les Intérêts', *Revue Française de Science Politique*, 46:3, 409–29.
McDonald, Maryon (2000). 'Identities in the European Commission', in Neill Nugent (ed.), *At the Heart of the Union: Studies of the European Commission*. New York: St. Martin's Press, 51–72.

McLaren, Robert I. (1997). 'Organizational Culture in a Multicultural Organization', *International Review of Administrative Sciences*, 63, 57–66.

McPherson, Miller, Lynn Smith-Lovin and James M. Cook (2001). 'Birds of a Feather: Homophily in Social Networks', *Annual Review of Sociology*, 27, 415–44.

Michelmann, Hans J. (1978). 'Multinational Staffing and Organizational Functioning in the Commission of the European Communities', *International Organization*, 32:2, 477–96.

Middlemas, Keith (1995). *Orchestrating Europe: The Informal Politics of the European Union*. London: Fontana Press.

Morgan, Gareth (1986). *Images of Organization*. London: Sage Publications.

Nugent, Neill (2000). 'At the Heart of the Union', in Neill Nugent (ed.), *At the Heart of the Union: Studies of the European Commission*. New York: St. Martin's Press, 1–27.

Page, Edward C. (1997). *People Who Run Europe*. Oxford: Clarendon Press.

Pampel, Fred C. (2000). *Logistic Regression: A Primer*. Thousand Oaks, CA: Sage Publications.

Pratt, Michael G. (2001). 'Social Identity Dynamics in Modern Organizations: An Organizational Psychology/Organizational Behavior Perspective', in Michael A. Hogg and Deborah J. Terry (eds.), *Social Identity Processes in Organizational Contexts*. Ann Arbor: Sheridan Books, 13–30.

Risse, Thomas (2004). 'European Institutions and Identity Change: What Have We Learned?', in Richard K. Hermann, Thomas Risse and Marilynn B. Brewer (eds.), *Transnational Identities: Becoming European in the EU*. Lanham, MD: Rowman & Littlefield Publishers, 247–71.

Selznick, Philip (1957). *Leadership in Administration: A Sociological Interpretation*. New York: Harper & Row.

Shore, Cris (2000). *Building Europe: The Cultural Politics of European Integration*. London: Routledge.

Spence, David, and Anne Stevens (2006). 'Staff and Personnel Policy in the Commission', in David Spence (ed.), *The European Commission*. London: John Harper, 149–84.

Stevens, Anne, and Handley Stevens (2001). *Brussels Bureaucrats? The Administration of the European Union*. Basingstoke: Palgrave.

Trondal, Jarle (2001). *Administrative Integration across Levels of Governance. Integration through Participation in EU-Committees*. Oslo: ARENA Report No. 7/2001.

Trondal, Jarle (2006a). 'Governing at the Frontier of the European Commission: The Case of Seconded National Experts', *West European Politics* 29:1, 147–60.

Trondal, Jarle (2006b). 'An Institutional Perspective on Representation. Ambiguous Representation in the European Commission', *European Integration online Papers* (EIoP), 10:4.

Appendix: Research Design and Methodology

The research questions have been answered by means of interviews with policy-making, that is, Administrator level (A-level)[13] European Commission officials. The interviews contained both structured and open questions derived from the literature and exploratory pilot interviews. To get the most interesting results with this number of informants, the study was limited to one policy area. Four DGs belonging to the 'Social Regulation'[14] family have been included in the sample: Employment, Social Affairs and Equal Opportunities; Environment; Health and Consumer Protection; Justice, Freedom and Security. Methodologically, obtaining a high response rate is crucial, and reducing the respondents' burden is one of the main factors that influence the response rate (Lohr 1999: 261). At the time of sampling, this group of DGs employed a total of 1100 A-level officials, more or less equally distributed across the DGs. This was an important factor in terms of distributing the respondent burden across DGs. Reducing the respondents' burden is one of the crucial factors that influences the response rate (Lohr 1999: 261).

Since the DG attachment is the central variable for testing the effect of organisational structure, it is vital to ensure an adequate representation of all the DGs to allow comparison between the DGs. To obtain a real 'miniature of the population' that reflects the population with respect to the size of the DGs, the sampling technique that has been used is a type of stratified random sampling called proportional allocation (Lohr 1999: 104). Proportionate stratified sampling typically results in more precise survey estimates by reducing sampling error (Edwards *et al.* 1997: 58–59).

The online Commission directory was utilised to compose the list of the population of officials from which a random sample of 120 officials has been drawn. A proportionally equal number of officials were thus randomly selected within each DG. The interviews were conducted within the span of a total of five weeks, during the two periods between 5–22 April 2005 and 23 May–3 June 2005. The resulting overall response rate (out of 118 officials[15]) was 69 per cent, i.e. 82 officials, which is considered to be a very good response rate (Babbie 1992: 267). Item non-response rate was very low: Only one of the 82 officials only responded to half of the survey questions and was excluded from most of the analyses.

First, some background information on the officials was gathered to account for potential explanatory factors that determine the shape of an official's network, based on the studies and questionnaires of Beyers and Dierickx (1997, 1998), Hooghe (2001), and Trondal (2001). These elements included multinational family background and experience, command of foreign languages, past work experience (in national or international organisations) and length of service.

In social network analysis, a network is a set of actors connected by a set of ties. A single focal actor is called an 'ego' and the set of actors that ego has ties with are called 'alters'. The ensemble of ego, his alters and all ties among these (including those to ego) is called an *ego-network* (Borgatti and Foster 2003: 992). Since ego-networks can be collected for unrelated egos, ego-network studies combine a network-theoretical perspective with the conventional, individual-oriented methods of collecting and processing data (ibid.).

To obtain the network of each official, the respondents were asked to reflect upon the officials they regularly turn to for information or advice, specifying that this does not (necessarily) involve the officials they have to contact due to their task description and obligations. The respondents were then asked to select the *three officials*[16] they considered to be the most important for conducting their policy-making work. The interviews focused subsequently on the attributes of and relationships with these three contact persons.

The structured interview questions were followed up by open questions concerning networks in the Commission, such as how Commission officials build their networks and more importantly to what extent, how, and why their networks affect policy-making processes. This qualitative data has been recorded, and the recorded material and the notes of the interviews have been transcribed. The results of the quantitative part of the survey were analysed using the statistical software package SPSS 12.0.1.

Who Consults? The Configuration of Expert Groups in the European Union

ÅSE GORNITZKA and ULF SVERDRUP

This article examines a crucial property of the European governance system. The EU is frequently understood as a governance system characterised by a strong degree of interpenetration of different levels of government and a plethora of interactions between EU institutions, national and sub-national administrations as well as organised non-state interests. The ubiquity of different kinds of public policy networks or expert groups involved in consultation, bargaining, deliberation and decision-making is believed to be a prominent feature of the European governance system (Eising and Kohler-Koch 1999; Kohler-Koch 1997; Kohler-Koch and Rittberger 2006). Nowhere is this kind of multi-level governance system as evident as in the numerous expert groups and committees of the EU. Such committees are in some sense the epitome of the European multi-level governance system at work. EU committees encompass an array of bodies that vary considerably in what they do, how they are organised, what role they play in EU policy-making and to which EU institution they are anchored. Several specific and detailed studies have provided information and insights regarding the functions and dynamics of these public policy networks (Beyers and Trondal 2004; Christiansen and Larsson 2007; Egeberg *et al.* 2003; Larsson and Murk 2007; Wessels 1997). Scholarly attention has been paid in particular to the role of committees in overseeing the execution of EU rules by the Commission (Dehousse 2003; Dogan 1997; Franchino 2000; Pollack 2003), and there have been attempts to assess the extent to which committees and consultative organs affect the democratic quality of the European Union (Joerges and Neyer 1997; Rhinard 2002; Vos 1997).[1]

The focus in this article is on the committees and groups organised by the European Commission, i.e. its expert groups. New data are now available that enable us to examine more critically the use of such committees in the EU and to answer some basic questions related to this aspect of the EU multi-level system. What is the extent of the expert consultative system? What is the distribution of expert groups? Are expert groups distributed equally across different policy fields, or is this form of multi-level governance concentrated in some specific policy fields? Are these groups best understood as loose networks in the sense that they are informal, flexible, dynamic, temporary and ever-changing, or are they part of a more formalised, organised, routinised and well-established consultation system? Previous studies have not given clear answers to such questions. For instance, Larsson and Trondal (2006) claim that not even the European Commission itself has adequate knowledge of the scale and activities of the expert groups.[2] In the absence of good data, scholars have been engaged in making 'guesstimates', ranging from 800 to 1,300 groups (Larsson and Trondal 2006) or vague statements such as 'there are probably more than 1,000 committees' (van Schendelen 1998: 5). The new quantitative data also allow us to examine some rudimentary hypotheses that can shed light on the pattern of distribution and the factors involved in creating, changing and maintaining this part of the EU governance system. This article is the first report from a larger and ongoing research project on the role of the expert groups in the EU, in which we will also examine the participation and sociometrics of this consultative system (Gornitzka and Sverdrup 2007).

Our approach is consistent with two recent calls in the literature on European governance. First, Johan P. Olsen argued that better understanding of the levels and forms of European integration requires the building of more detailed knowledge about institutional variations across sectors (Olsen 2007). Second, there have been arguments for gradually changing the research focus from explorative and descriptive case studies to larger N studies and a stronger focus on empirical studies (Broscheid and Coen 2007; Coen 2007; Franchino 2005). In addition to supporting such calls, we believe that a systematic and structured cross-sector analysis of the consultative system might help to provide meaning to the diverse and competing statements being made about the qualities and functions of the EU governance system.

Our argument is that the expert groups play an increasingly important role in the EU. We can observe a proliferation of this mode of governance across sectors. We find that the use of expert groups has developed into a routinised practice of the European Commission in order for it to connect to its environment and bring together various state and societal actors. Moreover, a great proportion of the expert groups have become permanent and lasting properties of the governance system. However, our data also show that the expert groups are remarkably unevenly distributed along different policy domains and areas. Distinct policy segments have different modes of connecting to their environment. While some areas are clearly multi-level in their governance structure, others are not. The high degree of sectoral differentiation is accentuated by the fact that we observe weak horizontal coordinating structures between the Directorates-General (DGs) in their use of expert groups. We argue that the heterogeneity in modes of governance across policy fields is not only a result of deliberate design attempts and differences in policy tasks, but also largely the result of different institutional and organisational factors, such as legal and administrative capabilities, as well as the gradual development of different routines and norms for connecting to the environment.

The article is organised as follows: in the next section, we discuss two theoretical perspectives that might explain the use of expert groups in the EU and comment on our data and methodology. We then present an empirical analysis of the distribution of the expert groups across time and discuss factors that can explain the segmented pattern of consultation. Towards the end of the article we show how our observations are further strengthened by analysing the degree of specialisation and the degree of institutionalisation of the consultative system.

Theoretical Approaches and Expectations

Expert groups are one of the three main types of committees organised by EU institutions. Together with the Council working parties and committees, and the comitology committees, they make up the EU's committees system (Hayes-Renshaw and Wallace 2006). Formally, an expert group is a consultative entity comprised of public or private sector experts, and the Commission is in control of its composition. Expert groups are comprised of members from national governments, academia and various interest groups. The main task of the groups is to advise the Commission on the preparation of legislative proposals and policy initiatives as well as on its tasks of monitoring and coordination or cooperation with the member states. Expert groups do not formally make political decisions, but feed the decision-making processes by giving expert advice, providing scientific knowledge, sharing practical experience and information, and serving as forums for exchange of information. The groups can be either permanent or temporary. The Commission creates its expert groups itself, which is also a characteristic that sets them apart from both the comitology and Council committees. A Commission expert group may be created in two different ways, either through a Commission decision or other legal act establishing the group or by a Commission service with the agreement of the Secretariat-General. Officially, the expert groups' task is to assist the Commission as a whole, but in practice the expert groups run by the DGs are mostly involved with the relevant field.

In sum, the Commission's committees constitute a highly complex system that defies any easy categorisations[3] and does not have a well-articulated set of rules to regulate its operations. Hence, we can expect to see multiple factors that come into play in creating, changing and maintaining this part of the EU governance system, some of which are singled out for analysis in this article. Here we approach the issue of expert groups in the EU from two perspectives; one emphasising the role of choice and design and the other emphasising the role of routines and institutional factors (March and Olsen 1998; Olsen 1997; 2001; 2002; 2007).

Design Perspectives

From a design perspective, expert groups are basically viewed as instruments for increasing effectiveness in decision-making. The European Commission is often faced with tasks that have considerable technical, political or legal uncertainty, and is therefore in need of assistance. By using expert groups, the European Commission is able to extract knowledge, expertise and information from actors in its task environments and potentially improve the quality of its decisions and reduce uncertainty. The participants in these groups bring relevant topics to the discussions, indicate potential risks, and sometimes suggest modes for easing transposition and implementation. Expert groups can be used in direct linkage to decision-making situations or as a tool for surveying and monitoring the environment. The setting up of expert groups can be regarded as a relatively risk-free strategy when entering into new or difficult territory. Typically one could expect that the more uncertainty, the more room for a problem-solving logic based on expertise (Radaelli 1999). From this perspective, it is assumed that the European Commission would design and shape its expert groups so that they correspond closely with its preferences and tasks. In addition, we expect that the expert groups are flexible and easily adaptable to new and changing tasks and preferences. Once the 'mission is accomplished' the expert groups will be dismantled.

The policy task argument. It follows from this approach that as long as we know and are able to identify the nature of the policy problem facing the DGs we should be able to predict the organisational solution to decision-making and thus the presence of expert groups. Although the idea is simple, defining and operationalising the type of policy and nature of the policy good is notoriously difficult (Lowi 1964). We take as a starting point the distinction between regulatory versus non-regulatory policies. This has had a recurring significance for explaining the shape of EU decision-making arenas and the relative power of EU institutions in general (Burns 2005; Majone 1996: 61–79). The main idea we pursue is an assumption that distributive policies will be subjected more often to consultations than other policy types. The following underlying mechanism creates the rationale for such a relationship.

When the services are engaged in managing large resources, they will have a particularly great need for information stemming from their tasks to ensure good design of their distributive policy, sound management of the funds, and proper implementation. These needs cannot easily be fulfilled by internal sources of information; hence the Commission services will pursue an extrovert information strategy. Previous studies have also shown that the European Commission often uses financial resources for stimulating cooperation with member state governments and for mobilising sub-national and non-state actors in transnational networks around joint problem-solving activities, particularly in areas such as R&D, trans-European networks and efforts to build a 'People's Europe', which are aimed at complementing market integration (Laffan 1997). It has also been argued that the EU distribution that takes place under the common agricultural policy has also been particularly prone to control by member states and affected interests (Burns 2005). In order to find the concentration of expert groups one should therefore 'follow the money'. *In principle, we would expect that policy areas or Commission services that are responsible for managing large sections of the budget would generate more expert groups than services that are in charge of managing fewer budgetary resources (Hypothesis 1)*. In order to test Hypothesis 1, we sorted various policies according to their share of the EU budget in 2006. In the EU most of the redistributive portion of the budget is devoted to three policy areas: agriculture, regional policy and the various social cohesion programmes.

Supply-side argument. Another, but related, version of this model is to view the expert groups not as a result of careful design by the European Commission, but rather as an instrument resulting from specific supply-side pressures. The more the EU gets involved in a policy area, especially in shaping policies, the more the actors tend to react by organising in order to promote, protest or defend their interests. And by doing so they demand the opportunity to participate in formulating problems and solutions, and engage themselves in the production of new rules in consultative organs such as the expert groups. Such processes of growth in involvement contribute in turn to the creation of new initiatives and new areas of participation, and thus to a dynamic of steadily increasing institutionalisation (Stone Sweet *et al.* 2001). From this perspective, the emergence of expert groups is seen as resulting from distinct pressures from different interest organisations or national interests which regard the expert groups as their instrument for influencing and controlling EU decision-making. We would expect a close relationship between the profile of the expert group system and the supply-side capacities. This kind of supply-side mechanism fits well with ideas of lobbying in the EU (Broscheid and Coen 2007; Coen 2007; Mahoney 2004) and with the observation made by Broscheid and Coen (2007) on an independent effect of the number of interest groups in a certain policy field and the establishment of consultative fora in different DGs. Their underlying argument is that the Commission creates the largest number of expert groups in areas overloaded with interest groups. In order to manage this overload, DGs create expert groups and extend privileges to a limited set of actors who have access to them. Hence, we expect to find that *the more interest groups are organised in a policy area at the European level, the more the relevant DG will tend to create expert groups (Hypothesis 2)*. In order to test this claim we included data on interest groups gathered from the so-called Connecs base[4] and compared this with the number of expert groups per DG.

Institutional Perspectives

An institutional perspective, by contrast, puts particular emphasis on the importance of historical developments, path dependencies and routines when explaining the patterns of distribution of the expert groups. It is assumed that the expert system in the EU, like other institutions in political life, depends not only on satisfying current environmental pressures and political concerns, but it also reflects an institution's origin, history and internal dynamics (March and Olsen 1998). Rather than seeing expert groups as carefully designed to meet specific tasks, the presence of expert groups are regarded as reflecting local rationality, sectoral specialisation and differentiated traditions and histories for relating to the environment. Changes and developments often occur through multiple learning processes, but not always in consistent ways (March and Olsen 1998). Rather than expecting a smooth and well-planned distribution of expert groups, a patchy picture is expected. This argument merges nicely with Kohler-Koch's observation that the EU is functionally segmented. She argues that the governance system in the EU is largely a result of processes of incrementally adding bits and pieces to the functional responsibilities of the Community. The result of such processes is not close co-operation to assure coherence, but rather patchwork policies in a highly segmented system (Kohler-Koch 1997), as well as a marked difference between DGs in their mode of policy-making (Christiansen 1997).

From this perspective, expert groups are seen as mirroring the long-term patterns of interactions between sectorally specialised DGs and their equally specialised and differentiated environments, as well as reflecting internal factors such as internal capacity, age of certain policy domains, and different norms, routines and experiences from consultation and cooperation that have evolved across time. In addition, it follows from this perspective that the use of expert groups over time has developed into a routinised activity with a high degree of institutionalisation. With the present data we cannot make a meaningful operationalisation of historical path dependency and local administrative cultures, yet we incorporate into our analysis two fundamental institutional conditions that determine an organisation's characteristics and that can be expected to account for the differences in density of the DGs' set of expert groups according to an institutional perspective. First, we explore the significance of the legal competencies that DGs operate under and then we look at the importance of their administrative capabilities.

The legal competence argument. A common-sense interpretation we find in some of the literature on EU governance is that the density of expert groups is largely a function of the allocation of competence in the EU. For instance, according to Nugent (2003: 130–131), 'One factor making for variation is the degree of the importance of the policy within the EU's policy framework – it is hardly surprising, for example that there should be many more agricultural advisory committees than there are educational advisory committees.' If we define the degree of importance of a policy area as the legal competence of the EU in the specific area, we can consider this mechanism more in detail. In a simple version of this perspective, we can expect this relationship to be linear: *the more exclusive legal competence allocated to the EU, the more expert groups (Hypothesis 3).*

The underlying idea is that the level and intensity of activity of the Commission are determined by the legal competence of the EU. Increased activity in turn triggers the activation of expert bodies. When competence is transferred from the national level to the European level, new opportunity structures are created at the European level, and new patterns of consultation emerge. The competence attributed to different policy areas is the fundamental legal parameters within which the DGs operate, independent of the budgetary means at the Commission's disposal for pursuing its policies. These competencies are unevenly distributed across the DGs' activity areas and have accrued to the European level at different points in the history of European integration. In order to operationalise this variable we have coded the policy fields according to treaty competence, ranging from 1 to 4. The treaties differentiate between areas of exclusive competence for the EU (coded as 1), areas of shared competence (coded as 2), areas where the EU has coordinating competencies (coded 3), and areas of supporting and complimentary competencies (coded 4).[5]

The administrative capability argument. From an institutional perspective we also expect that the administrative capacity of DGs will feature as a possible explanation for the variation in the use of expert groups. The European Commission consists of a small administration with limited staff and administrative capabilities, particularly when compared with the size of national governments. Still, there has been a continuous growth of new tasks delegated to the European Commission and a de facto extension of the basis for Community action. Expectations regarding the Commission's ability to manage new responsibilities and deliver results have also increased. Balancing task expansion with limited administrative resources has been an enduring theme in European governance. The expert groups can be seen as a form of outsourcing and a mechanism for coping with limited administrative capabilities. Participants in the expert groups can improve the ability of the European Commission to develop policies and monitor implementation by contributing their administrative resources and providing information, knowledge and expertise. Compared with establishing permanent, specialised organisations capable of fact-finding, rule-making and/or enforcement, such as by establishing European agencies or Commission joint research centres, using expert groups incurs less cost for Community budgets. Although expenses are reimbursed by the Commission, participating experts are unpaid. Consequently, the existence of expert groups does not require long-term budgetary commitments. It follows from such a perspective that we would expect there to be a relationship between internal administrative resources and the use of expert groups. *The smaller the internal administrative staff that the DG has at its disposal, the more expert groups it will create (Hypothesis 4).* In order to test this hypothesis we have gathered data on the size and distribution of the European Commission staff.

Data and Methodology

The empirical analysis presented in this article relies on data from our database of Commission expert groups. Our database provides information on key properties of these groups, such as the lead services in the Commission, the policy area and composition of the group in general terms, as well as the group's tasks and missions and their formal status. It classifies the participants into broad categories (scientists, academics, practitioners, industry, NGOs), but it does not contain any information on individual experts, nor does it contain information on the number of meetings and participation rates of the expert groups. When constructing the database we used the European Commission's register of expert groups. Information was downloaded from the register, coded and entered into our database in January 2007.[6]

The register's reliability as a source of information on expert groups is underpinned by the formal rules of the register. The register is partly a result of a commitment made by Commission President Barroso to the European Parliament in November 2004 to increase the transparency of the

Commission's operations and give a public overview of the advisory bodies that assist it in preparing legislative proposals and policy initiatives. According to the 'Framework Agreement on relations between the European parliament and the European Commission' (Article 16), 'The Commission shall inform Parliament of the list of its expert groups set up in order to assist the Commission in the exercise of its right of initiative. That list shall be updated on a regular basis and made public.'[7] As illustrated by its codification in the framework agreement, the importance attached to the registry for ensuring a constructive dialogue and flow of information between the European Commission and the European Parliament increases the reliability of the data. The Commission is formally obliged to enter reliable information and update the register, functions which are performed by permanent staff in the Secretariat General. The unit responsible for the register of expert groups was consulted in the creation of our database.

Distribution of Expert Groups

The Growth of Expert Groups

Our analysis shows that there were 1,237 expert groups organised by the European Commission in January 2007. This is a large number, and it is clearly in the upper range of previous estimates. The expert group system is without doubt a considerable supplementary administrative resource of the European Commission. In fact, there is about one expert group per eight persons working as an official in the European Commission.[8] By comparison there are 250 comitology committees and 162 Council committees/working parties;[9] hence Commission expert groups far outnumber the other parts the EU committee system.

There has been a significant increase in the number of expert groups over time. In 1975 it was reported that there were 537 groups, in 1990 the number had increased to 602 (Wessels 1998), and by 2000 the number had reached 851 (Larsson 2003). These measures indicate gradual and steady growth during the 25-year period, as new competencies and tasks have been added to the European Commission and the European Union. It is noteworthy that this gradual growth has been replaced by a more rapid and radical increase since 2000. In this period the number of expert groups has increased by more than 40 per cent.[10] The large number and the strong growth of the use of expert groups in the European Commission contribute to making this mode of interaction a significant element of the European governance structure, and a routinised and rather standardised mode of consultation. The extensive consultative structure also contributes to the impression of the European Commission as an open, extrovert and accessible administrative body, which is engaged in numerous consultations with a huge number of actors from multiple levels of governance.

Uneven Distribution across Policy Domains and Commission Services

Although the presence of expert groups is widespread throughout the European Commission, there are significant differences in the extent of consultation in different policy areas. In our data, we find three clear patterns regarding the distribution of the expert groups.

First, the expert groups operate primarily in the EU public policy domains (Table 1). There are hardly any expert groups in the field of internal administrative services, and there are few expert groups engaged with the general services. Hence, the DGs related to administrative affairs, budget and financial control, and the General Services such as the Legal Service, General Secretariat and Press and Communication, which are typically regarded as horizontally coordinating Directorates-General and services in the EU (Stevens and Stevens 2001), score low on coordination and cooperation with external experts. We also observe that very few (under 5 per cent) of the total number of expert groups are related to external relations policies.

Secondly, the distribution of expert groups is biased and unevenly distributed across the different DGs (Figure 1). More than 75 per cent of all the expert groups in the Commission are related to ten DGs. The data fall into three broad categories: DGs that organise many expert groups (more than 70), DGs in the mid-range (between 70 and 20), and DGs with just a few expert groups (fewer than 20). Within the first group we find three 'super users', consisting of DG Research, DG Environment and DG Enterprise, all having 120 or more expert groups. Taken together, these three DGs organise approximately 30 per cent of all expert groups. In addition, DG Taxation and Customs, DG Energy and Transport, DG Health and Consumer Protection, Eurostat and DG Education and Culture all have more than 70 expert groups each. In the second category we find the DGs that are responsible for what we might label 'classic' European affairs, such as economic and social policy, agriculture policy, internal market, fishery and regional policy. This biased distribution of expert groups clearly indicates strong sectoral differentiation between different DGs in their mode of governance. While extensive use of consultation with expert groups is a prominent characteristic of some policy areas, such as research,

TABLE 1
COMMISSION EXPERT GROUPS ACCORDING TO POLICY DOMAIN. N=1237

		Count	Valid percentage	Cumulative percentage
Valid	Policies	1,076	87.0	87.0
	General services	99	8.0	95.0
	External relations	54	4.4	99.4
	Internal services	8	0.6	100.0
	Total	1,237	100.0	

FIGURE 1
COMMISSION EXPERT GROUPS ACROSS SERVICE AND TIME

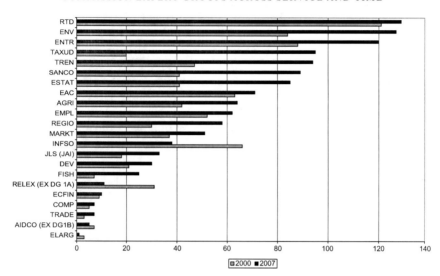

Source: Own data from 2007, data on 2000 based on Larsson (2003). Some services with fewer than five expert groups are excluded.

environment, energy and transport, this mode of governance is found much more seldom in other areas, such as trade, competition, economic and financial affairs.

A third striking feature regarding the distribution of the expert groups is the changes in the number of expert groups across time.[11] As illustrated by Figure 1, the overall trend is that there are more expert groups attached to most of the various DGs now than seven years ago. Very few DGs deviate from this pattern. In 2007, the median value was 27 expert groups per service compared to 19 in 2000. During a seven-year period the number of DGs with more than 80 expert groups has increased by more than 100 per cent, and four of the DGs have more than doubled their number of expert groups. The DGs that had the highest number in 2000 remain at the top in 2007, and we still observe considerable variation between the various DGs. However, there is also a clear move towards less differentiated distribution, indicating that this method of consultation and interaction between the Commission and its environment is becoming more widespread and standardised.

Explaining Uneven Distribution

What we have seen here is a strong sectoral differentiation in the DGs use of expert groups. Why are there more expert groups in some policy domains? What are the relevant dimensions of the policy sectors and political organisation that make such a difference for the way in which the Commission relates to external expertise? Let us now assess how and to what extent the four hypotheses can help to explain this pattern.

Task Matching – Policy Type Argument

Our data show that the DGs engaged in distribution do not have a large number of expert groups. As we can see from Figure 2, the DGs that are most involved in such polices, DG Agriculture, DG Regional Policy, DG Employment and Social Affairs, and DG Research, which together account for more than 85 per cent of the total EU budget, have only about 25 per cent of the total number of expert groups, and DG Research accounts for half of these. We can therefore conclude that our Hypothesis 1 is not supported.

However, the lack of support for our hypothesis could in fact be a misspecification of the nature of the policy task. When we fail to see the effect of distributive policy, it should not lead us to dismiss the idea that the nature of the policy domain significantly affects the pattern of expert group distribution.

In particular, one could argue that the Commission's choice for establishing a group is conditioned by the technical versus the political nature of the task rather than whether or not the DGs are tackling distributional or regulatory problems. One could also argue that the varying intensity of political conflict in policy-specific interest constellations impinges on the ability of the Commission to act (Scharpf 1999) and that international

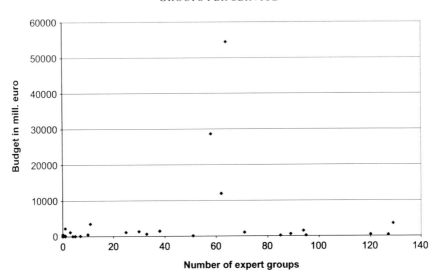

FIGURE 2
RELATIONSHIP BETWEEN EU BUDGET PER SERVICE AND NUMBER OF EXPERT GROUPS PER SERVICE

cooperation and integration are easier to achieve in fields seen as being technical with low intensity of political conflict. Technical issues typically require expertise, and expertise tends to subordinate national boundaries to shared professional concerns and epistemic communities (Haas 1992; March and Olsen 1998). The literature on international coordination has shown the crucial role of experts in political integration and transnational governance in general and in the EU in particular. It can be argued that regulatory policy rather than distributive policy is based on knowledge as a resource and aims at efficiency rather than fair distribution. Consequently, regulatory policy areas fit better in the realm of technocracy and the world of expert groups, which is relatively insulated from political conflict (Radaelli 1999).[12]

Although we recognise the significance of this distinction for explaining the variation in forms of consultation, we find it hard to operationalise and use policy type as an independent variable. First, coding the policy types according to their degree of technical specialisation requires detailed knowledge of the activities of each expert group, which is unavailable in our database. Using DG types as a proxy for 'type of task' is inadequate in this respect. Secondly, additional substantive challenges are posed by the fact that what is regarded as technical versus political issues changes over time. Politically salient issues can be decentralised into technical arenas in order to avoid politically sensitive conflicts. Sometimes policy labels shift as a result of deliberate choice, for instance when an issue is being 'decentralised' to a technical level in order to avoid political conflicts (Olsen 1983: 208–209), or the other way around, when a rather technical issue becomes highly politicised, for instance regarding stem cell research in the EU 7th Framework Program or statistical measures in the case of EMU. In other instances, the label attached to a policy can change rapidly as a result of external events or sudden crisis, such as in the case of BSE and Creutzfeld-Jacob disease. Studies of EU committee governance, in particular working groups under the Council (Fouilleux *et al.* 2005), also report that this distinction is continuously blurred and putative technical working groups are heavily involved in dynamic processes of politicisation and depoliticisation of public policy issues. If this is indeed the case, the distinction between technical versus political policy domains cannot be used as an independent variable for explaining the variation in the presence of expert groups.

Supply-Side Argument

As we see from Figure 3, the strong correlation between the number of interest groups and density of expert groups gives support to supply-side explanations. Nevertheless, we are uncertain how plausible it is to make conclusions about the causal mechanism of interest group overload based on this significant correlation.

FIGURE 3
RELATIONSHIP BETWEEN NUMBER OF INTEREST GROUPS AND EXPERT GROUPS IN DIFFERENT POLICY FIELDS

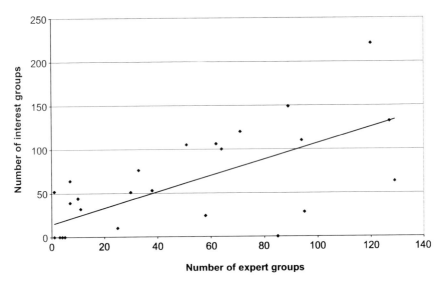

An alternative argument would be to say that it is the general level of activity within the EU that generates both the presence of interest groups *and* expert group density in different policy domains. It should also be noted that a large share of Commission expert groups *do not* include interest group participation (Gornitzka and Sverdrup 2007), and therefore their creation can hardly be seen as the Commission's means of managing interest group overload. Rather it might be the case that the creation of expert groups causes participatory overload as it opens up a 'can of worms' of potential participants that are deemed relevant and legitimate, from 27 member states and their respective national administrations, regional authorities, candidate countries, EEA members, interest groups and academics. Furthermore, there are some important DGs that deviate from the overall pattern. For DG Research, DG Taxation and Customs and Eurostat and DG Regional Policy, this correlation is not present. Rather than seeing the proliferation of interest group organisations as the main trigger for the establishment of expert groups, we would argue that the number of interest groups at the European level reflects more general sectoral differences in political organisation in Europe, as well as the fact that some policy areas are considered more receptive to influence and input than others.

Legal Competence Argument

In Figure 4 we present a scatter plot of the distribution of competencies and the number of expert groups. As we can see, our data do not support the

FIGURE 4
RELATIONSHIP BETWEEN LEGAL COMPETENCE AND THE NUMBER OF EXPERT GROUPS

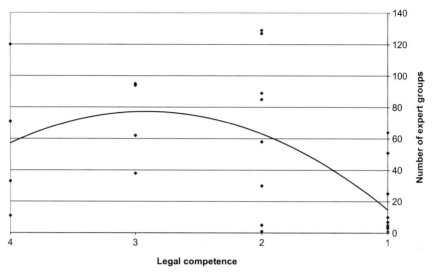

Note: 1 = exclusive, 2 = shared, 3 = coordinating, 4 = supporting/complementary.

argument of a linear relationship, in which increased EU competence in a policy field would lead to increased involvement of expert groups. In fact, we observe that most of the expert groups are operating in policy areas where competences are shared. The number of expert groups is rather low in policy areas of exclusive EU competence, such as agriculture and fishery policy. We also find relatively few expert groups in DGs in which primacy is given to market building and legal aspects, trade, competition and internal market issues (see also Table 4). This supports the argument that consultations have not developed in traditional areas of EU integration where the DGs can operate with high European legal capacity for action and correspondingly low national capacity (Scharpf 1999). These are all areas where the Commission DGs act in a management role with the day-to-day operation of policy areas where the European level has replaced the nation-state level (Shore 2000). The uneven integration (Olsen 2007) is reflected in an uneven distribution of consultations across levels of governance.

It follows from this discussion that there is no simple linear relationship between the quality of EU legal competence and the number of expert groups. If there is a relationship between legal competence and the density of expert groups in policy fields, it seems to bear more of a resemblance to a hump-shaped curve. This observation is consistent with a view of the Commission as the defender of the treaty and an organisation that seeks to maximise its autonomy within the conditions set by the treaty. In areas of exclusive competences the DGs can function as relatively independent actors in their day-to-day operations, but areas of mixed competences are the realm of multi-level policy-making and implementation where the Commission practices would involve the joint exercise of coordination and authority. These areas have developed issue-specific constituencies across multiple levels, involving multiple types of actors (Eising and Kohler-Koch 1999). At the other end of the scale, i.e. areas where there is very limited or no treaty basis for Commission action, there is no room for a structured interaction between levels of governance organised by the Commission.

The Administrative Capability Argument

In Figure 5 we present a scatter plot of the relationship between the administrative resources of a DG, defined as the size of the administrative staff, and the number of expert groups at its disposal. As we can see from the plot, we observe a relationship, but its direction is opposite to what we expected. The more internal administrative capacities a DG has at its disposal, the more expert groups it will create. Rather than being a substitute for its own administrative resources, the DG uses expert groups as a supplement to its own capacities. This is not consistent with the view that DGs will systematically pursue a 'self-reliance' strategy and only organise a multi-level administrative structure to compensate for a lack of in-house administrative capacity. Rather it seems that internal administrative capacity is a prerequisite for organising a large number of expert groups. None (with one exception) of the DGs with a dense set of expert groups (i.e., with more than 70 groups) has fewer than 500 officials. This observation suggests that expert groups are perhaps best seen as a tool for extending the DGs' capacity for action rather than limiting the DGs' autonomy vis-à-vis member states and interest groups.

However, we also see different types of relationships between internal administrative staff and the use of external expert groups. In the lower right-hand section with a low degree of internal resources but a high degree of expert groups, we find DG Environment and DG Taxation and Customs. In these policy areas the outsourcing hypotheses seem to fit the data very well. In the upper right-hand section we find the policy areas that mobilise many internal resources and many external resources. Not surprisingly, we find policy areas that have increased in importance during the last few years and areas that are of crucial importance to the current EU agenda, such as DG Research, DG Energy and Transport. In the upper left-hand section we find the DGs with a relatively high level of internal resources and relatively few expert groups, such as DG Agriculture, DG Information Society and DG External Relations. In the lower left-hand quadrant, we find policy areas that have relatively few internal resources and that make use of few external resources, including DG Justice and Home Affairs, DG Development and DG Fish and Maritime. In the centre and almost on the trend line we find DGs related

FIGURE 5
RELATIONSHIP BETWEEN ADMINISTRATIVE CAPABILITIES IN THE
COMMISSION DGS AND THE NUMBER OF EXPERT GROUPS (N=1233)

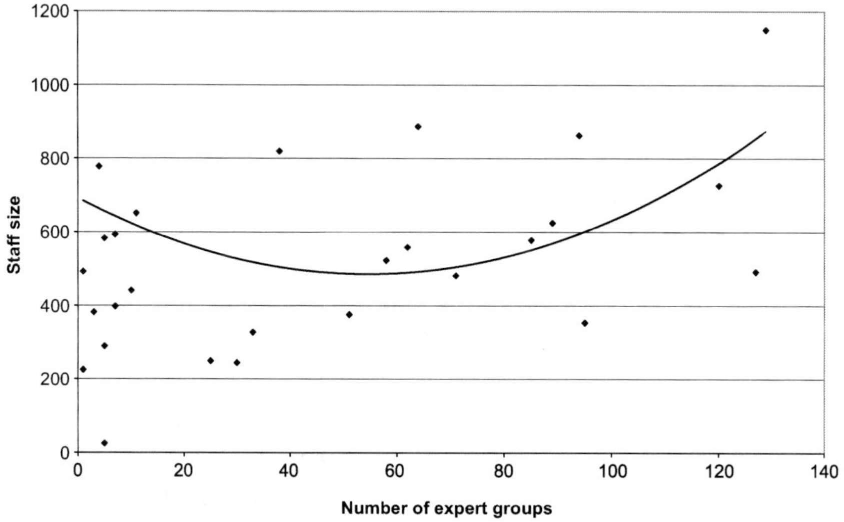

Note: DG for Translation and the joint research centres are excluded.

to traditional EU activities such as regional policy and employment, as well as health and consumer affairs.

Strong Sectoral Specialisation and Weak Horizontal Coordination

So far our analysis has clearly documented the heterogeneity and functional specialisation of the expert group system and how this system has developed according to the logic of sectoral specialisation. We have identified dimensions of the policy types and institutional characteristics that can account for some of this heterogeneity. We argue from this that we have pinpointed a part of the EU governance system in which centrifugal forces are at work. The sectoral differentiation we have observed speaks directly to an enduring tension in the organisation of governments between specialisation and horizontal coordination (Gulick 1937). In a purely functionally differentiated decision-making structure, the internal specialisation is matched by highly specialised external contacts, and there are few horizontally integrating forces and structures that ensure cross-sectoral coordination. Our findings fit well with the EU administrative history, in which the organisation has been based primarily upon the sectoral and functional principle, that is, on the purpose and nature of the subject area (Egeberg 2006). We observe this strong sectoral and functional differentiation throughout the whole EU governance system, in the Commission services, in the Council secretariat, in the various Council configurations, as well in the European Parliament, with its functionally differentiated standing committees. In this respect our findings confirm that expert groups contribute to this sectoral and functional specialisation.

However, to take our analysis a step further we also want to examine the degree of horizontal coordination and the degree of institutionalisation. One indicator of cross-sectoral coordination in relation to the expert groups is if we find that the various expert groups are associated with other DGs apart from its host DG. If this is the case, expertise provided by a group in one field is more likely to be used to influence policy-making processes in other fields and DGs as well, and possibly also contribute to increasing the likelihood of developing cross-sectoral politics in the Commission. The extent to which expert groups are set up in collaboration with other DGs and report back to different DGs is therefore also a measure of the (horizontal) permeability of organisational boundaries between the various Commission services.

We observe (Table 2) that only a small fraction of the expert groups are formally linked to DGs other than their host service. Four out of five of the expert groups have a single DG ownership and do not have any other associated DG. Moreover, in cases in which there is coordination across DGs, the number of DGs that are associated is very limited. Of the expert groups that are associated with other DGs in addition to their host DG, a majority is linked to one or two DGs, bringing the total number of more broadly, cross-sectorally anchored expert groups to only 85. We can therefore conclude that the Commission expert groups are not a key part of the horizontal coordinating mechanisms of the Commission. The sectoral and functional differentiation, which is a hallmark of the administrative history of the Commission (Cram 1994, 1997; Egeberg 2006; Stevens and Stevens 2001), seems to be further accentuated by the practice of interacting with extramural expertise structures through expert groups.

A High Degree of Stability and Institutionalisation

Growth and distribution across policy domains and DGs bear witness to how widespread this consultative system has become. However, this does not necessarily imply that these are stable and predictable structures which are unsusceptible to short-term fluctuations and shifts in attention and

TABLE 2
CROSS-SECTORAL COORDINATION OF EXPERT GROUPS. NUMBER OF COMMISSION EXPERT GROUPS ASSOCIATED WITH OTHER DGS IN ADDITION TO THEIR HOST DG

		No	Yes	... of which 1 DG	... of which 2 DGs	... of which 3 or more DGs
Valid	N	1,006	231	96	54	85
	%	81	19	8	4	7

legitimacy or governance fads. What is this system's degree of institutionalisation?

Our data allow us to measure the degree of institutionalisation in two ways. First, we make a distinction between formal and informal expert groups. Formal expert groups are established by a Commission decision or other legal acts, while informal groups are established by the DGs themselves in agreement with the Secretariat General and without reference to such a formal legal act. In principle, formal groups may be regarded as more institutionalised than informal groups. Secondly, we make a distinction between temporary and permanent groups. Expert groups that are either explicitly defined as permanent or that have been in operation for more than five years are coded as permanent groups. The rest of the groups are coded as temporary.

Our analysis shows that (Table 3) three-quarters of the Commission's expert groups are informal and half are temporary. In some senses we can view the expert group system as a rather flexible part of the administrative space in which groups can be established and dismantled without going through elaborate formal decision-making procedures, and therefore contribute to creating a dynamic, flexible and adaptive administrative system. However, our findings also show that a considerable part of this system has become institutionalised and is an important element of a routinised and rather stable administrative structure. The close to 400 expert groups that have become a permanent fixture of the EU without having been created by a formal legal act, along with the numerous formal expert groups, indicate a rather high degree of institutionalisation of the expert group system.

Most DGs balance between temporariness and permanence in their consultative system. Yet some DGs organise a strikingly stable set of expert groups, which is especially the case for Eurostat, DG Agriculture and DG Fisheries. At the other end of the scale we find DG Research, DG Taxation and Customs and DG Information Society, whose expertise system is predominantly temporary.

In sum, we have obtained some striking and robust findings regarding the distribution and degree of institutionalisation of the expert groups. The

TABLE 3
COMMISSION EXPERT GROUPS BY TYPE AND STATUS (N = 1237)

			Temporary	Permanent	Total
Type F/I	Informal	Count	557	389	946
		%	88.6	64.0	76.5
	Formal	Count	72	219	291
		%	11.4	36.0	23.5
Total		Count	629	608	1237
		%	100	100	100.0

large number of expert groups clearly shows that multi-level consultation is an important feature of the European governance system, and our data also show that this mode is gradually becoming even more important over time. Table 4 provides an overview of the distribution of the groups and the degree of institutionalisation. The obvious conclusion of these findings is that the extent and quality of the EU multi-level governance is radically different across different functional policy areas. While multi-level consultation is a dominant and routinised feature of some policy areas and in some services, it is a rather rare occurrence or it is used as a much more flexible tool in other policy areas and services.

The pattern we see in Table 4 has both unsurprising and puzzling traits. The position of internal administrative DGs in the left-hand column does not represent much of a theoretical puzzle. The reason that we find DG Trade and DG Competition in this group, on the other hand, is not that self-evident. In the middle column we find many of the main traditional areas subject to European integration and with a relatively high level of capacity to act at a European level, in particular agriculture, internal market and regional policy. We also see that many of the policy areas associated with the 'New Europe' or the European knowledge economy, such as research and education, are located in the right-hand column along with high-profile areas, such as energy and environmental policy. The degree of institutionalisation, on the other hand, also pairs policy areas that usually are not thought of as having much in common – such as taxation and research policy. Placing the policy areas in a two-dimensional space points us in the direction that both the nature of the policy area and institutional differences

TABLE 4
DISTRIBUTION OF EXPERT GROUPS AND THEIR INSTITUTIONALISATION
(NUMBER OF EGS PER DG IN PARENTHESIS)

		Number of expert groups		
		Few (fewer than 20)	Medium (21–70)	Many (71 or more)
Degree of institutionalisation	Low (0–33.3%)	RELEX (11) TRADE (7) COMP (7) BUDG (3) ELARG (1) DGT (1)	INFSO (38)	RTD (129) TAXUD (95)
	Medium (33.4–66.6%)	BEPA (5) SG (4)	EMPL (62) REGIO (58) JLS (33) DEV (30)	ENV (127) ENTR (120) TREN (94) EAC (71)
	High (66.7–100%)	ECFIN (10) OLAF (5) AIDCO (5) JRC (3) ADMIN (3) COMM (1)	AGRI (64) MARKT (51) FISH (25)	SANCO (89) ESTAT (85)

are factors that encourage, facilitate and restrain the Commission's use of expert groups.

Conclusions

Our analysis substantiates the idea that the European Union should be understood as a governance system characterised by interpenetration of different levels of government and non-state actors. We see this in the ubiquity of expert groups at the European level. The Commission's 1,237 expert groups are a key element in the multi-level European administrative space, outnumbering by far other types of committees in the EU system. Over time this particular mode of consultation has become more widespread and institutionalised. The number of expert groups has increased considerably, especially after 2000. Although the formal rules system regulating the creation and operation of expert groups is weak, the use of expert groups has become a standard way for a large proportion of the DGs to interact with their environment. We also see some convergence in consultative system(s) in the various DGs, as all the DGs, with the exception of two, have increased the number of expert groups they organise. While three-quarters of the expert groups are informal, half of them are permanent. These findings clearly support the claim that the EU can be understood as a relatively stable multi-level governance system.

The density and durability of the expert groups, on the other hand, vary considerably between different Commission services. Some DGs are clearly engaged in governance of this kind while other DGs are not involved in this mode of governance. As for the factors that can explain the observed heterogeneity in the organisation of expert groups across policy fields, we find some support for the design perspective. On the one hand, parts of the Commission's set of expert groups represent a deliberate attempt to match information systems and consultation to policy tasks. This is especially the case when we differentiate between internal/general services and sectorally oriented DGs. Most of the expert groups are found in areas of substantive European policy areas, especially in task areas related to research, environment and enterprise policy. In issue areas related to internal administration, general services, and external relations, there are few – if any – expert groups. The distinction between regulatory versus distributive policy can also account for some of the heterogeneity in the Commission's use of expert groups – contrary to our expectations, distributive policies do not entail more use of expert groups. We also find that external pressures in terms of the number of interest groups are significantly correlated with the Commission's DG propensity to establish expert groups. Moreover, much of the variation results from different institutional and organisational factors such as legal and administrative capabilities, as well as the gradual development of different routines and norms for connecting to the environment. Expert groups are typically established and drawn into the policy process in policy areas where legal competence is shared between the European and national level of governance, and the density of organised expert groups is highest in the policy areas where administrative and policy-making capacity has been amassed in the Commission.

One main pattern we observe is that expert groups contribute to the sectoral differentiation of EU decision-making, amplifying the sectoral organisation of the European administrative space. Cross-sectoral coordination of expert group activities is at a very low level. The world of expert groups unveils the Commission as a multi-organisation that is part of structured multi-level governance within sectorally defined boundaries. This underscores the significance of the basic organisational structure of the Commission, its institutional traditions and routines, as well as the legal parameters and administrative capacity of the various DGs for the way in which European multi-level governance is structured. We therefore argue that the EU is best understood as a functionally differentiated system with very different *modus operandi*. Different policy areas form issue- and policy-specific constituencies that evolve according to different logics. We have described the empirical variance in the Commission's expert group system and pointed to causal mechanisms and differentiating factors that can account for these differences. The findings emphasise the need to give due attention to the heterogeneity of European multi-level governance in the study of European integration and its institutions and to specify the institutional conditions and constellations of actors involved in governing Europe.

Acknowledgements

Draft versions of this article were presented at the ARENA seminar on 8 May 2007, at the CONNEX Conference: Institutional Dynamics and the Transformation of Executive Politics in Europe, Barcelona 7–9 June 2007, and at the 4th ECPR general conference, Pisa, Italy, 6–8 September 2007. We would like to thank Michael Bauer, Jeff Checkel, Thomas Christiansen, Pieter de Wilde, Morten Egeberg, Fabio Franchino and Johan P. Olsen for helpful comments.

Notes

1. Note that these studies focus specifically on comitology committees.
2. To our knowledge, the most comprehensive overview to date is provided by a Swedish governmental report prepared by Torbjörn Larsson (2003).
3. See Christiansen and Larsson (2007) for a discussion of the defining characteristics of the Commission's expert advisory groups.
4. Consultation, the European Commission and Civil Society (Coneccs) is the Commission's database of civil society organisations active at the EU level. http://ec.europa.eu/civil_society/coneccs/index.html.
5. For reasons of simplicity we use here the terms found in the unratified Draft Constitutional Treaty.

6. It does not cover all expert groups and committees that are linked to the Commission. The following broad categories of entities are excluded from the Commission's register and thus also from our database: 1) independent experts charged with assisting the Commission in the implementation of framework programmes for research and development; 2) Sectoral and cross-industry social dialogue committees, whose work is particularly aimed at the finalising of agreements implemented by the Council or autonomous agreements implemented by the social partners themselves and at adopting frameworks for action. There were about 70 such committees in 2004; 3) Comitology committees which are established by the legislator to assist the Commission in policy areas where the Commission is empowered to implement legislation (about 250 such committees in 2004); 4) Joint entities arising from international agreements (a total of 170 joint entities in 2004). These entities differ from expert groups in terms of their creation and competence: they are created in accordance with methods laid down in international agreements, and their role is to supervise their implementation: http://ec.europa.eu/transparency/regexpert/faq/faq.cfm?aide=2.
7. See full agreement at http://ec.europa.eu/dgs/secretariat_general/relations/relations_other/docs/framework_agreement_ep-ec_en.pdf.
8. Data on the European Commission was found in the Statistical Bulletin of Commission staff: http://ec.europa.eu/civil_service/docs/bs_dg_category_en.pdf.
9. Data for comitology committees from 2006 and for Council committees from 2005; in addition there were 121 sub-groups under the Council working parties and committees (Hayes-Renshaw and Wallace 2006).
10. Since there is uncertainty attached to the accuracy of the data from the years prior to the establishment of the register, some of this increase might reflect more rigorous methods for reporting.
11. As noted earlier, there is some uncertainty regarding the accuracy of the measure from 2000.
12. A similar argument is voiced in theory by Broscheid and Coen because they expect to see more expert groups in regulatory policies as the nature of the policy good in these policy areas affect limited sets of societal actors in combination with high demand for technical information. However, they fail to find support for this hypothesis in their data on expert fora creation; rather they find (insignificantly) more expert groups in distributive policy domains (Broscheid and Coen 2007).

References

Beyers, J., and J. Trondal (2004). 'How Nation States "Hit" Europe: Ambiguity and Representation in the European Union', *West European Politics*, 27:5, 919–42.

Broscheid, A., and D. Coen (2007). 'Lobbying Activity and Fora Creation in the EU: Empirically Exploring the Nature of the Policy Good', *Journal of European Public Policy*, 14:3, 346–65.

Burns, C. (2005). 'Who Pays? Who Gains? How Do Costs and Benefits Shape the Policy Influence of the European Parliament?', *Journal of Common Market Studies*, 43:3, 485–505.

Christiansen, T. (1997). 'Tensions of European Governance: Politicized Bureaucracy and Multiple Accountability in the European Commission', *Journal of European Public Policy*, 4:1, 73–90.

Christiansen, T., and T. Larsson, eds. (2007). *The Role of Committees in the Policy-Process of the European Union – Legislation, Implementation and Deliberation*. Cheltenham: Edward Elgar.

Coen, D. (2007). 'Empirical and Theoretical Studies in EU Lobbying', *Journal of European Public Policy*, 14:3, 333–45.

Cram, L. (1994). 'The European Commission as a Multi-Organization: Social Policy and IT Policy in the EU', *Journal of European Public Policy*, 1:2, 195–217.

Cram, L. (1997). *Policy-Making in the European Union*. London: Taylor & Francis.

Dehousse R. (2003). 'Comitology: Who Watches the Watchmen?', *Journal of European Public Policy*, 10:5, 798–813.
Dogan, R. (1997). 'Comitology: Little Procedures with Big Implications', *West European Politics*, 20:3, 31–60.
Egeberg, M. (2006). 'Balancing Autonomy and Accountability: Enduring Tensions in the European Commission's Development', in M. Egeberg (ed.), *Multilevel Union Administration. The Transformation of Executive Politics in Europe*. Houndmills: Palgrave MacMillan, 31–50.
Egeberg, M., G.F. Schaefer, and J. Trondal (2003). 'The Many Faces of EU Committee Governance', *West European Politics*, 26:3, 19–40.
Eising, R., and B. Kohler-Koch (1999). 'Governance in the European Union: A Comparative Assessment', in B. Kohler-Koch and R. Eising (eds.), *The Transformation of Governance in the European Union*. London: Routledge, 3–13.
Fouilleux, E., J. de Maillard and A. Smith (2005). 'Technical or Political? The Working Groups of the EU Council of Ministers', *Journal of European Public Policy*, 12:4, 609–23.
Franchino, F. (2000). 'The Commission's Executive Discretion, Information and Comitology', *Journal of Theoretical Politics*, 12:2, 155–81.
Franchino, F. (2005). 'The Study of EU Public Policy: A Survey', *European Union Politics*, 6:2, 243–52.
Gornitzka, Å., and U. Sverdrup (2007). 'The Sociometrics of EU Governance'. Unpublished paper, Arena – Centre for European Studies, University of Oslo.
Gulick, L. (1937). 'Science, Values and Public Administration', in L. Gulick and L. Urwick (eds.), *Papers in the Science of Administration*. New York: Institute of Public Administration, 191–5.
Hayes-Renshaw, F., and H. Wallace (2006). *The Council of Ministers*. Houndmills: Palgrave Macmillan.
Haas, P. (1992). 'Introduction: Epistemic Communities and International Policy Coordination', *International Organization*, 46:1, 1–35.
Joerges, C., and J. Neyer (1997). 'From Intergovernmental Bargaining to Deliberative Political Processes: The Constitutionalisation of Comitology', *European Law Journal*, 3:2, 273–99.
Kohler-Koch, B. (1997). 'Organized Interests in the EC and the European Parliament', *European Integration online Papers (EIoP)*, 1:9, 1–14.
Kohler-Koch, B., and B. Rittberger (2006). 'The Governance Turn in EU Studies', *Journal of Common Market Studies*, 44:1, 27–49.
Laffan, B. (1997). *The Finances of the European Union*. London: Macmillan.
Larsson, T. (2003). *Precooking in the European Union – The World of Expert Groups*. ESO DS 2003:16, Stockholm: Ministry of Finance.
Larsson, T., and J. Murk (2007). 'The Commission's Relations with Expert Advisory Groups', in T. Christiansen and T. Larsson (eds.), *The Role of Committees in the Policy-Process of the European Union*. Cheltenham, UK: Edward Elgar, 64–95.
Larsson, T., and Trondal (2006). 'Agenda Setting in the European Commission: How the European Commission Structure and Influence the EU Agenda', in H.C.H. Hoffmann and A.H. Türk (eds.), *EU Administrative Governance*. Cheltenham: Edward Elgar, 11–43.
Lowi, T. (1964). 'American Business, Public Policy, Case-Studies, and Political Theory', *World Politics*, 16:4, 677–715.
Mahoney, C. (2004). 'The Power of Institutions – State and Interest Group Activity in the European Union', *European Union Politics*, 5:4, 441–66.
Majone, G. (1996). *Regulating Europe*. London: Routledge.
March, J.G., and J.P. Olsen (1998). 'The Institutional Dynamics of International Political Orders', *International Organization*, 52:4, 943–69.
Olsen, J.P. (1983). *Organised Democracy: Political Institutions in a Welfare State: The Case of Norway*. Bergen: Universitetsforlaget.
Olsen, J.P. (1997). 'Institutional Design in Democratic Contexts', *Journal of Political Philosophy*, 5:3, 203–29.

Olsen, J.P. (2001). 'Organizing European Institutions of Governance: A Prelude to an Institutional Account to European Integration', in H Wallace (ed.), *Interlocking Dimensions of European Integration*. Houndmills: Palgrave, 323–53.

Olsen, J.P. (2002). 'Reforming European Institutions of Governance', *Journal of Common Market Studies*, 40:4, 581–602.

Olsen, J.P. (2007). *Europe in Search of Political Order. An Institutional Perspective on Unity/Diversity, Citizens/Their Helpers, Democratic Design/Historical Drift, and the Co-Existence of Orders*. Oxford: Oxford University Press.

Pollack, M.A. (2003). 'Control Mechanism or Deliberative Democracy? Two Images of Comitology', *Comparative Political Studies*, 36:1–2, 125–55.

Radaelli, C.M. (1999). 'The Public Policy of the European Union: Whither Politics of Expertise?', *Journal of European Public Policy*, 6:5, 757–74.

Rhinard, M. (2002). 'The Democratic Legitimacy of the European Union Committee System', *Governance – An International Journal of Policy and Administration*, 15:2, 185–210.

Scharpf, F.W. (1999). *Governing in Europe: Effective and Democratic?* New York: Oxford University Press.

Shore, C. (2000). *Building Europe: the Cultural Politics of European Integration*. London: Routledge.

Stevens, A., and H. Stevens (2001). *Brussels Bureaucrats? The Administration of the European Union*. Houndmills: Palgrave.

Stone Sweet, A., N. Fligstein and W. Sandholtz (2001). 'The Institutionalization of European Space', in Stone Sweet, A., W. Sandholtz and N. Fligstein (eds.), *The Institutionalization of Europe*. Oxford: Oxford University Press, 1–28.

van Schendelen, M.P.C.M. (1998). 'Prolegomena to EU Committees as Influential Policy Makers', in M.P.C.M. van Schendelen (ed.), *EU Committees as Influential Policymakers*. Aldershot: Ashgate, 3–22.

Vos, E. (1997). 'The Rise of Committees', *European Law Journal*, 3:3, 210–29.

Wessels, W. (1997). 'An Ever Closer Fusion? A Dynamic Macropolitical View on Integration Processes', *Journal of Common Market Studies*, 35:2, 267–99.

Wessels, W. (1998). 'Comitology: Fusion in Action. Politico-Administrative Trends in the EU System', *Journal of European Public Policy*, 5:2, 209–34.

APPENDIX

Service	Service	Expert groups (N)	Budget 2006 €m	Connecs	Legal	Staff
Personnel and Administration	ADMIN	3	660	0	1	670
Agriculture and Rural Development	AGRI	64	54,455	30	1	887
Europe Aid	AIDCO	5	0.1	0	2	583
Bureau of European Policy Advisors	BEPA	5	0.1	0	1	25
Budget	BUDG	3	1,160	0	1	382
Directorate General for Communication	COMM	1	205	0	1	492
Competition	COMP	7	99	0	1	593
Directorate General for Development	DEV	30	1,301	1	2	245
Directorate General for Translation	DGT	1	0	0	1	2,113
Education and Culture	EAC	71	1,008	12	4	482
Economic and Financial Affairs	ECFIN	10	468	0	1	441

(continued)

APPENDIX
(Continued)

Service	Service	Expert groups (N)	Budget 2006 €m	Connecs	Legal	Staff
Enlargement	ELARG	1	2,205	0	2	226
Employment, Social Affairs and Equal Opportunities	EMPL	62	11,934	36	3	559
Enterprise and Industry	ENTR	120	400	23	4	727
Environment	ENV	127	346	17	2	492
Eurostat	ESTAT	85	133	0	2	578
Fisheries and Maritime Affairs	FISH	25	1,074	1	1	250
Information Society and Media	INFSO	38	1,425	2	3	820
Justice, Freedom and Security	JLS	33	605	0	4	328
Joint Research Centre	JRC	3		0		1,710
Internal Market and Services	MARKT	51	75	1	1	376
European Anti-Fraud Office	OLAF	5	66	0	1	290
Regional Policy	REGIO	58	28,629	1	2	523
External Relations	RELEX	11	3,476	1	4	651
Research	RTD	129	3,526	0	2	1,150
Health and Consumer Protection	SANCO	89	559	3	2	625
Secretariat General/ Legal Service	SG	4	0	0	1	778
Taxation and Customs Union	TAXUD	95	130	0	3	354
Trade	TRADE	7	83	1	1	398
Energy and Transport	TREN	94	1,462	4	3	863
Directorate General Informatics	DIGIT	0	0	0	1	359
Humanitarian Aid	ECHO	0	515	0	2	154
European Personnel Selection Office	EPSO	0	0	0	1	106
Internal Audit Service	IAS	0	12	0	1	71
Office for Infrastructure and Logistics in Brussels	OIB	0	0	0	1	415
Office for Infrastructure and Logistics in Luxembourg	OIL	0	0	0	1	160
Publications Office	OPOCE	0	0	0	1	595
Paymaster's Office	PMO	0	0	0	1	234
Directorate General for Interpretation	SCIS	0	0	0	1	667
Legal Service	SJ	0	215	0	1	321
Total		*1,237*	*11,6226.2*	*133*		*21,693*

At a Critical Juncture? Change and Continuity in the Institutional Development of the Council Secretariat

THOMAS CHRISTIANSEN and SOPHIE VANHOONACKER

This article examines the historical trajectory and current challenges of a European institution that has remained under-researched: the General Secretariat of the Council of Ministers of the European Union. For most of the history of the integration process such a lack of attention might have been justified because of the limited role that the Council Secretariat appeared to play in EU politics. Recently, however, research on a number of issues – the management of EU foreign policy and the conduct of EU treaty reform – has demonstrated the contribution that this body makes to EU decision-making. We therefore believe that there is a strong case for developing a better understanding of the Council Secretariat.

The role of the institution[1] has changed over time, and it has expanded significantly in recent years – we will discuss the details of this expansion of tasks in detail below. What there has not been, however, is a formal reform of the institution, either recently or indeed at any point in its history.

Instead, the Council Secretariat has evolved gradually, in line with the changes that have occurred within the Council of Ministers (of which it forms a part) and of the wider changes which the Union has undergone. This presents the puzzle of an institutional development that only partially mirrors the shifting politics of the environment: there are institutional changes which need to be explained, but there is also a pattern of continuity which needs to be studied. It is against this background of seeking to account for both institutional change and continuity that we have chosen to approach the study of the Council Secretariat from the perspective of historical institutionalism.

Historical institutionalism seeks to explain institutional choices by examining the development of the institution over time. One of the key concepts that historical institutionalism employs towards this purpose is that of path dependency – the identification of a particular trajectory of the institutional development that has been formed through the historical continuity arising from past decisions. Such an approach allows us to gauge the relationship between continuity and change and to make statements about the reasons for both inertia and responsiveness of the institution in relation to the macro-social context within which it operates. The macro-social context here is the overall institutional evolution of the Union of which the Council Secretariat has been a part. Institutional arrangements, in this perspective, are the result of a 'logic of appropriateness' rather than the 'logic of consequences' posited by rational approaches (March and Olsen 1989).

The aims in this article are therefore threefold: first, we assess the nature of the previous path of institutional development in order to be able to make statements about the logic according to which this development has occurred; second, we examine the impact of the more recent developments to see whether these changes do indeed represent a significant change from the historical legacy of the institution – a development that could be classified as a 'critical juncture' in terms of the historical institutionalist perspective. Finally, building on this analysis of both long-term and recent developments, we briefly discuss the future challenges that the Council Secretariat is facing.

In order to address these concerns, the article proceeds as follows: the next section introduces the historical institutionalist approach, discussing the way in which this approach can add value to the study of the Council Secretariat. The subsequent section charts in some detail the historical evolution of this institution, a discussion that in turn provides the foundation for the following assessment of the way in which recent developments – in particular the rapid expansion of the foreign and defence policy role taken up by the Secretariat and the changes imposed on the institution through the Eastern enlargement of the Union – have, or have not, diverted the Secretariat from its traditional path of institutional development. The article concludes with a discussion of the future challenges that the findings presented here imply for the Secretariat.

A Historical Institutionalist Perspective on the Council Secretariat

Approaching the study of the Council Secretariat from a neo-institutionalist perspective means to start from the basic assumption that 'institutions matter'. The question is, of course, how they matter and in which way they have influenced decisions. This has been the subject of some debate and a number of different 'institutionalisms' have been advanced in order to provide answers to these questions (Hall and Taylor 1996). One of these, historical institutionalism, emphasises the temporal dimension in the search for an explanation about institutional choices (Hinnfors 1999; Pierson and Skocpol 2000; Blyth 2003). While there have been debates about the utility of historical institutionalism (Kay 2005), we believe that this approach is valuable in the analysis of the evolution of an institution such as the Council Secretariat that is part of the larger institutional development that the process of European integration constitutes.

Historical institutionalism is regarded as useful in this context because it seeks to provide an explanation not only of institutional change, but also of continuity. As we have argued above, and as we will demonstrate in more detail below, there is strong evidence to suggest that the Council Secretariat, as a sub-system of the broader institutional structure of the European Union, remained remarkably resilient to change over a long period of its history. In other words, the institutional parameters of the Council Secretariat did not necessarily change in line with the massive shifts that the Union underwent throughout its history. Instead, we appear to have witnessed a more gradual process of adaptation which allowed the Council Secretariat to remain fairly constant. It is against this historical background that recent developments, implying more substantial changes to the institution, need to be examined.

Historical institutionalism as an approach is well-equipped to confront the puzzle of institutional stability and change. It makes a number of assumptions, however, that have to be spelt out clearly in advance. The first set of assumptions concerns the interaction between structures and agency. Unlike other approaches that give priority, whether explicitly or implicitly, to one ontology or another, a historical institutionalist approach recognises both structures and actors to be mutually constituted. Actors are to some extent defined by their role in the broader structures within which they work and act, and even though their behaviour is not determined by these structures, their interests and their identity are shaped by them. At the same time, structures, and this includes both legal-institutional and ideational structures, cannot be seen as determining actors' behaviour, and even less so decisional outcomes, but instead are themselves subject to change under the behaviour of actors (Hall and Taylor 1996, 1998; Hay and Wincott 1998). Denying both actors and structures ontological priority, but instead regarding both as mutually constitutive of one another, is what requires us to look at the *process* of interaction. Only over time can it be fully understood how the interaction between structures and agency, and between interests, ideas and identities, pans out. It is on the basis of such a procedural approach that we can then make statements that provide an explanation of institutional evolution.

This recognition of the role of both actors and structures in the explanation of institutional developments is particularly pertinent in the case of the Council Secretariat. Here we have an institution which provides those working within it with a structure – a set of formal–legal rules as well as socio-cultural norms – but which at the same time is also an agent in the wider politics of the European Union. 'institutions...can shape and constrain political strategies..., but they are themselves also the outcome (conscious or unintended) of deliberate political strategies of political conflict and of choice' (Thelen and Steinmo 1992: 10) – this tenet of institutional analysis accurately sums up the situation concerning the Council Secretariat.

It is against this background that we can specify in more detail the nature of a historical institutionalist approach to the study of the Council Secretariat. The concept of path-dependency is crucially important in this context. Path-dependency emphasises the stickiness of prior institutional choices for subsequent institutional development. In brief, a previous decision to set up a decision-making environment in a particular way has a tendency to reproduce itself through a sequence of events which follow from the original institutional choices (Collier and Collier 1991). It is due to such stickiness of institutional choices and the inertia of bureaucratic processes that institutions evolve along a certain path – one that is foreshadowed by the original design and resilient to the kind of changes that the environment may experience. And it is precisely the observation of this process over time – the temporality of a historical institutionalist approach – that permits us to study whether, and how, such a dynamic has been unfolding.

At the same time, historical institutionalism is not blind to the possibility of change. However, from such a perspective one would expect for change to occur only under extraordinary circumstances, when changes in the external environment, for example in the preferences of the actors or in the macro-social context, are so significant that these overcome the stickiness of existing institutional arrangements. It is during such a critical juncture that we then witness institutional change and indeed periods of institutional instability, which ultimately establish a different development path for the institution (Thelen 1999). What constitutes such a critical juncture may be difficult to define in advance, but it can be seen as having occurred if the new or changing institutional development points in a direction marking a departure from the existing developmental path.

We also include in our approach an awareness of the ideas, values and norms that form part of the institutional culture and that contribute to the direction of the institutional environment. Recognition of the role of ideas and norms can also be regarded as being part of a historical institutionalist approach (Hinnfors 1999; Pierson and Skocpol 2000; Blyth 2003), but can also be seen as constituting the core of a separate, sociological institutionalist approach (Hall and Taylor 1996; Lewis 2006). This sensitivity to (unwritten) cultural norms and values is a key part of the sociological dimension of institutional analysis (Rosamond 2000). Ideas matter in this respect as part of a cognitive map that is being developed in an institution – a 'theory of the institution' about itself which then has consequences for the actions of individual actors (Jachtenfuchs 1997). In the case of the Council Secretariat, there are powerful self-referential concepts at work – the idea of being an 'honest broker' being one of them – that may heavily influence the way in which the institution and those working within it operate (Tallberg 2006: 45).

Rationalist, sociological and historical varieties of institutionalist analysis have recently been applied to the study of the Council Secretariat (Beach 2004; Hamlet 2006; Lewis 2006) – a trend that is an expression of the much wider debate about the different kinds of new institutionalism that have been advanced. We do not have the space here to go into this more general debate. Instead, it will be evident from what has been said above that we are opting for the historical and sociological rather than the rationalist variant of the neo-institutionalist approach.

The key element of such a historical and sociological institutionalist approach is the temporal tracking of institutional developments, identifying the way in which specific (and contingent) choices at the outset lead to a path-dependent trajectory, as well as a sensitivity to the occurrence of critical junctures. Looking towards a detailed analysis of the Council Secretariat, this implies an in-depth examination of the history of the institution, pinpointing those elements in the evolutionary path that have contributed to institutional stability and continuity. The subsequent section will provide this survey of the history of the institution. Based on the insights gathered in this way, we will then move on to answering some of the key questions that historical institutionalism poses. First, what have been the driving forces in the institutional development of the Council Secretariat? Second, to what extent have the changes in the macro-social context contributed to institutional stability and change? Third, what has been the effect of the ideas, values and norms that have been cultivated inside the institution? And, finally, what is the effect of the more recent developments in the European Union for the future evolution of the Council Secretariat?

The Establishment and Growth of the Council Secretariat

In examining the historical development of the Council Secretariat through the lens of the historical institutionalist approach, one may distinguish between three periods: first, the actual setting up of the institution in the foundation years of the integration process. It is during this period that key choices were made which – if the thesis of a path-dependent trajectory is correct – would result in subsequent events already foreshadowed by the initial institutional design. Second, a period of stability and growth during which the Secretariat also underwent significant changes, albeit without any formal reform of the institution. And, third, there is the more recent period which has been one of considerable turbulence, raising the question of whether the established developmental path is sustainable or whether, by contrast, the Secretariat is facing a critical juncture in its institutional life.

Institutionalisation

In order to account for the origins of the Council Secretariat one needs to go back to the very early period of European integration. The creation of a 'Secretariat' was one of the first decisions of the inaugural meeting of the Council of Ministers of the European Coal and Steel Community (ECSC) meeting in Luxembourg in September 1952. The provisional rules of procedure adopted on that occasion barely spent one line on this new body and defined its role as purely supportive: to assist the Council under the responsibility and guidance of the Presidency (Règlement intérieur provisoire). Originally the small Secretariat was based in Luxembourg. With the creation of the EEC and Euratom, its Secretary General, the Luxembourg diplomat Christian Calmes moved to Brussels to take over leadership of the Secretariat General of the European Communities. Until the merger Treaty of 1967, however, a small ECSC section was maintained in Luxembourg (Mangenot 2002; 2003a and b).

What needs to be noted in this context is the 'thinness' of the formal rules on which this institutional development was based. The Council Secretariat is not mentioned in the founding treaties (it was only introduced formally with the Maastricht Treaty). The Secretariat was however referred to in the Council's own Rules of Procedure (RoP), and changes to these internal RoP reflect the significance the Secretariat has had for the operation of the Council from the inception of the Communities. But even here references to the Secretariat were rather brief and cursory. Essentially, an institution was initially set up without clear formal rules governing its activities, and therefore the foundation was laid for unwritten rules, existing practices and bureaucratic reflexes to fill the normative vacuum.[2]

Against this backdrop, the Secretariat, interacting with other players such as COREPER, the Presidency, the High Authority and European Commission, explored its scope of manoeuvre and gradually the office took shape. In the early years it fulfilled primarily an organisational and administrative function. It was in charge of organising meetings, preparing agendas, translating and distributing documents, drafting minutes. Its main task was to create the conditions for a smooth running of the Council machinery (Hayes-Renshaw and Wallace 2006; Sherrington 2000; Westlake and Galloway 2004). This may be a low-profile job, but it was crucial for the efficiency of the day-to-day policy-making process.

Institutional Growth, Stability and Change

With the gradual extension of Community competencies, the first enlargement (1973) and the proliferation of meetings at various levels, the Secretariat's workload steadily increased. These new developments led to the creation of new Directorates-General and an increase in the number of staff (Mangenot 2002). By 1975, the number of A officials had grown from 5 (1953) to 161 and the total number of staff had expanded from 30 to 1,475.[3]

At the same time, there was a gradual evolution and expansion of the Secretariat's administrative function. Due to the regular rotation of the Presidency,[4] the Secretariat developed into the Council's institutional memory and also functioned as a bridge between various chairs. Its officials not only supported the Council in all its formations but also its preparatory bodies such as the Committee of Permanent Representatives (Coreper) and the working groups. As a result, the Secretariat also became a source of coordination, coherence and continuity in the Council's work. The Council decision of 1980, appointing the third Secretary General, explicitly referred to these tasks (Decision 80/918/EEC).

From the late 1960s onwards, we see the gradual development of an entirely new function which consists in helping the chair with the formulation of compromises. Following the 'empty chair crisis' (1965–66), the European Commission's position as a broker came under pressure and the Presidency gained more leverage in fulfilling this task (Kirchner 1992). As the Council Secretariat follows dossiers throughout the legislative process, it is well informed about the various national positions and well placed to advise the chair in forging deals. Also its legal and procedural expertise are key when advising the chair in possible compromise solutions, and increasingly the Presidency came to rely on the Secretariat for the drafting of text proposals or the provision of tactical advise. This did not imply, however, that the Secretariat could articulate its own position. The norm has been that its civil servants are impartial. They are expected to look for the common interest and facilitate the problem-solving process. As one senior official of the Council Secretariat remarked, 'I don't mind whether they decide to paint the room black or white, as long as the decision is taken in the correct way' (quoted in Schout and Vanhoonacker 2006: 1054). Whether there is scope for this brokering function, however, is contingent entirely upon whether the Presidency is willing to take its suggestions on board. As has been argued elsewhere, due to their limited resources, smaller member states tend to rely more on the work of Secretariat staff than larger ones (Christiansen 2002; Elgström 2003; Schout and Vanhoonacker 2003; Tallberg 2003).

A further development which strengthened the position of the Secretariat was the creation of the European Council (1974). In addition to being involved in the organisation and provision of secretarial services, the Secretariat, from 1982 onwards, started to play a key role in the preparation of the draft Presidency conclusions (Bulmer and Wessels 1987; Werts 1992; Mangenot 2002; Council 2006).[5] Its long-term experience with European negotiations implied that it was well placed to formulate a text supported by the large majority of the delegations. As a result of this role at the highest political level, the position of the Secretary General grew in importance, and the prestige of the function also reflected on his institution. Niels Ersbøll, former Permanent Representative of Denmark to the EC and Secretary General from 1980 to 1994, played a key role in giving shape to this new role. Coming from a small member state and extremely knowledgeable about EC affairs, he enjoyed the trust of the member states and managed to build up a central position in advising succeeding Presidencies in forging compromises. Another effect of the Secretariat's role in preparing European Councils was the establishment of direct contacts with the President of the European Commission (Mangenot 2002).[6]

In the 1990s, the Secretariat again received an important boost, not so much because it was given formal recognition in the Treaty on European Union (Art. 151, para. 2),[7] but mainly as a result of developments on the international and European scene. The fall of the Berlin wall opened the prospect of Eastern enlargement and simultaneously raised the need for a further deepening of European integration and the adaptation of its institutional framework. Through a series of IGCs (Maastricht, 1991; Amsterdam, 1996–97; Nice, 2000; Constitutional Treaty, 2003–04), the member states tried to strengthen the European construction by expanding its scope to new areas, by reinforcing the role of the European Parliament, and by reforming its institutional underpinnings and the decision-making process.

From the 1990s, the continuous process of treaty reform – which can also be seen as a process of the constitutionalisation of the European Union – created new opportunities for the Council Secretariat (Deloche-Gaudez 1994; Christiansen and Reh forthcoming). A small group of highly qualified officials, who mostly remained the same throughout the various IGCs, assisted the Presidency as the 'conference secretariat' with the taking of minutes, drafting of texts and the formulation of compromise proposals (Galloway 2001). Furthermore, the Secretariat also served as the IGC's legal service. In contrast to the SEA negotiations, where it shared this responsibility with the legal service of the Commission, the Council Secretariat now had the sole responsibility for this influential function (Christiansen 2001). Its procedural and legal expertise, its informational advantages and brokering capacities gave the Secretariat scope to play an active role in defining negotiation strategies, drafting treaty amendments and elaborating compromises (Beach 2005). But, as in the legislative process, the Secretariat's role was only as strong as the Presidency allowed it to be (Beach 2004, 2006).

Furthermore, the Secretariat was also affected by the changing institutional balance after Maastricht. With the introduction of the co-decision procedure, the Council and the EP became co-legislators, and had a shared interest to reach an agreement on legislation (Shackleton 2006). The increased institutional interaction intensified the Secretariat's contacts with the EP. As most dossiers span more than one Presidency, the Secretariat fulfilled an important bridging function, providing an element of continuity between the rotating chairs. In contrast to the country at the helm, its civil servants are well versed in this complex decision-making procedure and its many informal 'do's and don'ts'. The chair is assisted by the responsible Directorate General as well as by a special co-decision unit known as the '*dorsale*' or 'backbone'. The officials in the *dorsale* follow all legislative acts falling under the co-decision procedure and closely cooperate with their counterparts in the EP and the Commission.

With the entry into force of the Treaty on European Union, the Secretariat also started to play a role in the Treaty's newly established intergovernmental pillars of the Common Foreign and Security Policy (CFSP) and Justice and Home Affairs (JHA). Since the Single European Act (1987), there had been a small but independent secretariat for European Political Cooperation (EPC), the predecessor of CFSP (Sanchez da Costa Pereira 1988; Nuttall 1992). The 16 EPC staff members (6 diplomats and 10 secretaries) were based in the same building as the Council Secretariat, but were seconded and paid by their national ministries. They formed a separate entity with its own rules and internal codes. To emphasise its distinct intergovernmental character, the EPC unit was only accessible through a special combination lock (Nuttall 2000). With Maastricht the EPC secretariat was merged with the Council Secretariat and the Directorate General for External Relations (DG E) was reorganised into two directorates, one for external economic relations and one for CFSP. The latter was manned with a mixture of diplomats delegated from the national capitals (one per member state), civil servants of the Council Secretariat (11) and the Commission (1) (Nuttall 2000). The decision to work with seconded officials can be explained by the member states' reluctance to give up sovereignty in the sensitive area of foreign policy. In practice the links between Brussels and the national capitals were further strengthened.

In the new policy areas of CFSP and JHA, the rules of the game were not those of the supranational Community method, but of intergovernmental cooperation. Decisions were taken by unanimity, and policy formulation and implementation fell under the responsibility of the member states and the Presidency instead of the European Commission. Initially the role of the Council Secretariat was similar to that in other policy areas: supporting the chair and the Council with the organisation of meetings and the management of the negotiation process. This changed radically, however, when the European Council of Cologne in June 1999 decided to establish a European Security and Defence Policy (ESDP) and appointed Javier Solana as High Representative for CFSP and Secretary General of the Council Secretariat (Howarth 2001). Spurred by the poor EU performance in the Balkans, the member states agreed that the time had come to engage in a more operational foreign policy. They expressed the ambition to carry out the full range of Petersberg tasks as defined in the Treaty on European Union (TEU): humanitarian and rescue tasks, peace-keeping tasks and tasks of combat forces in crisis management, including peace-making. As a result, the Secretariat for the first time in its history was also entrusted with executive tasks.

Recent Developments: Towards a 'New Secretariat'?

The twin decisions of the Cologne European Summit in 1999 – establishing the ESDP and appointing Javier Solana as High Representative – constituted a watershed in the development of the Council Secretariat. By nominating a former Secretary General of NATO (1995–99) and former Spanish Minister of Foreign Affairs (1992–95), the office of Secretary-General was no longer headed by a top-level official or diplomat, but by a high-profile politician. Entrusted with the broad task of assisting the Presidency with the formulation, preparation and implementation of CFSP (Art. 26, TEU), Solana decided to concentrate fully on his foreign policy mission and left the day-to-day management of the Secretariat to the Deputy Secretary General Pierre de Boissieu. The vague formulation of his mandate provided him with sufficient latitude to strongly influence the shape and content of his new function. At the same time, the important internal responsibilities of the Deputy Secretary-General were recognised in the Treaty (Art. 207, TEU) and enhanced in the Council's internal RoP.

These developments had important implications for the administrative level of the Secretariat, in terms of its organisational structure, staff and responsibilities. In the monitoring and analysis of international developments, Solana was assisted by a newly created 'Policy and Early Warning Unit', better known as the Policy Unit. It fulfilled an early warning function in case of potential crises, and its staff could, in contrast to the rest of the Secretariat, take the floor in CFSP meetings. Apart from a small number of civil servants from the European Commission, the Council Secretariat and the WEU Secretariat, the unit was primarily staffed with seconded national diplomats. The analytical and strategic task of the policy unit was kept separate from the supportive task of DG E. In practice, this artificial distinction never worked, and from 2004 onwards members of the policy unit have been increasingly integrated in the respective geographical units of DG E (Duke and Vanhoonacker 2006).

DG E itself has been expanded with two new directorates, respectively dealing with defence questions (directorate 8) and with civilian crisis management and coordination (directorate 9). They are both predominantly staffed with seconded experts and diplomats. Furthermore, the Secretariat has also become the home of the EU Military Staff and the situation centre (SITCEN). Both fall directly under the authority of Solana. While the former plays a central role in early warning, situation assessment and strategic planning of operations, the intelligence officers of SITCEN analyse intelligence material and monitor potential crisis situations. For certain issues such as non-proliferation of weapons of mass destruction and human rights, Solana can rely on Personal Representatives. They play a coordinating role and assist him with the implementation of policy decisions.

The staff working in the area of CFSP and ESDP are divided from the rest of the Secretariat in two ways: through the strong presence in their ranks of seconded diplomats and experts, and through their role in the process of policy formulation and implementation. Formally the High Representative has no right of initiative, but by launching policy papers and bringing problem areas to attention, he can influence the agenda and steer the debates in a certain direction. The staff of the policy unit provide him with the background documents required to fulfil this agenda-setting function. Furthermore, the Secretariat also plays a role in the preparation and implementation of civilian and military missions. It draws up background documents and draft joint actions. Once the member states have agreed upon the launching of a civilian or military operation, it prepares an operational plan, in cooperation with the Commission and the Presidency. Also during missions it fulfils certain implementing tasks. Through the so-called Athena mechanism, for instance, it administers the financing of the common costs of military operations (Missiroli 2003).

The presence of men and women in uniform on the premises of the Secretariat and their close cooperation with NATO have also raised new challenges with regard to the security and protection of confidential information. The Justius Lipsius building failed the security test, and all ESDP-related departments are housed in a separate building in the Avenue de Cortenberg. This is not conducive to coordination with other departments dealing with external relations, but it symbolises very well the differences between the two worlds in which the officials from the Secretariat operate. The staff working in the first pillar still primarily fulfil the traditional administrative and advisory role, while those in the second pillar increasingly combine this with executive responsibilities. While the former group consists of civil servants who passed the *concours*, the second group is heavily dominated by seconded experts and diplomats. This is not only due to a lack of expertise in the Secretariat, but can also be explained by the desire of the national capitals to maintain direct control over this sensitive policy area. In 2007, the group of seconded staff numbered approximately 210 (25 in the policy unit, 165 military, and 20 police officers). In total they represented up to 28 per cent of the policy-making staff in the Secretariat.[8]

Although this intergovernmental approach is attractive for member states reluctant to pool sovereignty, it undeniably presents a number of pitfalls (Vanhoonacker and Dijkstra 2006). First, one can question whether the Secretariat is equipped to deal with its executive function. Traditionally, Council civil servants have been trained to provide logistic support and to assist the chair in managing the negotiation process. Most of them do not have a diplomatic background, and contrary to national foreign ministries, the Secretariat cannot look back on a long foreign policy tradition. Bringing in national expertise by seconding diplomats addresses this problem, but it also has drawbacks. More than 50 years of socialisation means that the Secretariat has developed its own administrative culture. Its staff adheres to well-established professional norms such as efficiency and impartiality and has internalised rules of appropriateness. National diplomats may not necessarily share or be aware of their way of thinking. Although research on the Commission has illustrated that delegated national civil servants are not immune to their new international environment, the process of adaptation takes time and can be the cause of tensions (Egeberg 2006; Trondal 2006). At this moment there is hardly any empirical data about the interaction between the Secretariat's traditional civil servants and the seconded staff. It is well known, however, that when in the early 1990s the CFSP unit was staffed with a mixture of seconded and Secretariat officials, the process of integration took time and was not without problems (Dinan 1999; Nuttall 2000).

The question of expertise is closely linked to that of access to information. The secondment of national diplomats in the Secretariat and the establishment of a Joint Situation Centre staffed with intelligence officers have considerably increased the information flow between Brussels and the national capitals. It remains the case, however, that the Secretariat, in contrast to the Commission, has no delegations in third countries. Whether or not the Secretariat is properly informed depends to a large extent on the goodwill of the member states and the European Commission.

Finally, the Secretariat's new executive role also demands improved coordination mechanisms, both internally as well as with the European Commission. The latter can look back on a long tradition of fulfilling executive tasks in the field of trade and development. It was not amused by the Secretariat's interference in the field of external relations and initially this led to bureaucratic turf battles (Spence 2006). This institutional rivalry was further fuelled by the fact that there are many grey zones and that foreign policy projects do not necessarily respect the demarcation between pillars. Gradually, however, both players have been able to find a *modus vivendi*, and modalities for cooperation and coordination have developed (Council 2003; Vanhoonacker forthcoming; EU crisis response capability revisited).

A Path-Dependent Development? Assessing the Historical Evolution of the Council Secretariat

Having reviewed the historical evolution of the Council Secretariat, we can now engage the questions raised previously. The first task in this respect is to identify the historical legacy that was created at the outset. A number of key factors can be identified in this regard – key factors which were contingent at the time (other choices would have been possible then), but which subsequently contributed to the institutional development that we have seen. These factors were, first, the creation of a small administration that would work with and under the supervision of the member states, in institutional opposition to the European Commission; second, the decision to give significant responsibilities to a rotating Presidency which is being assisted by the Secretariat; and, third, the decision to leave the work and the internal organisation of the Secretariat fairly unregulated for the first few decades of its institutional life.

The combined effect of these initial choices for the design of the institution was to steer it towards a particular kind of development. For example, having the role of 'assisting' the Presidency meant that the institution had to grow into a body that institutionalised permanency and whose staff would work in the 'shadows' rather than in the political spotlight, thus emphasising the supporting role and the impartiality of the Council Secretariat (Beach 2004; Christiansen 2002).

Working close to national civil services and being occupied largely with the legal aspects of the Community's legislative programme implied the import of a bureaucratic and legalistic culture into the staff of the Council Secretariat – which in turn became the source of the norms and ideational structures of the institution's staff. This pattern of the development of a normative foundation for the work of the Secretariat based on the professional standards of its staff was also the result of the under-specified formal underpinnings of this institution that we have observed. Finally, this original set-up also implied that with future enlargements the role of the institution would expand: a greater number of member states requires more resources spent on coordination, and new member states holding the rotating Presidency mean more scope for the expertise of the permanent Secretariat (Juncos and Pomorska 2007).

These observations demonstrate that the initial design of the institution had far-reaching consequences throughout its history. The increasing reliance of countries holding the Presidency, the gradual growth of the institution to reflect the expansion of competences and rising number of member states, and establishment of a certain *esprit des corps* among the staff of the Secretariat – these developments which are the hallmarks of the institutional life of the Secretariat all had their origin in the choices that were made at the outset of the institution. Institutional changes that happened to the Council Secretariat did not require any formal institutional reforms precisely because such changes inevitably followed from the choices that had been made initially.

This observation leads to the recognition that, beyond concrete legal and procedural choices that have had an indirect impact on the evolution of the Council Secretariat, we need to recognise the power of ideas that have helped to shape the institutional development of the Union. Here it may be worth pointing to the discourse about impartiality, the protection of diversity, the representation of national interests and the idea of 'intergovernmentalism' as a way of achieving both national protection and member state consensus. It has been on the basis of these discourses that the Council Secretariat has been receiving additional tasks and responsibilities, as it has been regarded as the institution that is more 'intergovernmental' than the Commission. Such a development demonstrates the effects of a 'logic of appropriateness', even if it contributed – ironically – to making the Council Secretariat more of a supranational institution.

The institutional evolution of the Council Secretariat can be linked to these initial choices and subsequent developments in the overall context of European governance. However, in addition to these external factors we also need to recognise the internal dynamics of the Council Secretariat itself. On the one hand, there has been the institutional self-interest to protect the institution, *inter alia* by expanding its role and establishing it as a key part of the EU's administrative system. Such institutional self-interest can operate in a number of ways, but in this context it might be important to point out that, as mentioned above, senior officials participated in the IGC secretariats at the Maastricht, Amsterdam and Nice Treaty negotiations, and that the subsequent expansion of Council Secretariat responsibilities might be linked to the involvement of senior officials from the institution in the IGCs through their work in the conference secretariat and/or the Council's legal service.

However, identifying such a path-dependent development should not imply that revolutionary changes might not occur. Radical changes to the institution would need to be seen as a critical juncture where a number of important factors imply a departure from the previous path. Our tracing of the history of the Council Secretariat, and, in particular, the identification of a number of important developments in the recent phase of integration, raises the question as to whether we are witnessing such a critical juncture now.

As we have seen in recent years, successive mergers and addition of new tasks have produced a dual administration within the Secretariat. The identity of the 'old' Secretariat is now under threat from the distinct approach of those in the 'new' Secretariat – the foreign policy and military machinery, which is concerned not with the quiet work in support of legislative procedures, but with the executive management of foreign and security policy. This requires more rapid reactions to changing circumstances, direct action by Council Secretariat staff and thus a public profile to the role of the institution that is totally alien to the 'old' Secretariat. The result of the presence of such differing, even conflicting, cultures within the institution is internal tension and potential fragmentation.

If this is a concern, then the impact of enlargement must also be considered. The arrival of new staff from the new member states, the growing size of the institution overall and the ensuing changes to the organisational structure have all combined to create the potential to unsettle the traditional beliefs and norms that have helped to maintain continuity in the Secretariat's institutional development. So far, the 2004 enlargement has left a strong mark on the internal processes of the Council Secretariat.[9] In this respect the Secretariat mirrors the developments elsewhere in the institutional architecture of the EU – generally the images of 'gridlock' or 'blockage' that accompanied accounts of the workings of the EU if Eastern enlargement was to occur without fundamental reforms have not been borne out (Best et al. 2008). There have, for example, been fewer promotions to senior positions of Secretariat officials from the new member states compared to the appointments in the European Commission, and the administration has resisted the imposition of the kind of quotas for new appointments from the new member states that were introduced in the Commission. However, further pressure for internal changes is to be anticipated given future enlargements and the need for geographical balance among senior levels within the administration.

Institutional cohesion, which for decades had been sustained by a common set of beliefs and norms about the role that the institution should be playing in the Union, is therefore under threat from a number of directions: the arrival of new kinds of professional logics (diplomats and military personnel) working alongside the older community of lawyers as well as the arrival of new staff as a result of enlargement. While the strains are already showing, the institution has so far managed to preserve an image of internal cohesion. The question is whether, or indeed for how long, such an image can be maintained if the internal tensions become greater and ideational cohesion is more seriously at risk. In this respect, the issuing of a 'mission statement' espousing the 'core values' of the Secretariat staff is a very interesting development (Council 2007). This brief, one-page document states that professionalism, impartiality and *esprit de corps* are the core values to which officials in the Secretariat adhere. These are indeed the values that we have also seen at work in the self-perception of the Secretariat throughout the decades, and as such this announcement does not appear as a break with tradition. However, the very fact that such a public statement was deemed to be necessary, implying that pure reliance on the long-established unwritten norms is apparently not sufficient any more, is a sign that the internal cohesion of the institution might be in doubt.

In sum, there have been significant changes to the way in which the EU has made its policies since the 1950s, but the adaptation of the Council Secretariat has not followed a clear path of rational decisions about this process; rather its path has been determined by gradual adaptation, unintended consequences and internal processes within the Council Secretariat itself. As such, the institutional development of the Council shows 'historical causes' rather than 'constant causes' at work (Collier and Collier 1991). These explanatory factors might be more difficult to identify when taking only a brief look at the current situation, but they quickly become evident as part of the temporal study that we have undertaken here.

In this context we have identified the period around 1999, and the Cologne European Council in particular, as a decisive moment in terms of a possible shift of the institutional development. Given the very different logics that have entered the Council Secretariat since then, this may indeed be seen as the kind of critical juncture that historical institutionalism regards as the point at which there is a departure from the previous path-dependent sequence of events. The changes taking place in the Secretariat can only be explained against the background of the changing European and international context. The collapse of the bipolar structure and uncertainty about the future of the transatlantic relationship gave an important impetus to the development of an independent European security identity and opened the door for eastern enlargement. Without this shock in the external environment, the 1999 developments in the Secretariat would not have taken place. At the same time, the preferences of the member states have also played an important role. It may have been more efficient to entrust the implementation of ESDP to the European Commission, but for most national capitals this was a bridge too far. In an attempt to maintain control over the sensitive foreign policy area, they opted for the expansion of the role of the Council Secretariat, a body over which national governments were considered to have a stronger influence. The lack of prior expertise was compensated by the delegation of national diplomats, a further device to keep a firm grip on ESDP's Brussels-based players. The Secretariat's own role in fostering the changes is negligible. Although it had gradually started to assume a modest foreign policy role since the Single European Act, it had always been a player at the service of the member states and, contrary to the European Commission, it did not have a voice of its own.

Conclusion

Our study underlines a number of points. First, path-dependency is there, but it only demonstrates the continuity of the work of the Council Secretariat in the absence of formal changes to the institution. Adaptation to changing circumstances occurs in a more informal manner, through gradual institutional changes and as unintended consequences of broader institutional developments, not as the result of strategic decisions to establish a particular institutional design.

Second, the nature of these unintended consequences is such that, over time, the institution may develop pathologies that reduce internal cohesion and effectiveness significantly. Cultural norms and common values that have been developed within the administration may clash with countervailing ideas as fragmentation occurs and internal tensions increase. The development of a dual administration since the late 1990s – traditional policy-making and legislative bureaucracy on the one hand, emerging diplomatic and military components on the other – may be an example of that.

Third, the changes the Council Secretariat has undergone since 1999 – creation of the post of HR, establishment of the EU military staff, arrival of the new member states – may in this respect come to be seen as a critical juncture that forces the Council Secretariat onto a different development path towards a much more politicised executive agency, from the established role of providing a more subtle influence in the legislative process. The additional tasks acquired in this period go hand-in-hand with a new set of ideas and norms that has entered the institution as a result of these changes.

The creation of the post of a High Representative of the Union for Foreign Affairs and Security Policy and the establishment of a European External Action Service (EEAS) under the Lisbon Treaty may be decisive in determining whether the early phase of the twenty-first century will turn out to have been a critical juncture for the evolution of the Council Secretariat. Should these changes be implemented, the 'outsourcing' of foreign policy-making and crisis management to such an external action service may go some way towards putting the 'old' Secretariat back on its established path. The crucial issue then will be the nature of the relationship between this EEAS, the European Commission and the High Representative, but presumably it will be outside the institutional logics of the Council Secretariat. This would be a significant change from the existing path of institutional development, but as such it would be a way to alleviate the tensions between the 'old' and 'new' parts of the Secretariat that we have explored in this article.

Acknowledgements

We are grateful for the useful comments we received from the conference participants as well as from the editors of this special issue, and we acknowledge the valuable research assistance provided by Johanna Oettel. The usual disclaimer applies.

Notes

1. While the Council Secretariat is not an official EU institution in the formal understanding of the treaties, it is treated here as an institution for the purposes of analysis.
2. A detailed analysis of the evolution of the Council's own rules of procedure demonstrates that these have developed in response to the changing external circumstances and reflect the growing importance of the Secretariat. Apart from a series of minor changes throughout history, there were six major revisions of the RoP which resulted in new versions being published in the *Official Journal*. This occurred in 1979, 1993, 1999, 2000, 2002, 2004 and 2006 – a development that reflects the increasing and accelerating juridification of the Council's work in the wake of successive treaty changes and enlargements. If the early period of the Secretariat's institutional life was fairly unregulated – the RoP foreseen by Art.5 of the Merger Treaty in 1965 were only adopted in 1979 – it allowed (or required) a process of institutionalisation along the lines of other, unwritten norms.
3. Growth in the total number of staff: 30 (1953); 264 (1959); 603 (1970); 1,475 (1975). Growth in the number of A officials: 5 (1953); 68 (1959); 94 (1970); 161 (1975) (Mangenot 2002).

4. In the ECSC the Presidency rotated every three months; in the EEC and Euratom there was a six-month rotation.
5. Before, it was the Permanent Representatives who prepared the draft conclusions.
6. Before, the contacts with the Commission only went through the Secretariat General of the Commission.
7. Art. 151, para. 2, TEU stipulates, 'The Council shall be assisted by a General Secretariat, under the direction of a Secretary-General. The Secretary-General shall be appointed by the Council acting unanimously. The Council shall decide on the organization of the General Secretariat.'
8. The total number of Secretariat officials involved in policy-making numbers 750 (this figure excludes secretarial staff and linguists) but includes military and police officers. There are 540 permanent AD officials; 140 of them (25 per cent) work for DG E.
9. We already mentioned the changes to the language regime which are, of course, a direct result of the Union's enlargement to 25/27 members. These changes are best understood, however, as changes affecting the Council as a whole, rather than changes of the Council Secretariat. Indeed, the language regime concerns arrangements for meetings of member state representatives such as ministerial councils and working groups. Within the administration of the Secretariat, a more informal and secular trend towards the replacement of French with English as the dominant working language is under way.

References

Beach, D. (2004). 'The Unseen Hand in Treaty Reform Negotiations: The Role and Influence of the Council Secretariat', *Journal of European Public Policy*, 11:3, 408–39.

Beach, D. (2005). *The Institutional Dynamics of the European Union*. London: Palgrave.

Beach, D. (2006). 'Oiling the Wheels of Compromise – The Role and Impact of the Council Secretariat in EU Treaty Reform'. Paper presented at the 47th annual international studies association convention, San Diego, CA, 22–25 March.

Best, E., T. Christiansen and P. Settembri (eds) (2008). *The Institutions of the Enlarged European Union-Continuity and Change*. Cheltenham: Edward Elgar.

Blyth, M. (2003). 'Structures Do Not Come with an Instruction Sheet: Interests, Ideas, and Progress in Political Science', *Perspectives on Politics*, 1:4, 695–706.

Bulmer, S., and W. Wessels (1987). *The European Council: Decision-making in European Politics*. Basingstoke: Macmillan.

Christiansen, T. (2001). 'Inter-institutional Relations and Intra-institutional Politics in the EU: Towards Coherent Governance?', *Journal of European Public Policy*, 8:5, 747–69.

Christiansen, T. (2002). 'Out of the Shadows: The General Secretariat of the Council of Ministers', *The Journal of Legislative Studies*, 8:4, 80–97.

Christiansen, T., and C. Reh (forthcoming). *Constitutionalising the European Union*. Basingstoke: Palgrave Macmillan.

Collier, R.B., and D. Collier (1991). *Shaping the Political Arena*. Princeton: Princeton UP.

Council of the European Union (1999). *Operation of the Council with an Enlarged Union in Prospect. Report by the Working Party set up by the Secretary-General of the Council*. Brussels, 10 March 1999 (SN 21139/99).

Council of the European Union (2003) *Suggestions for Procedures for Coherent, Comprehensive EU Crisis Management*. Doc. 11127/03, Brussels 3 July.

Council of the European Union (2004). 'Council Decision of 22 March 2004 adopting the Council's Rules of Procedure', *Official Journal*, L 106/22, 15 April.

Council of the European Union (2004). *Report from the Deputy Secretary General on the Management of the General Secretariat*. Brussels, 1 October.

Council of the European Union (2006). *Council Guide. I. The Presidency Handbook*. Luxembourg: Office for Official Publications of the EC.

Council of the European Union (2007). *Mission Statement of the General Secretariat of the Council*.

'Decision 80/918/EEC, Euratom, ECSC of 26 September 1980', *Official Journal*, No. L 261, 4 October 1980.

Deloche-Gaudez, F. (2004). 'Le Secrétariat de la Convention européene: un acteur influent', *Politique Européenne*, 3:1, 43–67.

Dinan, D. (1999). *Ever Closer Union: An Introduction to European Integration*. Palgrave: New York.

Duke, S., and S. Vanhoonacker (2006). 'Administrative Governance in CFSP: Development and Practice', *European Foreign Affairs Review*, 11:2, 163–82.

Egeberg, M. (2006). 'Europe's Executive Branch of Government in the Melting Pot – An Overview', in M. Egeberg, *Multilevel Union Administration. The Transformation of Executive Politics in Europe*. Basingstoke: Palgrave Macmillan.

Elgstrøm, O., ed. (2003). *European Union Council Presidencies. A Comparative Perspective*. London: Routledge.

'EU Crisis Response Capability Revisited' (2005). *Europe Report*, No. 160, 17 January.

Galloway, D. (2001). *The Treaty of Nice and Beyond – Realities and Illusions of Power in the EU*. Sheffield: Sheffield University Press.

Hall, P., and R. Taylor (1996). 'Political Science and the Three Institutionalisms', *Political Studies*, 44:4, 936–57.

Hall, P., and R. Taylor (1998). 'The Potential of Historical Institutionalism: A Response to Hay and Wincott', *Political Studies*, 46:6, 958–62.

Hamlet, L. (2006). *Delegation, Information and Supranational Entrepreneurship: The Use of the Council Secretariat by New EU Members*. Paper presented at the Annual Meeting of the International Studies Association, San Diego, USA.

Hay, C., and D. Wincott (1998). 'Structure, Agency and Historical Institutionalism', *Political Studies*, 46:5, 951–7.

Hayes-Renshaw, F., and H. Wallace (2006). *The Council of Ministers*. London: Palgrave Macmillan.

Hinnfors, J. (1999). 'Stability through Change: The Pervasiveness of Political Ideas', *Journal of Public Policy*, 19:3, 293–312.

Howorth, J. (2001). 'European Defence and the Changing Politics of the EU: Hanging Together or Hanging Separately?', *Journal of Common Market Studies*, 39:4, 765–89.

Jachtenfuchs, M. (1997). 'Conceptualising European Governance', in K.E. Jørgensen (ed.), *Reflective Approaches to European Governance*. London: Macmillan, 39–50.

Juncos, A.E., and K. Pomorska (2007). 'The Deadlock that never Happened: The Impact of Enlargement on the Common Foreign and Security Working Groups', *European Political Economy Review*, 6, 4–30.

Kay, A. (2005). 'A Critique of the Use of Path Dependency in Policy Studies', *Public Administration*, 83:3, 553–71.

Kirchner, E. (1992). *Decision-making in the European Community: The Council Presidency and European Integration*. Manchester: Manchester University Press.

Lewis, J. (2006). *Where Informal Rules Rule: The Role of the Council General Secretariat and Presidency in Everyday EU Decision Making*. Paper presented at the annual meeting of the International Studies Association, San Diego, USA.

Mangenot, M. (2002). 'L'affirmation du Secrétariat du Conseil de l'Union européenne : les transformations du rôle d'une institution non codifiée'. Paper presented at the 'VIIe congrès de l'Association française de science politique. Lille, 18–21 September.

Mangenot, M. (2003a). 'Une 'chancellerie du prince'. Le Secrétariat général du Conseil dans le processus de decision bruxellois', *Politique Européenne*, 11, 123–42.

Mangenot, M. (2003b). 'Gouverner l'Union européenne. L'institutionnalisation du Secrétariat general du Conseil', in R. Dehousse and Y. Surel (eds.), *Institutionnalisation de l'Europe*. Paris: L'Harmattan.

March, J., and J. Olson (1989). *Rediscovering Institutions*. New York: The Free Press.

Missiroli, A. (2003). 'Euros for ESDP: Financing EU Operations', *Occasional Paper, 45*. Paris: EU Institute for Security Studies.

Nuttall, S.J. (1992). *European Political Cooperation*. Oxford: Oxford University Press.
Nuttall, S.J. (2000). *European Foreign Policy*. Oxford: Oxford University Press.
Pierson, P., and T. Skocpol (2000). 'Historical Institutionalism in Contemporary Political Science'. Paper presented at the 2000 American Political Science Association annual conference. Washington, DC.
'Règlement intérieur provisoire pour le Conseil Spécial de Ministres de la Communauté du charbon et de l'acier' (1967), in L.J. Brinkhorst and R.H. Lauwaars, *Verdrag tot de oprichting van de Europese Gemeenschap voor Kolen en Staal*. Zwolle: Tjeenk Willink, 277–8.
Rosamond, B. (2000). *Theories of European Integration*. London: Palgrave.
Sanchez da Costa Pereira, P. (1988). 'The Use of a Secretariat', in A. Pijpers, E. Regelsberger and W. Wessels (eds.), *European Political Cooperation in the 1980s. A Common Foreign Policy for Western Europe*. Dordrecht: Kluwer Academic Publishers.
Schout, A., and S. Vanhoonacker (2006). 'Evaluating Presidencies of the Council of the EU. Revisiting Nice', *Journal of Common Market Studies*, 44:5, 1051–77.
Shackleton, M. (2006). 'The European Parliament', in J. Peterson and M. Shackleton (eds.), *The Institutions of the European Union*. Oxford: Oxford University Press.
Sherrington, P. (2000). *The Council of Ministers – Political Authority in the European Union*. London and New York: Pinter.
Spence, D. (2006). 'The Commission and the Common Foreign and Security Policy', in D. Spence with G. Edwards (eds.), *The European Commission*. London: John Harper.
Tallberg, J. (2003). 'The Agenda-shaping Powers of the EU Council Presidency', *Journal of European Public Policy*, 10:1, 1–19.
Tallberg, J. (2006). *The Power of the Chair: Formal Leadership in International Cooperation*. Paper presented at the Third Pan-European Conference in EU Politics, Istanbul, 21–23 September 2006.
Thelen, K. (1999). 'Historical Institutionalism in Comparative Politics', *Annual Review of Political Science*, 2, 369–404.
Thelen, K., and S. Steinmo (1992). 'Historical Institutionalism in Comparative Perspective', S. Steinmo, K. Thelen and F. Longstreth, *Structuring Politics*. Cambridge: Cambridge University Press.
Trondal, J. (2006). 'Governing at the Frontier of the European Commission: The Case of Seconded National Officials', *West European Politics*, 29, 146–60.
Vanhoonacker, S. (forthcoming). 'Co-ordination Challenges in ESDP', in H. Kassim, A. Menon and B.G. Peters (eds.), *Coordinating the European Union: Constructing Coordination and Coherent Action in a Multilevel System*. Oxford: Oxford UP.
Vanhoonacker, S., and H. Dijkstra (2006). 'Het EU Raadssecretariaat en het Europese Buitenlandsbeleid: Meer dan een griffier', *Internationale Spectator*, 60:12, 636–41.
Werts, J. (1992). *The European Council*. Amsterdam: North Holland.
Westlake, M., and D. Galloway (2004), *The Council of the European Union*. London: John Harper.

European Administration: Centralisation and Fragmentation as Means of Polity-building?

JOHANNES POLLAK and SONJA PUNTSCHER RIEKMANN

History has shown that all polity-building has also been administration-building. To what degree does this Weberian truth hold true for the European Union? Obviously supranational bureaucracy is not an exact replica of national bureaucracy. There are several reasons for this. First, the European Commission enjoys rights and powers which go beyond those of national bureaucracies. Secondly and somewhat paradoxically, the Commission is far too small to administer directly and effectively a polity of some 500 million citizens. In this respect it is largely dependent on national administrations. European administration is as multi-level as European governance. And, third, the administration of Europe is not a process that is evenly distributed across all policy areas. Nevertheless, the interaction of the national and supranational levels is said to have led to the 'fusion' of administrations (Wessels 1997), thus supporting the thesis that a Weberian approach to European polity-building is appropriate. However, if 'fusion' is defined as the result of the application of a common legal order, it does not necessarily entail administrative convergence in the sense of harmonised practices (Olsen 2007: 263–267). Differences may persist or even widen, either due to ideological resistance against centralisation or functional fragmentation. With regard to the Union, perhaps a mixture of both aspects applies.

As historical-comparative analyses show, European polity-building recalls early modern state-building in that both processes rest on the invention of a special kind of bureaucracy that could be defined as 'commissarial management' (Puntscher Riekmann 1998). This term encompasses not only administrative actions *strictu senso*, but also a political mission geared towards the 'ever closer union' of the members of the would-be polity (Joerges and Dehousse 2002; Olsen 2007). Hence, by promoting the 'idée directrice' of unification, such bureaucracy tends to foster centralisation. The European Commission has done so from Hallstein to Delors. Nevertheless, in the aftermath of Delors, the Commission lost clout. Whatever the impact of the scandals that shook the Santer Commission, new forms of policy-making and administration changed the landscape. First, Open Method of Coordination (OMC) has qualified the Commission's right of initiative formally and informally; second, the potent European Central Bank (ECB) has gained a central place in the institutional set-up; and, third, a plethora of agencies has been created according to functional needs as well as to sovereignty preserving attitudes of member states. The latter argument holds particularly true with regard to security agencies, which will play a special role in this article. However, centralisation and decentralisation appear as two sides of the same coin also in nation states where outsourcing of power to more or less independent agencies generally occurs in the name of efficient governance (Everson 1995, 2005).

If with regard to the Union it seems at least premature to imagine its finalité in terms of a full-fledged state, the evolution of its peculiar administrative space provokes some questions. What do all those instances of creation of supranational administrative bodies through agencification amount to? Where does the creation of a European administrative space, however centralised, multi-layered or fragmented, ultimately point? Our preliminary answers to these questions mirror the ambiguities of the Union itself. First, European integration has led to the emergence and fortification of a central 'commissarial management' exemplified by the Commission and its underworld of committees and working groups, luring national bureaucrats into supranational policy-making. Second, while the Commission over decades has broadly expanded its tasks, it has not sufficiently grown in size and has outsourced some of its powers to agencies. Third, the Council and the member states have created their own agencies, in particular with regard to issues relating to the core of national sovereignty, i.e. domestic and external security. Thus, the European administrative space, rather than gradually developing into a coherent whole, appears increasingly to be a mosaic with different forms of competences, decision-making procedures and accountability. By way of conclusion, we will also pose the question of the extent to which this creates problems for the democratic constitution of the emerging European polity. Is the administrative complexity detrimental to democracy, accountability and responsiveness? Or is the resultant 'integration by stealth' the trade-off we have to accept as it provides for the most efficient way to administer a diverse polity? (Majone 2005).

Administrative Techniques of Polity-building: Lessons from the Past

In his seminal work *Economy and Society* (1922), Max Weber has comprehensively shown that bureaucratic power is a crucial factor of statehood. He did not specifically focus, however, on the question of how states are built through the integration of different nations, territories, rulers, and their administrations. This was a subject dear to political theorists such as Tocqueville, Hintze and Schmitt as well as to the many modern historians who have described how the highly decentralised medieval political order had been transformed over the centuries into increasingly centralised nation states that pursued legal, politico-administrative and cultural homogenisation through a special bureaucracy referred to here as 'commissarial management'. The socio-economic basis for this enterprise was the building of a smoothly functioning single market in which economic actors were enabled to carry out transactions without barriers. Thus, negative integration has marked national state-building as much as positive integration, the latter gaining utmost importance only in the era of full-fledged industrialisation and the eventually emerging modern welfare systems. At the beginning of the national integration processes, political decisions were largely focused on two issues: the construction and imposition of a coherent fiscal system, necessary above all for a sovereign foreign and security policy, and the dismantling of barriers protecting provincial markets as well as specific production sectors. Thus, traditional politico-legal orders of the provinces were transformed and their lords and administrations lured into the new order or simply overruled (Puntscher Riekmann 1998).

The concept of commissarial management comprises three elements: (1) the relative independence of the administration, (2) an 'idée directrice' guiding its actions, and (3) the capability to orchestrate consensus.

(1) First and foremost, the commissarial type of bureaucracy must profess considerable independence from those who are to be integrated. In order to induce provincial or member states' elites to shift their loyalty to the new centre or level of policy-making, a novel and 'rootless' bureaucratic elite is needed in the first place. Ernst B. Haas' argument about this shift as being crucial for European integration also held true for past integration processes (Haas 1958). Thus, the kings of the Ancien Régime were eager to appoint commissioners without roots in

the provinces they were called to administer, whereas the European commissioners are not to represent the member states but European interests. Both must act in the name of the idea of the new political order which does not yet exist. Therefore, the French 'commissaires' and 'maîtres de requête' (and the correspondent commissioners in other European states), in their attempt to attract provincial rulers, administrations, parliaments and assemblies into the new order, continuously refer to the 'king' as its representative. To some extent the European Commission as well as the European Court of Justice use similar discursive techniques by reiterating their reference to the spirit of the treaties, in particular the 'ever closer community' (later the 'union') or the market freedoms.

(2) Commissarial management will only work if the new political order it represents is based on an 'idée directrice' capable of gaining the active consensus of elites or at least the permissive consensus of majorities. Peace, security and socio-economic modernisation form the core of any integration ideology. Relevant arguments have to be reiterated time and again, though, as they might lose their appeal once peace is established or modernisation becomes more difficult due to socio-economic developments. In Europe today the peace argument has quite obviously lost its appeal to younger generations who lack the war experience. However, new security issues related to international crime, terrorism or illegal immigration are important reference points in the creation of the relevant policies and institutions such as European agencies. Interestingly, the treaty negotiated at the IGC 2007 has moved security issues up to second place on the list of goals pursued by the Union, surpassing economic goals (Treaty Article 3, para 2). As for socio-economic modernisation, it appears to presuppose new orientations which might lead to the dismantling of national welfare systems rather than bolstering them (Leibfried 2005). Thus, contrary to the idea of peace and security, the 'idée directrice' of reforming the Union's economy to become the most competitive region in the world (Lisbon Agenda) may lead to contestation by those that deem themselves to be losers in the modernisation process.

(3) One central task of commissarial management is to orchestrate consensus and hence to ensure good implementation of decisions taken to advance integration. To achieve this, the EU has invented different techniques of 'sharing administration' (Vos 2005: 124): In particular, techniques ranging from centralisation (Commission together with the ECB as guardian of the single market, monetary union and the Stability and Growth Pact) to decentralisation (OMC, national courts as guardians of cartel law) have been tried out and complemented by a significant growth of regulatory agencies (fragmentation) to endorse efficient governance. These agencies are to prepare scientifically sound grounds for regulations which – away from

political contestation – may warrant modernisation and thus legitimise discourses of change. Their task, though, is first and foremost to inform political actors about the state of the art in a given policy field and the implications of change. Agencies are thus also collectors and producers of knowledge (Everson 1995, 2005; Majone 2002; Vos 2005) and may be defined as a lever of the commissarial management. However, and contrary to the so-called Meroni doctrine, the discretionary powers of regulatory agencies in particular in the second and third pillars are also growing, thereby deconstructing the power of the traditional commissarial management as embodied by the Commission and building new strata of administration.

The Maze of European Agencies

European Agencies (EA) are not a new phenomenon in the world of EU administrative politics, though it might be asked if today we are witnessing an 'epidemic of agency fever' (Christensen and Laegreid 2005: 15) or an 'explosion of agencies' (Chiti 2000). In general, the willingness to delegate authority to non-majoritarian institutions which fulfil public functions but are not directly accountable to voters or their representatives seems to be increasing (Majone 1999) due to the increasing need for regulation, information and coordination.

The first two EAs, the Centre for Development of Vocational Training (CEDEFOP) and the European Foundation for the Improvement of Living and Working Conditions (EUROFUND), were established as early as the mid-1970s. Contrary to national agencies, these two agencies did not constitute a challenge to the institutional arrangement of supranational politics since they only enjoyed very limited powers in clearly delineated policy fields. Following a decision taken by the heads of state and government in October 1993, the second generation of agencies emerged in the mid-1990s in the quest to finalise the internal market project. The European Environment Agency (EEA), the European Training Foundation (ETF), the European Monitoring Centre for Drugs and Drug Addiction (EMCDDA), the European Agency for the Evaluation of Medicinal Products (EMEA), the Office for Harmonisation of the Internal Market (OHIM), the European Agency for Health and Safety at Work (EUOSHA), the Community Plant Variety Office (CVPO), the Translation Centre for Bodies of the European Union (CDT), the European Monitoring Centre for Racism and Xenophobia (EUMC), and the European Agency for Reconstruction (EAR) were founded. These agencies introduced a new management dimension and were an answer to the desire for geographical devolution and the need to cope with new tasks of a technical and/or scientific nature. The third step towards agencification was taken at the beginning of the 2000s with the establishment of the European Food Safety Authority (EFSA), the European Maritime Safety Authority (EMSA), the

European Aviation Safety Authority (EASA), the European Railway Agency (ERA) and the Network and Information Security Agency (NISA). Recently, the European Agency for the Management of Operational Cooperation at the External Borders (FRONTEX) and European Centre for Disease Prevention and Control (ECDC) were founded. In addition, the European GNSS Supervisory Authority (EGSA), the Community Fisheries Control Agency (CFCA), the European Fundamental Rights Agency (EFRA), and the European Chemicals Agency (ECHA) are under planning (Geradin and Petit 2004: 36).

Of the above-mentioned Community agencies, those established in the second and the third pillars should be distinguished. The European Institute for Security Studies (ISS) and the European Union Satellite Centre (EUSC) were re-founded in 2002 after security matters were transferred from the WEU to the EU. In accordance with the requirements of the Nice Treaty, the European Defence Agency (EDA) was established in 2004 in the framework of a joint action of the Council of Ministers (OJ L 245). In the third pillar, we find the European Police College (CEPOL), the European Judicial Cooperation Unit (EUROJUST) and the European Police Office (EUROPOL). In addition to these agencies, the establishment of a mechanism for the creation of the Rapid Border Intervention Teams (RABIT) in the framework of FRONTEX should be mentioned as well several new multilateral cooperation agreements outside the EC/EU treaties such as the Prüm Convention (2005), the G6 (2003/06) and the European Gendarmerie (2006). FRONTEX is a special case, however, which we address in greater detail below.

In order to cut a path through the maze of abbreviations, the EAs can be distinguished along several criteria. In its communication on the 'Operating Framework for the European Regulatory Agencies', the European Commission (2002) suggested a rather simple categorisation: executive and regulatory. An equally simple differentiation was suggested by Chiti (2000): information function agencies responsible for the collection, management and dissemination of information, and executive agencies in charge of executing new EC regimes and service provisions. Geradin and Petit (2004) suggest a five-fold typology of EAs: (1) implementation agencies such as CPVO, OHIM and EMEA, (2) observatory agencies, such as the EEA and EMCDDA, whose main function is to collect, process and disseminate information, (3) cooperative agencies, such as CEDEFOP and EUROFOUND, which were established to provide a stage for social dialogue and the exchange of expertise, (4) executive agencies, for example the EAR, which operates as a subcontractor to the European Commission with limited discretionary powers for the management of Community programmes, and finally (5) network agencies, such as the EMSA and EASA, which were assigned the task of ensuring the safety of economic activities. This categorisation highlights the wide range of fields and functions encompassed by the agencies (Geradin and Petit 2004: 46).

What all these agencies have in common is that they have their own legal personality and a certain financial autonomy; they are established by legislation (normally Council regulation or, in the case of EUROPOL, a Convention of Member States; in the case of the EDA a Council Joint Action) for the performance of technical, scientific and managerial tasks (European Commission 2002). In line with the Commission's White Paper on Governance, emphasising the need for more agencies, the agencies have become a frequently used tool of regulation and administration.[1] One can expect that the more frequent use of agencies will also lead to a European agency model. However, this is not the case so far given their diversity in terms of functions, organisation and power.

It is true that (nearly) all the agencies were created by regulation in order to perform tasks clearly specified in their constituent acts, that all have legal personality and that their primary function is to support the policy-making process through the provision of information. But they differ considerably with regard to their organisational and financial autonomy, their accountability procedures (see e.g. Christensen and Lagreid 2005; Curtin 2005; Flinders 2004; Vos 2005) and, in the case of the vibrant third pillar, their participants. While, for example, EMEA's executive director is appointed by the management board acting on the recommendation of the Commission, the CPVO president is appointed by the Council from a list of candidates which is proposed by the Commission after obtaining the opinion of the CPVO's administrative council. The composition of the management boards, governing boards or administrative councils of the EAs also varies: member state representatives and Commission representatives (e.g. EEA) or representatives of governments, employee and employer organisations and Commission representatives (e.g. CEDEFOP, EUROFUND) and sometimes third states can be included too (e.g. EMSA). All of these account for their actions by delivering annual reports and, in some cases, the EP can invite the respective director to provide a special report or even to conduct hearings (e.g. EASA, ERA, FRONTEX). Internally, technical or scientific committees complement the ERA structure (e.g. EMCDDA, EFSA).

The wide variety of agency formats is not only the result of their respective functions and policy fields but also a 'trial and error process' – a process well known from state-building history. As long as the final outcome is contested, various tools are used to further the different and sometimes contradictory interests of the participants. More importantly, we are confronted not with the building of only one administrative space mainly as an extended arm of the Commission, but with the creation of two. Even if the member states retain legal and political control over the agencies in the second and third pillars, an increased, institutionalised cooperation takes place, thereby creating a horizontal fusion of national administrations.

Reversing such close cooperation would entail considerable costs in terms of money, loss of knowledge and political ramifications.

In the expanding body of literature on the ERA, we find several justifications for the establishment of agencies (e.g. Geradin and Petit 2004; Groß 2005). (1) The efficiency argument: removing agencies from the direct and possibly partisan control of the ministry by giving them autonomy and responsibility for regulatory tasks while still holding them accountable is expected to improve efficiency and thus enhance regulation. (2) The capacity argument: easing the workload of the central administration frees up capacity to concentrate on the core tasks. (3) The epistemological argument: given the sheer and increasing size of administrative tasks, the central administration is in need of additional expertise. This expertise ensures that policy solutions are prepared in an unbiased, objective and efficient way. (4) The trust or isolation argument: since today all political institutions are more or less regarded as breeding grounds for party politicians who do not exactly enjoy the highest esteem in the population, the objective administering of a polity may help to regain lost trust. Hence, agencies increase policy credibility by insulating certain core functions from political manipulation. (5) The legitimacy argument: a smooth-running administration increases the general level of legitimacy.

Also well known are the counter-arguments to the alleged benefits of agencies. (1) The fragmentation argument: central policy capacity might be reduced by the growth, dis-aggregation, and structural devolution of single-purpose organisations. Horizontal and vertical coordination problems can increase (Christensen and Laegreid 2005).[2] (2) The separation argument, which was already levelled against David Mitrany's functionalist approach: the clear demarcation of an administrative and a political sphere is hardly possible. (3) The not-so-independent argument: in practice, agency boards are brimming with member states representatives and party politicians (Thatcher 2005).[3] (4) The accountability argument: trust requires control, especially in the case of independent agencies. But how can we ensure that this very independence is not used to implement policies which are alien to the common good? Given the sheer number of EAs, the accountability deficit (Baldwin et al. 1998) of the EU will increase since efficient control requires a strengthening of the central EU bodies (Everson 1995). (5) The hollowing-out argument: the establishment of non-majoritarian institutions has undermined the possibility of holding political representatives accountable since due to lack of time they only implement the policy suggestions delivered by agencies. Thus, vertical accountability is weakened (Lodge 2001).

However, these pro- and counter-arguments do not provide clear indications as to the nature of the European administrative space. We will try to answer the question by assessing security-related agencies in terms of centralisation and fragmentation.

An Area of Freedom, Security and Justice?

The thesis about the Union's drive towards polity-building through the fusion of administrations gains particular substance in the field of internal security. Here, too, we witness ambivalent strategies. Attempts at centralisation by commissarial management and subsequent fragmentation can be observed as much as the inverse process in which the Council and member states start with fragmented approaches and over time yield to centralisation. However, this policy field is in such a state of flux that assessments must be made with caution. The emerging area of freedom, security and justice (AFSJ) – as conceived in TEU since Maastricht, further developed in the subsequent treaty revisions of Amsterdam and Nice and considerably extended in the Lisbon Treaty – reflects the increasing involvement of EU institutions in core functions of statehood (Lavenex and Wallace 2005: 458). Modern statehood was by and large the answer to specific questions of insecurity due to the demise of the feudal order in Europe, whereas the Union's gradual and incremental expansion of measures in the field quite obviously aims at coping with current threats to internal security. Since the 1970s, the fight against terrorism has been the major driving force for cooperation (Knelangen 2006: 140), which in the wake of '9/11' led to the proliferation of relevant European legal acts and agencies geared towards supranationalisation (intergovernmental as well as communitarised) of one of the most important policy fields pertaining to the member states and indeed defining the core of national sovereignty. The growing dialectics between internal and external security measures demonstrate the intensification of European polity-building even if it might come along haphazardly, incoherently and be void of a political will pursuing a federal finalité. Thus, whereas the academic literature comparing, for instance, EUROPOL to the American FBI, might still be ahead of real developments (Occhipinti 2003; Ellermann 2006), the growth of institutions and legislation in the field is impressive: 'At the beginning of the 1990s justice and home affairs ... did not yet exist as a policy-making area; since then it has been the fastest growing such area' (Monar 2002: 63).[4]

Police cooperation in Europe goes back to 1975 and the ministerial working group TREVI, which had been set up to exchange experience with regard to terrorism that haunted some European states at the time. With terrorist activities as executed by the Italian Brigate Rosse or the German RAF withering, this approach lost importance after the mid-1980s. However, with the dismantling of internal borders after Maastricht, organised crime advanced onto the internal security agenda and became increasingly important after the late 1990s in connection with criminal issues related to Eastern enlargement and migration (Lavenex and Wallace 2005). Concomitant with the project of a borderless single market, the Schengen process emerged (1985). First conceived as a bilateral and later multilateral agreement, Schengen gradually became part and parcel of EU/EC treaties.

The treaty revision of Amsterdam marked a significant differentiation between issues such as asylum, immigration and visa which were communitarised, whereas police and justice cooperation remained anchored in the third pillar, governed by intergovernmentalism and hence unanimous decision-making. However, Title IV TEC stipulated that unanimity was to end in 2004, whereas those matters remaining in Title VI TEU could be decided by a qualified majority on the basis of article 34(2)(c) relating to measures implementing a Council decision. Additionally, article 34 (3) mentions the special hurdle of a double majority to be composed of 62 votes and a minimum of ten member states (Monar 2002: 66). The Treaty of Nice (2003), on which Union governance rests today, has left this construction largely untouched (Knelangen 2006: 141) with the exception of the new article 67(5) TEC introducing qualified majority voting for asylum policy measures and civil law cooperation. Although the Council agreed on 22 December 2004 to decide by qualified majority starting from 1 January 2005, it appears from a motion for a European Parliament resolution of 19 December 2006 that the 'passerelle' offered by article 67 TEC has not been adequately used. The Treaty establishing a Constitution for Europe (2004), while abolishing the pillar construction, still stipulated a degree of intergovernmentalism in fields pertaining to the AFSJ, as does the Lisbon Treaty, which oscillates between the two poles (Carrera and Geyer 2007).

However, in spite of the persisting institutional ambiguities in the AFSJ, we observe a remarkable picture of bustling activity. Activities encompass legal acts ranging from programmes to action plans to decisions and the creation of new agencies as well as the widening or consolidation of the activities of existing agencies. As for programmes, the first one was established in 1999 by the Tampere European Council, followed by the Hague programme in November 2004 to run from 2005 to 2009. The Hague programme 'covers all aspects of policies in the area of freedom, security and justice, including the external dimension, in particular fundamental rights and citizenship, asylum and migration, border management, integration, the fight against terrorism and organised crime, judicial and police cooperation, and civil law' (European Commission 2006: Chapter IV). It is accompanied by a strategy on drugs established by the European Council in December 2004 and by a joint Commission and Council action plan (2005) that sets the priorities for the implementation of The Hague programme. A brief look at the activities carried out during 2005 and 2006 helps to demonstrate the great leap forward taken by political actors in this area and relevant policy fields, inefficiencies and persisting hurdles to qualified majority voting or to police and justice cooperation notwithstanding.

Under the pressure of threats beginning with '9/11' and culminating in the terrorist attacks on Madrid in 2004 and London in 2005, as well as the enhanced migration towards the Union, the whole discourse on justice and home affairs has changed and gained momentum. Justice and home affairs councils now meet at least eight times a year. Related topics appear on the agenda of European Council meetings, sometimes even dominating them (e.g. Council meeting 14–15 December 2006). Real integration, though, appears to be more cumbersome than in many other policy fields in that programmes and action plans do not easily result in concrete legislation, while the latter often suffers from poor or late implementation through national legislation.[5]

The EU Plan of Action on Combating Terrorism adopted at a special meeting of the European Council held at Brussels on 21 September 2001 (Council Document SN 140/01) was intended to make a strong statement in the wake of Al-Qaeda's terrorist attack against the United States of America. But the details of the action plan addressed the member states more than the Union by reiterating the need for better cooperation through the creation of conditions to further mutual trust between national administrations. It did not aim at institutional centralisation, let alone at harmonisation of criminal law or criminal law proceedings. The theme was facilitating cross-border cooperation and strengthening national authorities (Knelangen 2006: 143). However, the action plan laid the foundations for a framework decision on the fight against terrorism of 22 June 2002 (OJ L 164), which in turn led to a common definition of terrorism. This was accompanied by another framework decision on joint investigation teams (OJ 162 20 June 2002). Last, but not least, the implementation of the action plan occurred concomitantly with a more or less generally accepted need to cooperate with US authorities. However, cooperation existed mainly between the member states and the US due to the lack of European central authorities, EUROPOL being the exception. Thus, US representatives were invited to attend working groups of the Council. In December 2001, an agreement between EUROPOL and the US administration on information exchange was signed. Controversies arose between some member states and the US, in particular due to different perceptions of data protection, investigation methods and the death penalty (Knelangen 2006: 148). Within the Union the action plan led not only to reiterated rhetoric about better coordination of EUROPOL, Eurojust and the Task Force of Chiefs of Police, but also to the creation of a team of 30 experts on terrorism stemming from national police and intelligence. Yet the efficiency of these steps is not to be over-estimated. As a matter of fact, the task force was terminated by the end of 2002 (ibid.).

It goes without saying that success in combating crime in general, and terrorism in particular, depends first and foremost on information. Europeanisation of intelligence, although of paramount importance, remains a difficult matter. Distrust between national intelligence organisations looms everywhere. Upgrading SitCen (Situation Centre) within the Secretariat General of the Council is perhaps as far as the member states can go for the time being. Its main task is to evaluate terrorist threats in conjunction with national intelligence organisations within and outside the

EU and EUROPOL. As data exchange among all member states proved difficult, the big five (Germany, France, Spain, Italy, UK) decided to form a vanguard in this respect and to enlarge in 2006 by including Poland. Their cooperation aims at implementing measures related to the fight against terrorism and transnational crime, immigration policy and the construction of European criminal databases (Bossong 2007: 2). Almost simultaneously, other member states, overlapping somewhat with the G6, formed the Prüm Group, named after a convention signed at Prüm on 27 May 2005. The Prüm Convention stipulates cross-border police and justice cooperation to combat terrorism, crime and illegal immigration. The first signatory states were Germany, Austria, Benelux, Spain and France, joined later by Finland, and negotiations with Italy, Portugal, Slovenia and Poland are underway. The UK has also shown signs of interest (Kietz and Maurer 2007: 1). Central to the Convention, which has been dubbed 'Schengen III' or 'Schengen Plus', is a simplified procedure of data exchange and operative cooperation between police, justice and immigration authorities. Similar to Schengen, the Prüm Convention is intended to function as a motor for deeper integration and to eventually become part of the acquis. However, as we will argue in the concluding section, such initiatives raise questions about the coherence of the Union's institutional and legal framework and, perhaps more importantly, about the democratic quality of decision-making.

Incoherence and hybridisation, though, are problems that haunt the AFSJ in particular. So far, it is hard to tell whether they are a corollary to integration in this relatively new and sensitive policy field, which will eventually be overcome, or whether we are confronted with a new trend in the Union's workings. Certainly, with EUROPOL, Eurojust and the European Police College, we witness the emergence of central agencies; they are, however, holding only coordinating functions and weak powers as to information exchange as well as to police operations. However, the Lisbon Treaty has yet to enter into force and other means of upgrading EUROPOL were envisaged. Such upgrading may prove to be difficult if we consider that in 2006 not even the three protocols of 2000, 2002 and 2003 added to the convention establishing the agency and enhancing its effectiveness had been ratified by all member states.

The Lisbon Treaty of October 2007 explicitly refers to a Council decision on EUROPOL in Article 69 (k). In line with the will of the member states, on 20 December 2006 the European Commission had presented a proposal for a Council decision to establish the European Police Office (COM 2006/817 final, 2006/0310 (CNS)). In its explanatory memorandum, the Commission holds that such an approach is necessary in order to improve EUROPOL's effectiveness in times of increasing threats of terrorism and that the legal act of a Council decision does not require ratification by the member states. The same procedure had already been applied in the creation of Eurojust and CEPOL. In the case of EUROPOL, improved data sharing under the principle of availability is the main goal as stated by the Hague

Programme. Moreover, the Commission proposes to finance EUROPOL from the Community budget, thus putting the agency on an equal footing with the other two security agencies, while also increasing the role of the European Parliament in the control of EUROPOL. The Commission stresses the will of the member states, whose justice and home affairs ministers under the Austrian presidency in June 2006 had agreed to the following statement: 'Competent Council bodies should commence work in order to consider whether and how to replace by 1 January 2008, or as soon as possible thereafter, the EUROPOL Convention by a Council Decision as foreseen in Article 34(2c), where possible on the basis of a concrete initiative or proposal' (quoted in Kietz and Maurer 2007, 4). Interestingly, the Commission had not organised consultations with stakeholders, as this had already been done by the Austrian presidency and at various levels, including technical and data protection experts.

FRONTEX represents another case of hybridisation. Whereas the agency's precursor started as an intergovernmental enterprise called Integrated Border Management (IBM) in 2002, it was transformed into an agency proper in 2004 and instituted in the framework of the first pillar. This implies funding out of the Union's budget and Community procedures for decision-making and accountability, including reporting to the European Parliament as well as the involvement of the ECJ. However, at the same time FRONTEX is far from becoming an autonomous European border guard as it is highly dependent on member states' resources. Whereas the Commission has advocated a centralised model from the outset, the Council continues to envisage joint teams of operation. As a result, FRONTEX suffers from divided loyalties and dedication, which became highly visible in August 2007 when its director announced that joint operations had to be stopped due to material shortages (Agence Europe, 27 August 2007 (9488)).[6]

The Democratic Challenge

As stated above, more or less independent regulatory agencies are not a new invention of the EU, but have existed for quite some time in all modern democratic states, the USA, France and UK being important cases in point (Everson 1995; Gerardin and Petit 2004). So what is wrong with them or how is the democratic challenge to be assessed? As a matter of fact, the ideal of good governance and thus of enhancing legitimacy through better output is one rationale for establishing regulatory agencies in the member states as much as in the European Union. It is in this vein that Majone suggests (2005, 2006) that citizens are prepared to tolerate the delegation of power to the supranational level (and subsequently to its agencies) in the name of appropriate problem solving. However, even if we put aside the fact that Majone does not give any evidence for such tolerance, it may be questioned whether citizens are at all aware of the existence of the maze of agencies we described above, let alone the institutional variety in which they act. In particular, their different procedures of accountability as well as ports of access are largely ignored. Yet the greatest problem may not even lie in the complexity of structures and procedures. In fact, in most cases these can quite easily be detected by studying the website of a given agency. Access and accountability could and should be improved by proper reporting to the European Parliament and to national parliaments alike. Parliaments should be given the right of control and courts the right to scrutinise and sanction wrongdoing.[7]

However, what appears to be much more puzzling is the evolutionary potential of agencification in that it enhances integration by stealth in second and third pillar policies. It is indeed these core policies in which European integration is geared towards polity-building in the classical sense of the term. Together with the single market, monetary union and competition policy, a complex web of power has emerged that impinges on national political orders and deconstructs their democratic institutional set-ups without appropriately compensating the losses at the European level. It appears that the rejection of the constitutional treaty by the French and the Dutch 'Noes' was driven in part by fears of further deepening of integration without open discussion about where the Union is heading. In particular, the Dutch resistance can be explained in this vein (Flash Eurobarometer 2005). Integration by stealth is no longer an undisputed option for member states. Thus, even if security issues rank high among the general public, the incremental shift of competences to the European level and relevant agencies may need greater democratic legitimacy. What appears to be legitimised by permissive consensus (guided by what Majone believes to be central to the citizens, i.e. their quest for optimal output) may quickly erode when a crisis or serious problems occur.

The European Union is still far from commanding stable loyalty from its citizens. Contestation of specific Union policies is always prone to contestation of the new polity as well. Hence, it becomes all the more important to clarify institutional responsibilities, competences, and procedures by way of constitutionalisation if democracy is to be achieved in the Union. It may be concluded, therefore, that there is nothing wrong with regulatory agencies as long as they are created on the basis of treaty provisions, their tasks and procedures are clearly spelt out and their actions are controlled by the representative organs of the Union as well as of member states, in particular by parliaments and courts. One major problem ensuing from agencification is the hybrid forms agencies may take between supranational and intergovernmental provisions, thus diluting not only accountability and responsibility but also efficiency. The case of FRONTEX may serve as an important case in point: constructed as a first pillar institution but dependent on member states for financial and material resources, it may not be able to fulfil the tasks demanded of it by the citizenry.

Conclusions

While political science is still trying to theorise a model of agencification and struggles to find a general definition of it (Christensen and Lagreid 2001; Hood et al. 2001), it seems clear that additional agencies will be created with the aim of improving European governance. This development mirrors the processes we know from nation-states. However, this article not only tried to give an overview of the agencies established in different policy fields and pillars of the EU, but also how integration by supranational centralisation through commissarial management has been complemented over time by fragmentation through agencification. We then asked what influence this compounded administration has on the development of a European administrative space as a means of polity-building and on its democratic quality.

The following answers are tentative and require further investigation. First, the complex and diverse organisation of the EAs confirms the existence of multiple principals (being themselves only indirectly accountable to the European citizens) in the EU governance structure. Second, the lack of clear procedural rules and conditions for the establishment of EAs partly constrain the right of the European citizens to decide what portion of authority they want to transfer to a particular agent. Third, given the fact that a strict delineation of policy fields is hardly possible, agencification might create competition among the EAs and between the Commission and EAs. For instance, how are functions and competences among the different agencies in the AFSJ to be clearly demarcated and duplication or even competition to be avoided?[8] Apart from the potentially positive effects of competition, it can create unintended consequences such as blame shifting or shirking of responsibilities and thus greatly affect accountability. Fourth, who decides on which grounds what agencies are to be established? Some policy fields might receive preferential treatment, i.e. they are 'freed' from political influence and handed over to expert management. Given the inherent economic bias of the EU, this potentially amounts to a severe obstacle to efforts targeted at a political Europe. The existence of compounded administration also affects constraints and opportunities for social organisation because it adds to the administrative repertoire interests have to face.[9] Another question relates to the tension between efficiency and democracy/legitimacy. And, finally, we need to ask what the complexity of the emerging administrative space is good for and, for that matter, how we can assess its efficiency and democratic quality.

It is premature to assess where the creation of regulatory agencies in the European Union is actually leading. In particular, with regard to the security-related agencies, much more research on the basis of plausible hypotheses is needed to draw sound conclusions. Hypotheses apt to demonstrate the polity-building thesis should focus on the decision-making competences of the regulatory agencies, as well as on the actual effects of homogenisation or alignment of security-related competences in the fields of military procurement, common foreign actions, police operations, justice practices, and, last but not least, on the need for personnel and financial resources resulting thereof. In terms of democracy, studies should focus on the involvement of the European and national parliaments and their committees (and eventually the institution of the ombudsman), in particular regarding not only procedures of responsibility, and thus of transparency and accountability, but also the legal provisions on which specific actions are grounded. With regard to the rule of law and the respect for fundamental rights in the collection of personal data, the role of the ECJ and national courts will be crucial beyond the control exercised through specific advisory boards created within the agencies.

This article focused on the newly created agencies in the third pillar. The reason lies in the premise that in historical polity-building processes security issues have always been at the core of such enterprises. As a matter of fact, they were the driving force of modern state-building par excellence. Although the European agencies in this field are established by intergovernmental decision-making, it is their potential for further integration and thus polity-building which is of interest here. If historical tendencies are to be repeated, it would imply the continuation of the 'integration by stealth'-method. This may, however, lead once again to negative referenda in one or more member states.

Notes

1. The Meroni-doctrine no longer being regarded as an obstacle (see Dehousse 2002; Everson 1995).
2. See also the OECD report (2002).
3. See also Kreher (1997), who holds that agencies were not created to avoid control by one political party or to make administration more efficient but to improve collaboration between the member states.
4. It should be added that the FBI had not been built in one day either and that throughout its history it has had to cope with 50 different criminal law systems and state police organisations.
5. To give but one example: the European arrest warrant had been on the agenda since the Tampere European Council in 1999. It encountered massive opposition from the Italian government protracting negotiations until 2001 when the Council of Laeken could finally conclude the relevant framework decision (Knelangen 2006: 146). However, it took another three years for implementation as Italy only in April 2005 transposed the arrest warrant into national legislation (European Commission 2006: Chapter IV). Yet in spite of the fact that until February 2005 some 2600 such warrants had been issued, the European Commission still had to notify that in nine Member States implementation was not in line with European norms.
6. In October 2007 the EP budget committee has voted to double the FRONTEX budget but nevertheless decided to vote in favour of freezing one-third of the agency's administrative budget until it has improved efficiency, which largely depends on states' participation in missions and the means implemented by these states as part of the policies concerned. This development is an instance of the ambiguity about centralisation and fragmentation which characterises the process of agencification in AFSJ.

7. With regard to accountability in terms of efficient control and sanctions, see Bovens (2006) and Puntscher Riekmann (2007).
8. In particular if we consider such duplication and rivalry between the various agencies in the USA which created remarkable problems in the combat on terrorism (Ellermann 2006).
9. There is a clear resemblance between our term 'compounded administration' and the concept of federalism as in Tuschhoff (1999).

References

Baldwin, R., C. Scott and C. Hood, eds. (1998). *A Reader on Regulation*. Oxford: Oxford University Press.
Bossong, R. (2007). 'The European Security Vanguard? Prüm, Heiligendamm and Flexibel Integration Theory', LSE/Challenge Working Paper, January 2007, http://www.lse.ac.uk/Depts/intrel/pdfs/EFPU%20Challenge%20Working%20Paper%207.pdf.
Bovens, M. (2006). 'Analysing and Assessing Public Accountability. A Conceptual Framework', EUROGOV No. C-06-01.
Carrera, S., and F. Geyer (2007). 'The Reform Treaty and Justice and Home Affairs. Implications for the *Common* Area of Freedom, Security and Justice', CEPS Policy Brief, 141, August 2007.
Chiti, E. (2000). 'The Emergence of a Community Administration: The Case of European Agencies', *Common Market Law Review*, 37:2, 309–43.
Christensen, T., and P. Laegreid (2001). *New Public Management. The Transformation of Ideas and Practice*. Aldershot: Ashgate.
Christensen, T., and P. Laegreid (2005). 'Agencification and Regulatory Reforms', Paper prepared for the SCANCOR/SOG workshop on 'Autonomization of the State: From Integrated Administrative Models to Single Purpose Organizations', Stanford University, 1–2 April 2005.
Curtin, D. (2005). 'Delegation to EU Non-majoritarian Agencies and Emerging Practices of Public Accountability', in D. Geradin, R. Muñoz and N. Petit (eds.), *Regulation through Agencies in the EU. A New Paradigm of European Governance*. Cheltenham: Edward Elgar, 88–119.
Dehousse, R. (2002). 'Misfits: EU Law and the Transformation of European Governance', *Jean Monnet Working Paper* 2/02.
Ellermann, J.U. (2006). *Europol und FBI. Probleme und Perspektiven*. Baden-Baden: Nomos.
Everson, M. (1995). 'Independent Agencies: Hierarchy Beaters?', *European Law Journal*, 1:2, 180–204.
Everson, M. (2005). 'Good Governance and European Agencies: The Balance', in D. Geradin, R. Muñoz and N. Petit (eds.), *Regulation through Agencies in the EU. A New Paradigm of European Governance*. Cheltenham: Edward Elgar, 141–63.
European Commission (2002). 'Commission Communication, The Operating Framework for the European Regulatory Agencies' COM (2002) 718 Final 11.12.2002, Brussels.
European Commission (2006). General Report 2006, http://europa.eu/generalreport/en/2006/rg57.htm.
Flinders, M. (2004). 'Distributed Public Governance in the European Union', *Journal of European Public Policy*, 11:3, 520–44.
Geradin, D., and Petit, N. (2004). *The Development of Agencies at EU and National Levels: Conceptual Analysis and Proposals for Reform*, Jean Monnet Working Paper 1/04, New York.
Groß, T. (2005). 'Die Kooperation zwischen europäischen Agenturen und nationalen Behörden', *Europarecht*, 40:1, 54–68.
Haas, E. (1958). *The Uniting of Europe: Political, Social and Economic Forces, 1950–1957*. London: Stevens.
Hood, C., H. Rothstein and R. Baldwin (2001). *The Government of Risk. Understanding Risk Regulation Regimes*. Oxford: Oxford University Press.

Joerges, C., and R. Dehousse (eds.) (2002). *Good Governance in Europe's Integrated Market*. Oxford: Oxford University Press.

Knelangen, W. (2006). 'Die innen- und justizpolitische Zusammenarbeit der EU und die Bekämpfung des Terrorismus', in E. Müller and P. Schneider (eds.), *Die Europäische Union im Kampf gegen den Terrorismus: Sicherheit vs. Freiheit?* Baden-Baden: Nomos, 140–62.

Kietz, D., and A. Maurer (2007). 'Folgen der Prümer Vertragsavantgarde: Fragmentierung und Entdemokratisierung der europäischen justiz- und Innenpolitik?', *SWP Diskussionspapier* der FG 1, 2007/01, January 2007.

Kreher, A. (1997). 'Agencies in the European Community – A Step towards Administrative Integration in Europe', *Journal of European Public Policy*, 4:2, 225–45.

Lavenex, S., and W. Wallace (2005). 'Justice and Home Affairs', in H. Wallace in W. Wallace and M. Pollack (eds.), *Policy Making in the European Union*, 5th ed. Oxford: Oxford University Press, 457–80.

Leibfried, S. (2005). 'Social Policy', in H. Wallace, W. Wallace and M.A. Pollack (eds.), *Policy-Making in the European Union*. Oxford: Oxford University Press, 243–78.

Lodge, J. (2001). 'From Varieties of the Welfare State to Convergence of the Regulatory State? The Europeanization of Regulatory Transparency', *Queen's Papers on Europeanization*, 10/2001.

Majone, G. (1999). 'The Regulatory State and its Legitimacy Problems', *West European Politics*, 22:1, 1–24.

Majone, G. (2002). 'Delegation of Regulatory Powers in a Mixed Polity', *European Law Journal*, 8:3, 319–39.

Majone, G. (2005). *Dilemmas of European Integration: The Ambiguities and Pitfalls of Integration by Stealth*. Oxford: Oxford University Press.

Majone, G. (2006). 'The Common Sense of Integration', *Journal of European Public Policy*, 13:5, 607–26.

Monar, J. (2002). 'Decision-making in the Area of Freedom, Security, and Justice', in A. Arnull and D. Wincott (eds.), *Accountability and Legitimacy in the European Union*. Oxford: Oxford University Press, 63–80.

Occhipinti, J.D. (2003). *The Politics of EU Police Cooperation. Towards a European FBI*. Boulder: Lynne Rienner Publishers.

OECD (2002). *Distributed Public Governance: Agencies, Authorities and Other Autonomous Bodies*. London: OECD.

Olsen, J.P. (2007). *Europe in Search of Political Order*. Oxford: Oxford University Press.

Puntscher, Riekmann, S. (1998). *Die kommissarische Neuordnung Europas. Das Dispositiv der Integration*. Wien and New York: Springer.

Puntscher Riekmann, S. (2007). 'In the Search of Lost Norms. Is Accountability a Solution to the Legitimacy Problems of the European Union?', *Journal of Comparative Politics*, Special issue ed. by Antje Wiener, 13:1, 121–37.

Thatcher, M. (2005). 'Independent Regulatory Agencies and Elected Politicians in Europe', in D. Geradin, R. Muñoz and N. Petit (eds.), *Regulation through Agencies in the EU. A New Paradigm of European Governance*. Cheltenham: Edward Elgar, 47–66.

Tuschhoff, C. (1999). 'The Compounding Effect: The Impact of Federalism on the Concept of Representation', in J.B. Brzinski, T.D. Lancaster and C. Tuschhoff (eds.), *Compounded Representation in Western European Federations*. London: Frank Cass, 16–33.

Vos, E. (2005). 'Independence, Accountability and Transparency of European Regulatory Agencies', in D. Geradin, R. Muñoz and N. Petit (eds.), *Regulation through Agencies in the EU. A New Paradigm of European Governance*. Cheltenham: Edward Elgar, 120–37.

Wessels, W. (1997). 'An Ever Closer Fusion? A Dynamic Macropolitical View on Integration Processes', *Journal of Common Market Studies*, 35:2, 267–99.

Delegation of Powers in the European Union: The Need for a Multi-principals Model

RENAUD DEHOUSSE

The creation of autonomous administrative structures is one of the most interesting developments of the past 15 years in European public administration. While only two semi-autonomous agencies had been created prior to the 1990s, their number had reached 28 at the end of 2007. This figure includes the various organisations established under the label of 'decentralised agencies', as well as the 'Union agencies' set up in the second and third pillars, such as the Institute for Security Studies, EUROPOL or EUROJUST. A few others are currently in the process of being established. Although this decentralisation is no longer new, it seems to have accelerated in recent years. Eight autonomous agencies were established during the Delors years, while another ten were created by the Prodi Commission. During the same period (2001–2005), five agencies were created in the second and third pillars of the EU. According to the 2007 budget, 3,588 administrative posts are assigned to these bodies – a significant number when compared to the overall size of the EU Commission (19,370 agents in 2007). Moreover, if one compares the cumulative figure for agencies staff to the number of posts created within the Commission since 1992 (5,886), we see that over a third of the executive positions created during that period have been assigned to regulatory agencies. The cumulative budget of EU agencies for 2007 amounted to over €1 billion. Several of the most recent structures enjoy powers that were explicitly denied to their predecessors. The European Agency for Reconstruction (EAR) has been entrusted with the task of distributing EU money in the former Yugoslavia, while the Aviation Safety Agency (EASA) enjoys, in practice if not in law, a degree of regulatory autonomy, as we shall see. As noted in a 2005 report by the French Senate, more autonomous organs had been created by the EU in the previous 50 months than in the preceding 50 years (Sénat 2005).

With the benefit of hindsight, it is tempting to regard this development as a long-term trend inspired by the will to reform European public administration and to gloss over the reasons prompting such a shift. The reality, however, is much more complex. As those who have been following the situation know, the creation of European agencies was a fairly haphazard development. None of the main institutional actors deliberately planned or defended it as the best way forward. Proposals to establish an agency were often met with resistance from one side or the other and usually gave rise to fairly intense inter-institutional bargaining. During the drafting of its White Paper on European Governance, disputes over the path that should be followed by the Commission concerning this very issue resulted in a substantial re-writing of the initial draft, the final version presenting a classical defence of the 'Community method' (interview at the Commission, November 2001) even though this 'hierarchical' approach was somewhat at odds with the philosophy underpinning the white paper (Scott 2002).

Thus far, the movement that led to the establishment of EU agencies has been analysed mainly along functional lines by taking adaptations of the principal–agent model developed in American literature in order to analyse the delegation of powers by the Congress towards administrative agencies. The necessity of bringing expertise to the public policy process or ensuring its credibility features prominently amongst the motivations attributed to those who promoted this new trend at the European level. However, despite its unquestionable relevance, the principal–agent model, in its standard form, is analytically inadequate as it does not take into consideration some of the peculiarities of the EU setting. The most important of these is the absence of a clearly defined 'principal' since European institutional architecture has been carefully designed to avoid any concentration of power.

For instance, following a basic interpretation of the principal–agent model, it would be difficult to explain the recurrent tensions between the Commission and the Council of Ministers over the composition of agency administrative boards or the ambivalence of the Commission, which has long appeared reluctant to accept delegations of power and yet has continued to propose the establishment of new agencies. Nor would one be able to understand the multiplicity of controls to which European agencies are subjected. The main contention of this article is that in order to make sense of both the decision to delegate powers to and the institutional design of EU agencies, one must keep in mind the absence of a defined hegemon within the EU, which is itself a by-product of the multi-level character of that system.

The article is organised as follows. The next section reviews the two kinds of principal–agent models that have been used thus far to analyse the delegation of powers either to supranational bodies in general or to European agencies in particular. The article then addresses the central issue of who can be regarded as the 'principal' within the EU setting and discusses the need for a 'multi-principals' model. Next, the discussion highlights the explanatory potential of this model in relation to regulatory politics and accountability issues. The final section questions the lasting character of this model in light of recent inter-institutional struggles.

Delegation of Powers to Supranational Institutions

Two basic models, both inspired by the rational choice approach to political institutions, seem to be relevant for examining the process whereby specific powers are entrusted to EU administrative agencies.

A number of scholars have examined the reasons that push states to transfer either more or less extended powers to supranational bodies. Adopting an international relations perspective, they argue that delegation is a way to reduce the transaction costs that are associated with the adoption and implementation of transnational policies. More specifically, supranational agents may solve problems resulting from incomplete information by providing decision-makers with the technical information they need, in particular when complex technical issues are at stake. They may also help to ensure the credibility of commitments adopted at the supranational level by monitoring states' compliance with joint decisions, enforcing the latter if needed, or exerting independent regulatory powers over powerful economic principals (in the case of competition policy) or in strategic policy sectors, such as monetary policy (Majone 1996; Moravcsik 1998; Pollack 2003). From this perspective, the EU member states are naturally regarded as principals, and the key question is to what extent supranational agents may take advantage of their discretionary powers to pursue their own policy preferences and promote integration against the wishes of national governments – an issue which, as is known, occupies a central place in European integration literature (Bauer 2002; Pollack 2003). Extrapolating from this perception, one may ask what motivations have propelled the same principals, i.e. national governments, acting in their capacity as members of the Council of Ministers, to transfer a growing number of powers to EU administrative agencies.

This interpretation of the delegation problem, however, is confronted with radically different alternatives. Adopting a comparative politics perspective, other analysts have suggested that delegation may be regarded as a process whereby directly elected legislatures transfer policy-making authority to non-majoritarian structures for reasons akin to those mentioned above. To the extent that this model may be applied to the EU, the principals are the EU institutions sharing legislative power: the Council of Ministers, acting together with the Parliament in cases where co-decision is required (Kelemen 2002). A variant of this model has been advanced by the European Commission. In its White Paper on Governance and in the various position papers that followed, the Commission has – implicitly, but nonetheless clearly – presented itself as the principal that must evaluate the possibility of delegating a share of its powers to autonomous bodies, which will assist in completing its tasks. It has repeatedly stressed the necessity to preserve 'the unity and integrity of the executive function' to ensure 'that it continues to be vested in the chief of the Commission if the latter is to have the required responsibility of vis-à-vis Europe's citizens, the Member States and the other institutions' (Commission 2002: 1). Similarly, in the 2005 draft Inter-institutional Agreement, agencies are described as mere auxiliaries of the Commission. They must 'provide the Commission, in particular, with the experience and expertise it needs so that it can fully meet its responsibilities as the Community executive'. From this viewpoint, agencies are only supposed 'to *help* regulate a particular sector at European level and to *help* implement a particular Community policy' (Commission 2005: 5; emphases added). In a speech delivered at a meeting of agency directors, Commission President Jose Manuel Barroso made it clear that the Commission regards itself as a political principal that agencies must assist, while also acknowledging that this partnership may entail some responsibilities on the part of the Commission (Barroso 2006).

The same vision has been forcefully defended by the Commission's legal service. It finds support in the celebrated *Meroni* ruling, in which the European Court of Justice narrowly defined the range of powers that may be delegated to other actors. Delegation, the ECJ stated, is permissible only when 'it involves clearly defined executive powers, the exercise of which can, therefore, be subject to strict review in light of criteria determined by the delegating authority'. Conversely, the delegation of 'a discretionary power, implying a wide margin of discretion' is to be excluded in all cases (*Meroni v. High Authority*, [1957–58] ECR 133, at 151–152). Not surprisingly, therefore, the legal community tends to reason as if the creation of autonomous administrative agencies should be mainly regarded as a transfer of authority from the Commission to these bodies (Chiti 2000; Géradin *et al.* 2005; Lenaerts 1993; Yataganas 2001).

Confronted with alternative models, one may be tempted to solve the contradiction by arguing that both of them may be relevant, although in distinct cases. Thus, the 'intergovernmental' model is clearly helpful for making sense of 'history-making' decisions, such as the establishment of the Commission itself, the ECJ or the European Central Bank, whereas the 'comparative politics' version might be used to analyse the problems surrounding the establishment of administrative bodies by the EU legislature.

However, in practice, both models appear to be relevant for understanding the logic that has led to agency creation. First, the role of the European Commission in the agency-creation wave of the 1990s cannot be ignored. The Commission proposed the establishment of the agencies, greatly shaped their structure and powers, and often provided them with their first director (Hauray 2006). In recent times, Parliament's influence greatly shaped the politics of agency design (Kelemen 2002). In other words, contrary to what a purely intergovernmental model would suggest, supranational institutions have played a substantial role in that process. Conversely, more often than not, the powers entrusted to European agencies were previously held by national authorities rather than by the Commission. Prior to the establishment of the European Medicines Agency (EMEA) or the Office for Harmonisation in the Internal Market (OHIM), marketing authorisations for medicinal products were delivered and trademarks were registered by national bodies rather than the Commission. To the extent that there was delegation, it entailed a vertical transfer of powers (from the national to the EU level) rather than a horizontal one (from Community institutions to specialised agencies). Outside of the 'executive agencies' created in the wake of the Kinnock reform to relieve the Commission of routine executive tasks, instances of actual transfers of powers from the Commission to bureaucratic structures remain very rare. The European Agency for Reconstruction is an exception in that it enjoys budget implementation powers that are normally vested in the Commission, according to the EC Treaty.

Consequently, drawing a clear line between the two strands of analysis would cause us to ignore an important part of the story. In truth, the creation of agencies requires an agreement between actors of various types, each with their own interests. A proposal to this effect must be tabled by the Commission and accepted by national governments and, to an increasing extent, by the European Parliament. Failing to acknowledge the wide variety of actors that participate in the final decision would make it difficult to account for the manifold tensions surrounding agency creation. It would also lead the current debate on inter-institutional agreement regarding agencies, proposed by the Commission in 2005, to seem incomprehensible. Why would a single principal want to codify delegation practices? In contrast, I would argue that recognising the multiplicity of principals enables us to understand some key structural features of the decentralised bodies that have been established and the variety of controls to which they have been subjected.

The difficulties that may be encountered when trying to identify precisely the principals and the agents have been noted in the literature on delegation. Thatcher and Stone Sweet (2002) have stressed, for example, that principals are not always unified, which increases the complexity of dealing with changes in preferences. 'Composite principals', they write, 'that is, a principal comprised of multiple actors whose collective makeup changes periodically through, for example, elections, may not possess stable, coherent preferences over time. Instead, they may be competitive with one another over some or many issues, as when member states in the EU disagree on matters of policy that fall within the agent's mandate' (ibid.; 6). They also discuss the case of multiple agents, i.e. situations in which 'the initial act of delegation may parcel out – among multiple actors – the functions normally associated with the principals' (ibid.). Interesting as they may be, neither of these hypotheses actually corresponds to what occurs when autonomous administrative structures are established at the EU level. The problem here is not the time consistency of principals' preferences, but rather the fact that different principals, each with their own preferences, must agree in order for the new body to be created. In Kelemen's words, the issue lies in understanding 'how conflicts between the EU's primary legislative actors – the Council and the Parliament – and its primary executive actor – the Commission – have influenced the design of new bureaucratic agencies' (Kelemen 2002: 93).

A Political System without a Principal

The delegation issue cannot be analysed without considering the basic principles that underpin the European Union's institutional architecture. European integration is an unprecedented attempt to build a form of continental order without recreating the hierarchical power structure of states. Balance and compromise are the main features of this system. Balance among the various countries that joined the Community, and later the Union, was a key concern for the founding fathers. No country, large or small, was to be in a position to be able to impose its own views. Hence, the elements that explain the originality (and, arguably, the effectiveness) of the European model. Significant powers have been delegated to an independent executive and an independent judiciary, the composition of which, however, is conceived in such a way that national interests cannot be ignored, and weighted voting has been allowed in the main decision-making body, the Council of Ministers, with a high majority threshold, which makes decisions by consensus well-nigh unavoidable.

Balance amongst the institutions is another way to further the same goal. Many of the original features of EU decision-making are also inspired by the same anti-hegemonic objective. The much-criticised monopoly of initiative bestowed upon the Commission, for example, was requested by the smaller member states in order to counteract the influence of larger countries within the Council of Ministers (Küsters 1990). Equally important, if one intends to preserve the decentralised character of the system, is the fact that national governments, through their role in the European Council and the Council of Ministers, play a central role in EU decision-taking. In other words, there is a direct link between the distribution of powers at the EU level and its character as a system of multi-level governance. Because the institutions of the Union had been deliberately designed to be able to represent a variety of interests, preserving the distribution of power effectuated by the Treaty of Rome was necessary to avoid any kind of capture by specific interests. The attention given to the principle of 'institutional balance' in the case law of the Court of Justice therefore appears quite justified (Majone 2005).

In sum, the absence of a principal within the EU institutional scenario is not an accident; rather, it is a corollary of the spirit that inspired European construction itself. Even today, with a directly elected European Parliament, it would be incorrect to regard the Commission as enjoying a type of popular mandate authorising it to implement a political programme of some sort. European election campaigns continue to be dominated by national issues. Despite the steady growth since the Maastricht Treaty of the Parliament's role in appointing the Commission, the composition of the executive still seems to owe more to national government preferences than to the decisions of the legislature (see however Hix 2006 for a contrasting view).

The implications of this situation for the issue of delegation are twofold. First, the multiplicity of principals should not be viewed as an anomaly or a transitional situation. Quite the contrary; this is perfectly in tune with the central, anti-hegemonic principle that represents the cornerstone of the European institutional architecture. Second, our interpretation of the principal–agent model must be adapted to this situation. As a rule, delegation decisions require the support of several principals, each with their own preferences and each anxious to exert some degree of control over the agent. The problem of control will therefore present itself in an atypical fashion. Given the variety of the principals' preferences, the link between the former and the agent's performance, as well as the principals' capacity to control the agent, is likely to be diluted. Our attempts to understand the politics of delegation and to evaluate their outcome must take these elements into account.

The Politics of Delegation in the EU

How does the multiplicity of principals affect delegation issues? The variant of the principal–agent model proposed here may enable us to understand a number of features which are at odds with the 'standard' delegation model, in which there is (at least for Europe, where parliamentary government is the rule) a clear chain of command leading to governments and political parties, and ultimately to the people. Tensions among principals explain a number of stable elements in the otherwise haphazard process that has led to the mushrooming of various kinds of agencies. These tensions have affected both delegation decisions and the institutional design of the agencies. The existence of several principals also has implications for how the accountability debate must be framed. Lastly, I would argue that in such a context, the creation of strong regulatory agencies is unlikely.

The multiplicity of principals has largely shaped the politics of agency creation. Each of the principals is somewhat reluctant to relinquish power (as with all principals, in general). However, their main concern is not what the P-A literature describes as 'agency drift', that is, the idea that agents will pursue a political agenda that differs from that of its principal. What the principals fear most is the emergence of a variant of 'political drift', in which agencies are somehow 'captured' by one of their institutional rivals in the leadership contest. Thus, as a rule, even where national governments accept the necessity of enhancing European cooperation, they tend to oppose the granting of more significant powers to the Commission. Similarly, when the first European agencies were established, the national governments insisted that they be subject to intergovernmental control so as not to threaten national administrations. EU agencies were therefore established as the hubs of networks bringing together national administrations (Dehousse 1997).

The Commission, naturally inclined to maximise its own power like most bureaucratic structures (Majone 1996), fears the emergence of potential rivals that will be more exposed to member states' influence. From the Commission's perspective, delegation is often only a second-best alternative, which it will accept only if convinced that an extension of its own powers is not likely to be approved by the Council. Thus, in the field of food safety, it supported the establishment of an independent authority only once it realised that the national governments were unwilling to enlarge its prerogatives (Kelemen 2002). The Commission's 2001 White Paper on European Governance clearly illustrates this 'official' point of view. While highlighting in classic fashion the advantages of agencies (sectoral expertise, increased visibility and cost savings), it dwells at greater length on the limits that should surround the delegation of powers if the balance between the institutions is to be respected. 'Agencies can be granted the power to take individual decisions ... but cannot adopt general regulatory measures', nor can they 'be given responsibilities for which the Treaty has conferred a direct power of decision on the Commission (for example, in the area of competition policy).' They 'cannot be granted decision-making powers in areas in which they would have to arbitrate between conflicting public interests, exercise political discretion or carry out complex economic assessments'. Finally, of course, 'agencies must be subject to an effective system of supervision and control' (Commission 2001: 24).

This lukewarm view is often shared by the European Parliament, which fears being deprived of its hard-won legislative powers by the regulatory agencies despite the fact that its own influence over the Commission has been growing during the past decade. A Parliamentary report summarises the Parliament's position concerning the issue as follows: Since 'the Commission bears ultimate political responsibility for the management of Community activities', it follows that 'the autonomy of the new regulatory agencies should be exercised under the direct supervision of the Commission and monitored politically by the European Parliament on the basis of the powers vested in it by the Treaty' (European Parliament 2003). From this perspective, the 'enemy' is represented by the member states' intergovernmental bias since, unlike the Commission, national representatives are not under the Parliament's authority.

These contrasting fears largely explain the complex institutional architecture of EU regulatory agencies. First, agency creation has often led to protracted negotiations and elaborate compromises between the various branches of the legislature. At the time the EASA was established, for instance, some 150 amendments were presented (Schout 2007). The reason is easy to understand since the greater the specifications of agency objectives, the easier it is for principals to control them. Similarly, although the establishment of these new structures has been criticised as a somewhat slapdash process (Commission 2005; Sénat 2005), there are a number of recurrent features to be found within their configuration and functioning, all of which appear to be directly linked to a willingness to preserve the existing balance of power in the Union.

In the principal–agent literature, the power to appoint the heads of an agency's executive is regarded as a standard control mechanism. At the EU level, this power is generally fragmented. Most often, directors are appointed by the agency's administrative board based on a proposal from the Commission; in other cases, he or she is appointed by the Commission based on a proposal from the administrative board or by the Council on the basis of a list of candidates drawn up by the administrative board or the Commission. The Council enjoys more autonomy for so-called 'Union agencies', created in the fields of foreign policy or justice and home affairs, in which it may be regarded as the main principal (Curtin 2006; Craig 2007: 151). The Parliament's role in the appointment process is less prominent, except for a few agencies whose work is of direct interest to the populace at large, such as the European Food Safety Authority (EFSA) or the European Centre for Prevention and Control of Diseases (ECDC). This is generally justified by referring to the Parliament's nature as a control institution, the Commission being perceived as the main holder of executive power (See e.g. European Parliament 2003: 9).

Agency administrative boards are composite structures. While there are several possible variants, they are generally comprised of at least one representative for each member state. This occasionally leads to rather peculiar situations. For example, Hungary and Malta are entitled to appoint one person on the board of the European Maritime Safety Agency or the European Railway Agency, respectively, even if their representative's expertise in those fields can be assumed to be limited. Likewise, in its first period of activity, EUROFOUND, the working conditions agency, had more board members than staff (Schout 2007: 6). To date, the only exception to the principle of intergovernmental control is the Food Safety Authority, created in 2002 after a series of food-related scares. Given the public's alarm, the Commission was able to successfully invoke the necessity of enhancing the agency's independence to ensure the credibility of the new structure and effectively convinced national governments to do away with the classical 'one state, one vote' rule as regards the administrative board. Yet this is the one exception that proves the rule, for even in this unusual case, the members of the management board are appointed by the Council of Ministers from a list drawn up by the Commission. The essence of the compromise is therefore clear: One must avoid concentrating the power to appoint in any one of the would-be 'principals'.

In similar fashion, principals seem to have found it appropriate to confine agencies to a secondary role, at least formally. The majority of the organisations created since 1990 have an information-gathering mission, such as the European Environment Agency in Copenhagen. They may assist the Commission in implementing programmes and policies, as the European Training Foundation in Turin or the European Reconstruction Agency in Thessaloniki. They may even go so far as to prepare decisions to be taken by the Commission, as is the case for the London-based European Medicines Agency. Yet most have been denied any independent decision-making power. At times, the reluctance to delegate was quite explicit, as is demonstrated by the regulation establishing the Lisbon Drug Monitoring Centre: '[T]he Centre may not take any measure which in any way goes beyond the sphere of information and the processing thereof' (Article 1 (4) of Council Regulation EEC 302/93, OJ [1993] No. L36/1).

In other cases, the principals' attitude was more ambivalent. As regards the licensing of pharmaceuticals, for instance, the Commission's initial proposal provided the possibility for the EMEA to make autonomous decisions regarding certain procedural matters, such as the format of the application for marketing authorisations. Yet the regulation that was ultimately adopted denied the Agency even this limited degree of autonomy (Dehousse 2003). Likewise, despite Commission President Romano Prodi's call for the creation of a 'strong' food safety regulator in the wake of manifold food-related scares, the Commission's own proposal demarcated the necessity of drawing a clear distinction between risk evaluation, during which a specialised agency could play a useful role, and risk management, which was to remain in the hands of the EU's 'political power', i.e. the Commission (Lafond 2001).

As a result, only a handful of agencies, such as the Office for Harmonisation in the Internal Market in Alicante, the Community Plant Variety Office in Angers or, more recently, the Aviation Safety Agency in Cologne, have been granted the power to take individual decisions on the grounds that such decisions do not entail significant discretionary powers.

Needless to say, the power to adopt formal rules of any kind is always denied to those bodies. The EASA, however, has been entitled to adopt non-binding 'guidance material' (Art. 13 (b) of Regulation 1592/2002, OJ L 240 of 7 September 2002), which, coupled with the authority to issue individual decisions, approaches independent regulatory power, as demonstrated by the Commission's experience in the field of competition policy. Moreover, when it advises the Commission on the rules to be adopted to implement the air safety regulations, the technical part of its opinions, in particular the part dealing with the construction, design and operation of aircraft, cannot be altered by the Commission without prior collaboration with the Agency (Article 12b).

The fact that the Agency's influence has been somewhat disguised, however, suggests there is strong resistance against a formal grant of regulatory authority. As a rule, agency heads themselves are mere executive directors, as the agency's work programme is defined by the administrative board. Indeed, in defining the profile of a good executive director, Fernand Sauer, founding director of EMEA (widely regarded as one of the 'strongest' EU agencies), indicated that networking skills were essential since directors are engaged in permanent negotiations, be they with the Commission, the Parliament, the member states, or stakeholders of some kind (Sauer 2007).

This reluctance to establish strong regulators is often justified by legal constraints. The *Meroni* doctrine of the European Court of Justice is religiously referred to as a justification for preventing any form of delegation that could undermine the Commission's own executive authority. Although the validity of the *Meroni* precedent in the European Community is questionable (Dehousse 2003), it is nevertheless interesting to note that the Commission has departed from legal orthodoxy on various occasions, as seen earlier. It is therefore tempting to conclude that the law provides a useful (and flexible) pretext for concealing the Commission's deeper motivations, which are linked to an eagerness to assert its authority as the EU executive – an authority that has been regularly challenged by national governments.

Be that as it may, the absence of formal authority does not necessarily mean that agencies are deprived of any influence. Indeed, in analysing the practice, one notes, for instance, that EMEA recommendations are systemically rubber-stamped by the Commission (Hauray 2006). This is hardly surprising. If an institution pooling the best expertise available at the European level warns against the dangers of a given pharmaceutical, the 'political power' could not ignore its advice without taking substantial risks. Giandomenico Majone has correctly pointed out that, provided the regulatory bodies manage to acquire (and preserve) credibility, they may acquire significant influence, even when endowed with mere advisory or information functions (Majone 1997). But are all European agencies, with their multiple principals, strong enough to acquire that type of influence?

Does the Multiplicity of Control Channels Make Agencies More Accountable?

In several respects, the creation of an agency can be seen as an advantage in terms of accountability. The very fact that an administrative body is established, endowed with a legal personality, subject to legal rules and provided with budgetary resources triggers a variety of control mechanisms that would be hard to conceive of with a loose regulatory network or with an intergovernmental committee, which remains the most likely alternative to an agency. Indeed, the number and variety of control devices used to monitor EU agencies' action is impressive, particularly when compared to those capable of forcing 'comitology' committees to account for their decisions.

Agencies are required to present an annual activity report describing how they implemented their yearly programme. Community contributions to the agencies are included in the general budget, which is prepared by the Commission and approved by the Council and the Parliament. As of 1 January 2003, the financial discipline governing agencies financed by the EU budget (a large category, since only two, the Office for Harmonisation in the Internal Market and the Plant Variety Office, are entirely self-financing) has been made stricter. Agencies are subject to the authority of the Commission's Financial Controller, whereas the discharge for the implementation of their budgets must be given each year by the European Parliament upon the recommendation of the Council (Financial Regulation 1605/2002 of 25 June 2002, OJ L 248 of 16 September 2002). Judicial control mechanisms have been provided for those agencies with the power to adopt individual decisions, such as the OHIM or the EASA. The Ombudsman has also used its powers of control to recommend that agencies adopt rules on transparency and access to documents.

In the principal–agent literature, accountability mechanisms are mostly viewed as a method by which the principal can ensure that the agent follows the instructions it has been given rather than developing its own priorities. As suggested above, in a system with multiple principals one of the main fears is that an agency will be subjected to undue influence by a rival in the contest for political leadership. The variety of accountability mechanisms is such that it is seems unlikely that this kind of 'capture' would occur. As a rule, national administrations are represented on the administrative board of agencies, as is the Commission, which often plays a role in the appointment of directors and can present its opinion on annual work programmes. Since the setting up of the first agencies in the 1990s, the European Parliament has used its 'power of the purse' to make its voice heard. For example, when unsatisfied with the policy pursued by some agencies, the Parliament did not hesitate to freeze a substantial part of the agencies' budgets until they complied with its demands (Brinkhorst 1996).

Should one conclude from this state of affairs that we are in a situation similar to the description of US agencies offered by Terry Moe (1987), according to whom in many instances 'no one controls the agency, and yet the agency is under control' (p. 295)? While this is a possible conclusion, it is far from certain. Indeed, the sheer complexity of control mechanisms may render improbable their utilisation and therefore diminish their deterring power. Even on the national plane, typical control devices such as the power to dismiss the director, change an agency's enabling legislation or cut its budget are rarely used, for their use may be politically costly (Thatcher 2005). How probable is it that the situation will be different at the European level, where the number of veto players is higher? As all three political institutions enjoy some influence over agency action, the sanction of possible mistakes seems rather unlikely. In its 2005 draft inter-institutional agreement, for instance, the Commission contemplated the possibility of amending or repealing the act establishing an agency if it is unsatisfied with the way the agency accomplishes its tasks. However, for such a threat to be carried out the Commission will normally require the support of the EU legislature, i.e. the Council and the Parliament; the opposition of either of these institutions would prevent the sanctions from being carried out. In other words, agencies remain immune to reform unless faced with a broad consensus (Williams 2005). Likewise, the threat of reducing an agency's subsidy will not be credible unless it receives a positive echo from within the two branches of the budgetary authority.

This is not to say that agencies are impervious to any control. Indeed, the fact that the Commission and the national administrations contribute to their internal functioning (rather than acting merely as forces of external control) suggests that agencies are unlikely to adopt a policy that would cross any red lines defined by their principals. Yet it is interesting to note that the logic of collective control by multiple principals has been taken to such an extent that it may actually weaken the possibility of sanctioning their agent's misconduct.

A Lasting Compromise?

It may of course be thought that the 'tug-of-war' between the institutions is merely a transitory phase linked to the relative novelty of the European regulatory system and that the situation will gradually stabilise with the emergence of a hierarchy of sorts amongst the various principals. However, there are many indications to the contrary. First, polycentricity has, if anything, been aggravated by the emergence of the European Parliament, which has used its increasing legislative powers to acquire more influence in the creation and operation of Community agencies (Kelemen 2002). Secondly, attempts to modify the current balance of power generally meet with strong resistance.

The evolution of the European Aviation Safety Agency is quite significant in this respect. Both the Commission and the aviation industry pushed in favour of the establishment of a strong European regulator to discipline member states and to provide a 'one-stop shop' to the industry. As we saw, the agency was endowed with quasi-regulatory powers. Yet budgetary constraints and member states' influence have led it to operate as a typical EU agency, i.e. largely as a network operator in a system that has obvious similarities with comitology (Schout 2007: 5).

Similarly, subsequent to its White Paper on Governance, the Commission issued a communication (Commission 2002), which was then followed by a draft inter-institutional agreement (IIA) on regulatory agencies (Commission 2005). The declared ambition of this proposal is to clarify the framework within which agencies should operate, setting conditions for their creation, operation and control. The Commission's approach may be regarded as confirmation of the relevance of the 'multiple principals' perspective advocated here. As suggested above, the resort to an inter-institutional agreement would hardly make sense if there were but one principal. The rationale offered by the Commission to explain its initiative is that the institutional architecture is so disorganised, given the contrasting views of the various actors that may influence agency creation, that 'the situation...is rather untransparent, difficult for the public to understand, and, at all events, detrimental to legal safety' (ibid.: 2).

The Commission's draft lays down several basic principles that must be respected upon the establishment of an agency. The Commission declares itself committed to a thorough impact assessment in order to analyse any problems to be resolved, whether the regulatory agency is likely to provide an adequate response, and under what conditions. To facilitate the agency creation process, the IIA recommends that a single 'legal policy' be adopted to avoid endless inter-institutional debate. The Treaty provision forming the legal basis of the policy in question should be used as the foundation for establishing an agency rather than Article 308, the EC Treaty's 'implied powers' clause. Likewise, the vexing question of the agency seat should be settled in the basic act or in the following six-month period.

While these proposals were the centre of some debates, the majority of the criticism was directed towards the Commission's propositions regarding the structure of the agency, which were strongly opposed by several member states. The Commission suggested that, in general, not all of the member states should be represented on the administrative board of agencies unless they are 'involved in the exercise of executive powers by the Member States'. It also recommended that 'the two branches of the Community executive', namely the Commission and the Council, should be equally represented on the board. The Parliament, it maintained, should not be involved as this 'would cast doubt on the Parliament's ability to perform external controls objectively'. Understandably, these proposals were viewed as an attempt to limit the national governments' room for manoeuvre both during the creation of an agency and in its day-to-day operations. Such an interpretation prompted the legal service of the Council to challenge the legality of the draft IIA on the grounds that it 'goes way beyond the establishment of arrangements for cooperation between the institutions: it concerns the adoption of "*supra-legislative*" substantive legal rules, in the sense that their purpose would be to bind the legislator in the future by a procedure not laid down in the Treaties' (Council 2005; emphasis original). Several governments also objected to what appeared to them as an attempt by the Commission to modify the current balance of power within the European regulatory system (Assemblée nationale 2006). It appears, therefore, that the current 'multi-principals' compromise is here to stay (see Craig 2007: 183, for a similar conclusion). Whatever one may think of the existing design of EU agencies, it is strongly anchored in the contemporary institutional culture of the Union.

Conclusion: Multiple Principals, Weak Agents?

This article has argued that it is difficult to make sense of the development of a galaxy of European regulatory agencies without analysing the environment in which this development has flourished. The absence of a clear institutional hegemon within the EU system has allowed the three 'political' European institutions to influence the rules governing the structure and functioning of agencies and their operation. The Commission has played a key role in the establishment of agencies; the European Parliament has acquired significant authority due to the increase in its legislative and budgetary powers; several member states have made it quite clear during negotiations on the draft IIA on regulatory agencies that they do not intend to relinquish the various powers of control that they currently enjoy. The respective influence of these actors may change. The parliament has gained more influence over time, while the Council has reserved itself a more important role in relation to second and third pillar agencies. But the multipolar character of the process has not been altered. None of the existing agencies can be depicted as a mere instrument in the hands of any one of the 'political' institutions. It is true that this type of polycentricity is not unknown on the domestic plane, where tensions may exist between, for example, the parliament and the executive when the creation of autonomous agencies is debated (see e.g. Shapiro 1997). Yet there is, at the very least, a difference in degree. In a system of multi-level governance such as the EU, it may be regarded as the cornerstone of the structure.

Given the existence of multiple principals, each with their own interests, it would have been quite surprising to witness the emergence of strong regulators. Indeed, the reluctance to delegate far-reaching powers to EU agencies represents one of the cornerstones of the present system, as well as being an essential element of the institutional discourse. Multiple accountability channels have been established in order to ensure that agencies do not overstep the boundaries assigned to them. The weakness of the powers they enjoy often leads some to regard agencies as irrelevant. Formal powers, however, tell us only one part of the story. There is already evidence that some of the existing structures, such as the EMEA, have become highly influential and are indeed the de facto decision-makers in their field. Furthermore, external events may create such pressure for change that the principals will find it politically costly to resist. A series of food-related scares have prompted national governments to allow more autonomy to be granted to the Food Safety Authority than to other agencies. Similar future events may raise questions as to the appropriateness of the current status quo. The main limitation of the current arrangement is the extreme dilution of power that it causes. The broad consensus required for both the establishment and the control of EU regulatory bodies has resulted in the creation of bodies the formal powers of which remain fairly limited. The risk is, of course, that this will generate a situation in which no player feels overall responsibility and the avoidance of blame is the main concern of all parties. The future will tell whether the 'multiple principals' system of the EU is as stable as it currently seems.

References

Assemblée nationale (2006). 'Rapport d'information sur les agences européennes déposé pour la délégation de l'Assemblée nationale pour l'Union européenne par M. Christian Philip', député, N° 3069, 3 mai 2006.

Barroso, José Manuel (2006). Discours prononcé le 23 février 2006 devant les directeurs d'agences, cited in Assemblée nationale, 'Rapport d'information sur les agences européennes déposé pour la délégation de l'Assemblée nationale pour l'Union européenne par M. Christian Philip', député, N° 3069, 3 mai 2006, 95–9.

Bauer, Michael (2002). 'Limitations to Agency Control in European union Policy-Making: The Commission and the Poverty Programmes', *Journal of Common Market Studies*, 40:3, 381–400.

Brinkhorst, Laurens J. (1996). 'The Future of European Agencies: A Budgetary Perspective from the European Parliament', in Alexander Kreher (ed.), *The New European Agencies*, EUI Working Paper RSC n. 96/49, 75–81.

Chiti, Edoardo (2000). 'The Emergence of a Community Administration: The Case of European Agencies', *Common Market Law Review*, 37, 309–43.

Commission (2001). *European Governance. A White Paper*, COM(2001)428 final 25 July 2001.

Commission (2002). Communication on the operating framework for the European regulatory agencies, COM(2002)718 final of 11 December 2002.

Commission (2005). Draft Interinstitutional Agreement on the Operating Framework for the European Regulatory Agencies, COM(2005), 59 final of 25 February 2005.

Council (2005). Opinion 7861/05 of the legal Service on the Draft Interinstitutional Agreement on the operating framework for the European regulatory agencies – choice of legal act and legal basis, 6 April 2005 (08.04).

Craig, Paul (2007). *European Administrative Law*. Oxford: Oxford University Press.

Curtin, Deirdre (2006). 'Framing Accountability of EU Administrative Actors', Paper presented at the CONNEX workshop on accountability, Lausanne, July 2006.

Dehousse, Renaud (1997). 'Regulation by Networks in the European Community: The Role of European Agencies', *Journal of European Public Policy*, 4:2, 246–61.

Dehousse, Renaud (2003). 'Misfits: EU Law and the Transformation of European Governance', in Christian Joerges and Renaud Dehousse (eds.), *Good Governance in an Integrated Market*. Oxford: Oxford University Press, 207–29.

European Parliament (2003). *Report on the Communication from the Commission: 'The Operating Framework for the European Regulatory Agencies' (COM(2002) 718 – 2003/2089 (INI))*, drafted by Ms. Teresa Almeida Garrett, EP Doc. 15-1471/2003 final, 4 December.
Géradin, Damien, Rodolphe Munoz and Nicolas Petit, eds. (2005). *Regulation through Agencies in the EU. A New Paradigm for European Governance*. Cheltenham: Edward Elgar.
Hauray, Boris (2006). *L'Europe du médicamen*. Paris: Presses de Sciences Po.
Hix, Simon (2006). 'Why the EU Needs (Left–Right) Politics: Policy Reform and Accountability are Impossible Without It', Notre Europe Policy Paper No. 19, Paris: Notre Europe.
Kelemen, R. Daniel (2002). 'The Politics of "Eurocratic" Structure and the New European Agencies', *West European Politics*, 25:1, 93–118.
Küsters, H.J. (1990). *Fondements de la Communanté économique Européenne*. Brussels: Labor.
Lafond, François (2001). 'The Creation of the European Food Authority: Institutional Implications of Risk Regulation', Notre Europe, European Issues, No.10, Paris: Notre Europe.
Lenaerts, Koen (1993). 'Regulating the Regulatory Process: "Delegation of Powers" in the European Community', *European Law Review*, 18:1, 23–49.
Majone, Giandomenico (1996). *Regulating Europe*. London: Routledge.
Majone, Giandomenico (1997). 'The New European Agencies: Regulation by Information', *Journal of European Public Policy*, 4:2, 262–75.
Majone, Giandomenico (2005). 'Federation, Confederation, and Mixed Government: A EU-US Comparison', in Anand Menon and Martin Schain (eds.), *Comparative Federalism: The European Union and the United States in Comparative Perspective*. Oxford: Oxford University Press, 121–47.
Moe, Terry (1987). 'Interests, Institutions and Positive Theory: The Politics of the NLRB', *Studies in American Political Development*, 2, 236–99.
Moravcsik, Andrew (1998). *The Choice for Europe. Social Purpose and State Power from Messina to Maastricht*. Ithaca, NY: Cornell University Press.
Pollack, Mark (2003). *The Engines of European Integration. Delegation, Agency and Agenda-setting in the EU*. Oxford and New York: Oxford University Press.
Sauer, Fernand (2007). 'Management Perspectives: Establishing a Focus for EU Agencies', Paper presented at the European Institute for Public Administration, Maastricht, 29 January.
Schout, Adrian (2007). 'EU Agency: Design or Default?', Paper presented at the CONNEX workshop on 'European Risk Governance; its Science, its Inclusiveness and its Effectiveness', Maastricht, 14–16 June.
Scott, Colin (2002). 'The Governance of the European Union: The Potential for Multi-Level Control', *European Law Journal*, 8:1 (March), 59–79.
Sénat (2005). 'Les agences européennes: l'expert et le politique', Rapport d'information no.58, présenté par Mme Marie-Thérèse Hermange au nom de la délégation du Sénat pour l'Union européenne, 27 octobre.
Shapiro, Martin (1997). 'The Problem of Independent Agencies in the United States and the European Union', *Journal of European Public Policy*, 4:2, 276–91.
Thatcher, Mark (2005). 'The Third Force? Independent Regulatory Agencies and Elected Politicians in Europe', *Governance*, 18:3, 347–73.
Thatcher, Mark, and Alec Stone Sweet (2002). 'Theory and Practice of Delegation in Non-Majoritarian Institutions', *West European Politics*, 25:1, 1–22.
Williams, Garrath (2005). 'Monomaniacs or Schizophrenics? Responsible Governance and the EU's Independent Agencies', *Political Studies*, 53, 82–99.
Yataganas, Xenophon (2001). 'Delegation of Regulatory Authority in the European Union: the Relevance of the American Model of Independent Agencies', Jean Monnet Working Paper 3/01.

Reshaping European Regulatory Space: An Evolutionary Analysis

MARK THATCHER and DAVID COEN

In the last 20 years, EU regulation has been transformed.[1] Its scope has expanded from a concentration on competition policy to coverage of many sectors, from telecommunications to food, while its depth has increased tremendously, as detailed legislation has been passed. Much work has focused on increased demand for EU regulation, be it from firms, governments or the European Commission (on regulation, see notably Bergman *et al.* 1999; Majone 1996, 2005; Gatsios and Seabright 1989). But, for regulation to be implemented, appropriate institutions for the greatly enhanced EU regulation also have to be established. This article looks at such institutions, notably concerning regulation of markets.

Implementation of public policies always raises questions of discretion and diversity. But, in the case of the EU, there are two other reasons for implementation being crucial. One is that there is a strong tension between the creation of a single European market through centralised EU-level legislation and its decentralised implementation by national-level authorities (see Armstrong and Bulmer 1998; Majone 2005; Young 2005; and, for cross-sectoral analyses, Schmidt 2002; Thatcher 2007). EU legislation is frequently broad and difficult to implement, and conditions in national markets vary, so the same rules must be applied differently to achieve a similar objective. Hence it is difficult to monitor whether EU regulation is being implemented consistently with respect to obtaining a single market. Worse still (for achieving a single market), there are strong national traditions of protecting domestic firms, while member states have incentives to aid domestic suppliers by cheating on the implementation of EU regulation, from late transposition or misinterpretation of EU rules to outright non-enforcement.[2] Most visibly, the sheer variety of national institutions responsible for implementing EU legislation makes consistency across member states very difficult. For instance, many countries regulate markets through national ministries and independent regulatory agencies (IRAs), but there are considerable differences in their institutional form, ambitions, capacity and relationships with politicians, incumbent suppliers and new entrants (see Coen and Thatcher 2005; Coen and Héritier 2005; Gilardi 2005; Levi-Faur 2005; Thatcher 2002a,b). Consequently, there is a real risk of conflict between the principles of a single market – notably equality of treatment among firms and ending barriers to entry – and its administration by a multiplicity of member states.

A second reason for the importance of implementing institutions for EU regulation is linkage to major analytical questions about the development of the EU. The dominant neo-functionalist and inter-governmental bargaining theories, whilst differing in their explanations of European integration, emphasise rational actors (such as transnational firms, the European Commission, the European Court of Justice or national governments) demanding further integration due to the advantages they derive.[3] They present the development of the EU in terms of transfers of powers from member states to EU bodies such as the Commission or European Court of Justice to respond to these demands. However, recent work has suggested that existing institutions mould the evolution of European integration. Thus, for instance, integration may occur due to 'policy transfer' between different sectors and between the national and supra-national levels (Bulmer and Padgett 2005; Bulmer et al. 2007; and see Börzel 2001 on uploading and downloading). Equally, it may occur as informal practices grow up that are then formalised (Coen and Héritier 2005; Héritier 2007). Finally, initial steps may lead to implementation gaps resulting in further integration (Kelemen 2004). More generally, historical institutionalist studies have argued that institutions change gradually and sometimes in path-dependent ways, as existing structures limit and shape new ones (see Mahoney 2000; Pierson 2000; Streeck and Thelen 2005; Thelen 2004; for path dependency or past legacies in the EU, see Kelemen 2005; for an analysis of the occurrence of path dependency see Capoccia and Kelemen 2007).

Evolutionary change can occur through 'layering' (creating new institutional elements in old regimes), displacement of existing institutions within a regime, 'drift' (deliberate neglect of institutions) and conversion of existing institutions for new functions (Streeck and Thelen 2005; Thelen 2004).

Examining the regulatory institutions for implementation allows us to consider whether, how and why existing structures affect the development of the EU and whether the institutional outcomes of debates is classic European integration with transfers of powers to the Commission and ECJ, or whether new forms of governance are in fact being used. At first sight, the prospects for comprehensive reform of European regulatory institutions should be better than in many other domains such as national welfare policies, offering a 'harder' case for historical institutionalist claims of evolutionary institutional change. One reason is that regulation at the EU level is less detailed and more recent than at the national level. Moreover, the 1980s onwards have seen radical changes in regulation in EU member states, showing the potential for comprehensive change (see Majone 1997; Thatcher 2007). Furthermore, the article illustrates how tensions between centralised rule-making and decentralised implementation have given rise to significant and repeated debates since the 1990s about the creation of new institutions to ensure effective implementation of EU regulation and hence which modes of integration and governance should be used.

The article argues that European regulatory space has not been radically and comprehensively but has in fact followed an evolutionary development involving gradual reshaping through a series of steps, with previous stages influencing later stages and institutions being built on existing structures. Initial reforms were very limited, despite talk of 'Euro-regulators'. Thereafter, further steps have taken place: new coordinating institutions have been created, and have been given formal powers. There has been a thickening of organisations and rules concerning regulation. In short, a process of 'institutionalisation' has taken place (see Armstrong and Bulmer 1998; Bulmer 1994; Stone Sweet *et al.* 2001). Each phase has prepared the ground for the following one through several mechanisms: actors created in one phase then became significant in pressing for movement towards further changes; experimentation with different institutional arrangements has occurred both within and across sectors; dissatisfaction with the results of one stage led policy-makers to seek further reforms; learning took place, thereby also altering actor preferences. As a result, evolution has taken place through 'layering', as new institutional coordination mechanisms have been developed in addition to existing ones, and through 'conversion', as existing regulatory organisations have been given expanded and different functions and powers. Evolutionary change has not been due to exclusion of past policy options from discussion: on the contrary, past institutional options are rejected in one stage but return for consideration in later stages. Instead, change has been gradual because, in part at least, new regulatory organisations have shaped institutional choices, suggesting that as institutionalisation of European regulatory space grows, it becomes more difficult to make radical changes.

The outcome of institutional evolution has been a gradual strengthening of networks of national policy-makers (in this case, independent regulatory agencies) for implementing EU regulation. Those institutions have become more formalised and centralised. But, there has been no movement towards a neat and tidy regulatory space. Instead, that space is filled with multiple organisations and is strongly marked by past steps. Indeed, evolution has been far from painless or consensual: rather it has involved strong debates about the extent of centralisation of powers at the European level and the respective roles of the European Commission and national and EU regulatory agencies, showing that implementing institutions link to wider political battles about integration and the form of the EU.

This overall conclusion is important both empirically and theoretically. Regulation is the EU's core activity and hence the choice of modes of coordination for EU legislation goes to the heart of European integration. It raises uncomfortable issues: the extent to which the EU should seek uniform administrative arrangements and application of European legislation across 27 member states; the allocation of responsibilities for different elements of policy-making between organisational levels; relationships between the Commission and national actors; how to avoid implementation gaps; the development of coordination mechanisms outside the formalised comitology procedures used for legislation. At the theoretical level, the article suggests that new work on evolutionary change can be usefully applied at the EU level. Indeed, analysing EU developments as the product of incremental change, collisions and compromises between organisations and endogenous processes may offer a better paradigm to understand the institutionalisation of Europe than 'grand bargains' or rational design of an overall system.[4]

We begin by setting out the choice of different institutional models for European regulatory space in economic markets, which lie at the core of the EU. The models range from the Commission leaving implementation to national bodies at one extreme to a single EU-wide regulator responsible for implementation throughout the EU. But beyond this dichotomy between supranational and national regulation, newer hybrid forms of coordination have emerged, such as informal forums, European networks of regulatory agencies or different forms of 'Euro-regulators'. Then, using process tracing in three economically and politically key sectors – financial services, telecommunications and electricity – we show how each step has prepared the ground for further reforms and how institutional 'layering' and 'conversion' have taken place. Equally, we underline that past choices return to the agenda, indicating continuing pressures for comprehensive change, but that existing institutions limit and reform, so that abrupt alterations are rejected. The three phases we identify consist of EU-supervised national implementation, informal networks of independent regulators and forum governance, European networks of national regulators. We end by looking at current debates on creating 'Euro-regulators' and then draw wider conclusions about the evolution of European regulatory space and the analysis of the development of the EU.

Institutional Choices for Structuring European Regulatory Space

Debates about administrative arrangements to coordinate the implementation of regulation across the EU have seen discussion of several models. Unfortunately, labels such as 'Euro-regulator' have been used without adequate definition, and indeed sometimes with diverse meanings over time. This section sets out different institutional choices by looking at seven major models that have been given serious attention for the implementation of EU regulation (as opposed to passing EU legislation). The models concern the formal 'regulatory space' in Europe, i.e. the structures for taking decisions about implementing EU legislation concerning regulation of markets.[5]

The seven models (summarised in Table 1) are stylised and based on five factors that structure regulatory space: the principals, i.e. the actors who formally delegate powers over implementation (if any); the participants in decisions about implementation (who may be agents if there is formal delegation); the allocation of powers and responsibilities for the implementation of EU legislation; possible mechanisms of implementation, dealing with issues of consistency and interpretation of discretion across EU member states (these can range from informal learning and norms to explicit but non-binding benchmarks/guidelines right up to legally binding decisions and standards and rules); which actors have controls over actors responsible for implementation decisions.[6]

The models themselves are subject to many variations but a schematic typology is presented. They are presented in an approximate hierarchy of increasing centralisation of coordination, starting with implementation in the hands of national bodies and ending with a single EU regulator, but it should be noted that this refers to formal powers – whether control in practice would be more centralised in one model than another is a different issue.[7] Finally, it should be noted that many of these regulatory options can be layered upon each other over time as they are not mutually exclusive and can operate in parallel.

EU monitoring and supervision involves the classic EU method whereby the EU delegates responsibility for implementing EU regulation to national regulatory authorities (NRAs – public bodies designated by member states, hence normally including government departments and independent regulatory agencies). The European Commission and behind it the European Court of Justice are responsible for ensuring that NRAs correctly implement EU regulation through monitoring and supervision; ultimately this can mean infringement proceedings against member states for failure to

TABLE 1
TYPOLOGY OF INSTITUTIONS OF THE EUROPEAN SPACE FOR IMPLEMENTING REGULATION

Type of coordination	Principals and legal basis	Participants	Allocation of powers and responsibilities	Mechanisms of implementation	Allocation of formal controls
EU supervised national implementation	EU Treaty	NRAs, Commission and ECJ	NRAs implement, European Commission and ECJ oversee	Legal infringement proceedings	Commission and ECJ
Forum Governance	None formally – no formal delegation	NRAs, Commission, suppliers, users and user groups	None formally	No legally binding measures; learning and norms, and benchmarking	None since no formal delegation
Informal networks of IRAs (NIRAs)	None formally – no formal delegation	IRAs	None formally	No legally binding measures; learning, norms, and benchmarking	None since no formal delegation
European Networks of Regulators (ERNs)	EU Commission and national governments and regulators, using EU secondary legislation	Designated national regulators (e.g. IRAs) and Commission)	National IRAs, with guidelines set by ERN	Advice to Commission on legislation; setting formal guidelines, learning, norms, and benchmarking	Commission and national regulators
European Regulatory Agency (ERA)	EU Commission and national governments and regulators using EU secondary legislation	Designated national regulators (e.g. IRAs, national government officials), Commission and sometimes European Parliament	Commission or NRA, except for 'technical' decisions	Specific Decisions, advice to Commission approval (or veto); setting formal guidelines; learning, norms, and benchmarking	Commission, member states, European Parliament

(*continued*)

TABLE 1
(Continued)

Type of coordination	Principals and legal basis	Participants	Allocation of powers and responsibilities	Mechanisms of implementation	Allocation of formal controls
Federal European Regulatory Agency (FERA)	EU Commission and national governments using Treaty amendment	Representatives of member states/IRAs	FERA with NRAs being subordinate in FERA's domains	Setting standards and rules and taking decisions in individual cases within its domain; learning, norms, and benchmarking	National governments; possibly also European Commission and European Parliament
Single European Regulator (SER)	EU Commission and national governments using Treaty amendment	European officials	SER – NRAs abolished	Setting standards and rules and taking decisions in individual cases	National governments; possibly also European Commission and European Parliament
Direct regulation by the European Commission	National governments through EU Treaty	European Commission	European Commission	Setting standards and rules and taking decisions in individual cases	European Court of Justice

comply with EU law. Informal methods such as benchmarking or discussions of national officials may occur, but they are not supplied institutionally and hence rely on the initiative of individual actors. Indeed, national agencies may in practice become 'double-hatted' as they also become 'agents' of the Commission with which they develop links (see Egeberg 2006). National governments have controls over EU institutions such as the European Commission and ECJ, as well as over NRAs.[8]

Forums are informal consultative groups. They do not enjoy formal delegation of powers and hence lack formal principals and controls (although informal delegation of functions, for instance by the Commission or national regulatory authorities, may take place). Their participants can be drawn from across a sector – both public and private and from EU and national levels. They offer a form of informal sectoral governance (cf. Kohler-Koch and Eising 1999). They can coordinate through informal mechanisms such as policy learning or setting benchmarks and norms. Such forum governance relies heavily on soft law through norms becoming accepted via a process of policy iterations between participants.[9]

Informal networks of independent regulatory agencies (NIRAs) are also informal groupings that do not have formal delegation. But they have a much narrower membership than forums, since they consist of independent regulatory agencies that enjoy domestic independence from national governments and exclude officials from ministries and the European Commission or the private sector. They also rely on informal mechanisms to influence national IRAs such as learning, norms and benchmarking, perhaps even aiding the development of a European regulatory 'epistemic community'.[10] However, unlike forums, they provide a more institutional setting for the IRAs, encourage contact via regular scheduled meetings, and reduce collective action problems by having a narrower and hence less diverse membership in the form of IRAs.

European Regulatory Networks (ERNS) are composed of designated regulators – usually but not necessarily national independent regulatory agencies, and sometimes also Commission officials. ERNs are created through a 'double delegation' – from both the Commission and national regulators, as each delegates formal coordinating functions and powers, such as setting standards or rules for implementation to the ERN (see Coen and Thatcher 2008). Both can be expected to have formal controls over ERNs. The ERNs enjoy formal powers and are more formalised and institutionalised modes of coordination of implementation compared with forums and informal NIRAs. For instance they have a more homogenous and defined membership (national officials), usually have a small secretariat and working groups and provide formal access to the Commission debates via consultation and regular plenary sessions. The role of ERNs is to coordinate national bodies that continue to implement EU legislation alongside the ERN. ERNs do so both through participating in formal rule-making (e.g. by setting or advising on standards) or through facilitating learning and best practice through regular interaction and discussion among national regulators and the Commission.

European Regulatory Agencies (ERAs) also involve a double delegation from the Commission and national regulators and/or governments. However, unlike ERNs, European Regulatory Agencies can make recommendations that are then subject to Commission acceptance (formally, they make proposals to the Commission), whereas ERNs can only offer advice on legislation. ERAs can be divided into three groups according to their powers: those offering advice, especially technical and scientific, to the Commission; those carrying out inspections; those empowered to adopt legally binding individual decisions (Majone 2005: 94). ERAs are established by secondary legislation to fulfil specific tasks and enjoy a limited degree of autonomy from the Commission (see Kelemen 2005: esp. 175–177). They also have management boards composed of representatives of national governments, the Commission and sometimes the European Parliament rather than just national IRAs, underlining the greater degree of integration and independence from national bodies. Nevertheless, ERAs face important constraints. They can only apply rules to specific decisions rather than making rules: the 'Meroni' doctrine of non-delegation, at least as currently interpreted, prevents the Commission from delegating rule-making powers. They also rely on national bodies for information and expertise, and sometimes for undertaking functions that the ERA delegates to national members. Examples of ERNs include the European Food Safety Authority or the European Agency for the Evaluation of Medicinal Products (EMEA), or the European Aviation Safety Authority or the Trademark Office (see Dehousse 2002; Kelemen 2002; Majone 2005: 83–99; Nicolaides 2006; Vos 2000; for the EMEA see Gehring and Krapohl 2007).[11]

Federal European Regulatory Agencies (FERAs) do not yet exist. They would have powers to make rules and set standards for implementation throughout the EU; national regulatory authorities would continue to exist but they would be subordinate to the FERA in the FERA's domains. A FERA could be composed of representatives of each member state; the European Central Bank offers an analogous body. Powers would be transferred from both the Commission and national governments and hence they would be its principals. The creation of Federal European Regulatory Agencies would require treaty amendment to be agreed by national governments (at least if the Meroni doctrine that the Commission cannot delegate rule-making powers remains as currently interpreted); governments would be expected to have controls over such agencies, as well as the European Parliament and perhaps the Commission. A Federal European Regulatory Agency would undertake implementation by setting detailed EU-wide rules and standards and taking decisions on matters within its jurisdiction (which would be defined by the treaty amendments) as well as informal mechanisms of coordinating national regulatory authorities. The rationale for such bodies has been argued to be increased policy-making efficiency, especially in complex and technical policy domains, as well as insulating national bodies from domestic pressures.[12] If the US experience in sectors such as telecommunications and energy were copied, lower-level regulatory agencies would continue to exist and to have powers in certain fields, notably intra-national issues, but questions that affect inter-(member) state trade would be under the jurisdiction of the FERA.

A *Single European Regulator* (SER) differs from a FERA in being the sole body responsible for implementation and being composed not of representatives of national regulatory agencies but of officials who are chosen to serve the EU as a whole. SERs do not exist and would be a radical step in that national regulatory authorities would be abolished, ending issues of coordination of such bodies (but perhaps transforming them into intra-organisational ones) and instead the SER would take all decisions on individual cases concerning implementation of EU regulation. Creating an SER would require Treaty amendment and would involve transferring powers from both the Commission and member states, which hence would be its principals. It would also necessitate resources, since the body would cover implementation across the EU. National governments would be expected to have controls over the SER, and perhaps also the Commission and the European Parliament. The closest analogous body is the Securities and Exchange Commission (SEC) in the US, which regulates securities markets.

Direct regulation by the European Commission is rare, since the organisation is small. It has been used in certain parts of competition policy, notably cross-border mergers and acquisitions over certain thresholds, abuse of a dominant position and state aids. Yet a major part of the Commission's regulation, namely vetting agreements between firms that have the potential to affect inter-state trade, were handed to national competition regulators in 2002, greatly reducing such direct regulation (see Wilks 2005 for an analysis).

European Regulatory Space in Network Industries

Network industries such as securities trading, telecommunications and electricity offer good examples of regulatory space, due not only to their importance but also as classic examples of governing EU regulation. Traditionally, regulatory space in Europe was dominated by nation states. Most network suppliers were publicly owned. Formal regulatory powers lay in the hands of ministries, which in practice enjoyed very close links with the state-owned suppliers. The EU played almost no role in regulating network industries; thus, for instance, the EU telecommunications ministers met twice between 1959 and 1977 (Schneider and Werle 1990: 87); almost no EU sectoral legislation was passed, and network industries were seen as outside competition law. Insofar as international coordination took place, it took the form of intergovernmental organisations that were composed of national representatives and had no powers to impose decisions; examples included the CEPT in telecommunications, which went beyond the EU, or IOSCO in securities.

However, from the 1980s onwards, new European administrative structures were created to regulate network industries. Although the timing of each phase has varied a little across different network industries, we see a repeated pattern, suggesting a cross-sectoral logic rather an industry-specific one. In part, the changes arose from the combination of three developments, namely the growth of EU regulation, privatisation of suppliers and modification of national regulatory structures. However, a fourth factor was endogenous processes from each previous phase of changes in the EU's regulatory space. We show how these processes contributed to an evolutionary pattern of development, with experimentation, layering of institutions, and gradual change.

Given the array of acronyms, Table 2 sets out the key types of regulator and specific regulatory organisation.

TABLE 2
ACRONYMS IN EUROPEAN REGULATORY SPACE

Acronym	Full name	Brief description
Types of regulator		
IRA	Independent Regulatory Agency	National agency for regulation with considerable formal independence from elected politicians
NRA	National Regulatory Authority	Organisation responsible for implementing EU regulation – may be an IRA or a government department
NIRA	Network of independent regulatory agencies	Informal network of national IRAs without formal delegation – e.g., CEER in energy or IRG in telecommunications
ERN	European Regulatory Network	Network of IRAs created by EC law
ERA	European Regulatory Agency	EU body able to make recommendations to the European Commission
FERA	Federal European Regulatory Agency	EU body with power to impose decisions concerning implementation on IRAs – none yet created
SER	Single European Regulator	Body responsible for implementing EU regulation in the EU – none yet created
Specific regulatory organisations		
FESCO	Forum of European Securities Commissions	Informal NIRA for securities, created 1997, replaced by CESR
CESR	Committee of European Securities Regulators	ERN for securities, created 2001
IRG	Independent Regulators Group	Informal NIRA for telecommunications, created 1997
ERG	European Regulators Group	ERN for telecommunications, created 2002
CEER	Council of European Energy Regulators	Informal NIRA for energy, created 2000
ERGEG	European Regulators Group for Electricity and Gas	ERN for energy, created 2002

Phase 1: EU-Supervised National Implementation

In the late 1980s and 1990s, the EU began to pass sector-specific legislation in network industries, beginning with telecommunications and soon expanding to electricity, gas and securities (Bulmer *et al.* 2007; Coen and Thatcher 2000; Levi-Faur 2005; more specifically, for telecommunications see Humphreys and Simpson 2005; Thatcher 2001; for energy see Eberlein 2003; Eising and Jabko 2000). Significant legislation for postal services and the railways only began in the late 1990s (see Héritier 2005).

The EU's expanding regulatory framework was binding on member states and was composed of three elements. First liberalisation, i.e. ending domestic legal monopolies, initially in particular market segments but later throughout industries, including domestic users. But the EU did not just 'deregulate', for a second element was 're-regulatory rules' that governed market competition and set conditions for suppliers and public actors (cf. Vogel 1996). Key rules covered access to infrastructures, cost-based tariffs and universal service.

The third element concerned implementation and is most directly relevant to this article. EU legislation placed duties for enforcing liberalisation and especially re-regulation on 'national regulatory authorities' (NRAs). It insisted that these NRAs be separate from suppliers, thus ruling out ministries that both regulated and contained suppliers (often the case in telecommunications and postal services). The legislation did not require member states to establish independent regulatory agencies (IRAs), although the Commission often encouraged this. Indeed, this period was characterised by a variety of regulatory solutions in the domestic markets, ranging from IRAs and government departments or agencies with varying links to elected politicians in telecommunications, to IRAs, self regulation and voluntary access agreements in energy markets (Levi-Faur 2001; Thatcher 2002b, 2007).

Thus, in this first phase, EU regulation sought to open national markets through liberalisation and re-regulation but left the institutional architecture of implementation to member states. There were few instruments to coordinate national regulatory authorities or to ensure consistent implementation of EU law, a major issue for the EU given that most of its legislation was very broadly defined in line with 'the politics of compromise' among member states and also between EU institutions.[13]

Phase 2: Informal networks of Independent Regulators (NIRAs) and Forum Governance

In the 1990s, concerns emerged about lack of coordination among national regulators, uneven implementation across member states and the need for more policy learning between national officials. Directives were seen as too rigid and 'old-fashioned' and instead new modes of ensuring better implementation of EU regulation were sought (Interview senior financial regulator 1; Börzel 2001). Moreover, the 1980s had seen the abandonment of attempts to create very detailed EU legislation to harmonise standards, using instead the 'new approach' of only setting minimum harmonisation standards. This left member states considerable discretion over implementation, especially of 're-regulatory' measures governing how competition should operate, such as interconnection or networks or licensing, and provision of services beyond competition such as universal service (Pelkmans 1987).[14] But variation in the forms of national regulatory authorities created problems of coordination throughout the EU (Interview with Commission official 1). Moreover, this 'patchwork regulatory environment' provided opportunities for industry, NRAs and member states to establish regulatory advantages at the expense of a consistent European single market.[15]

One possible response was to greatly centralise regulatory powers. Thus, for instance, in telecommunications there was support within the Commission (including Martin Bangemann, Commissioner responsible for telecommunications) for a powerful EU 'licensing committee' or a European-level agency to ensure even and effective implementation of EC regulation (Commission 1992; *Agence Europe* 10 March 1995, 24 May 1996, 25 February 1997; *Financial Times* 3 July, 30 September 1996, 19 December 1997). The European Parliament called for a Euro-telecoms authority or Committee to prevent separate and different regulatory areas developing (*European Voice* 17 April 1997; Coen and Doyle 2000; *Agence Europe* 11 April 1995, 20 February, 24 May, 21 December 1996, 24 February 1997). But no European agencies were established. The key reason was opposition by member states, many of which feared loss of control over their domestic markets and increased foreign competition to national firms, and hence preferred national IRAs. For their part, those new IRAs were attempting to establish their political position in domestic markets which Euro-regulators could have threatened (Humphreys and Simpson 2005: 102–106; *Agence Europe* 25 February 1997; *Financial Times* 19 December 1997; Interviews with Commission official and NRA). As Bangemann observed later, 'It would have been too much to ask of member states...to impose a European Regulator on top of liberalisation' (*Financial Times* 19 December 2007: 3).

Instead, two forms of more centralised coordination emerged in the late 1990s in response to not only exogenous pressures from creating the 'single market', but also endogenous pressures to coordinate markets arising from the previous regulatory patchwork and the desire to avoid European regulators. One was informal sectoral governance groups, notably the Florence Forum for electricity in 1998 (Eberlein 2003), followed by the Madrid Forum for gas in 1999. The creation of these forums was led by the Commission. It, politicians, and industry saw them as a low cost institutional design options thanks to their low political saliency (*Financial*

Times 1 February 2000; Eberlein 2003). The initial aim was to provide a neutral and informal EU-level forum for discussion of issues and exchange of experiences concerning the implementation of the EU electricity and gas directive and the development of a single EU energy market (Electricity Directive 96/92/EC; Gas Directive 98/30/EC). The new forums included a wide range of participant, e.g. Commission officials, national regulators (both IRAs and government officials), firms, trade associations, consumer groups, commercial experts and academics. They met once a year in Florence and Madrid, respectively, and had no permanent secretariat. Instead, the Commission offered its assistance in the day-to-day issues and NRAs continued to develop independent regulatory solutions.

The second form of coordination was new informal networks of independent regulators (NIRAs). Their creation was led by national IRAs, but also encouraged by the Commission. Each saw advantages: for IRAs they were a means of cooperating with overseas IRAs, but without being controlled by the Commission; for the Commission, they seemed a step forward towards greater integration (Interview, senior French financial regulator March 2007). In securities trading, French and Italian regulators initiated an informal network of regulators called FESCO (Forum of European Securities Commissions) (Interview senior French financial regulator 1 March 2007 and senior former British financial regulator September 2007). A similar group of IRAs was created in 1997 for telecommunications, the IRG (Independent Regulators Group), although for this group the European Commission took a stronger role in its initiation (Humphreys and Simpson 2005: 86–87). A network of independent energy regulators was created in 2000, when ten national IRAs established the CEER (Committee of European Energy Regulators) (*Financial Times* 1 March 2000). This was later than the other utilities, due to the initial move for forums, but occurred when IRAs became dissatisfied with the forums as being too slow, cumbersome and lacking in enforcement capacity (Interview European Commission official 2007). Its objectives were to enhance cooperation among national energy regulators and cooperation with the EU institutions. These groups involved informal meetings of national IRAs to exchange experiences. They had no formal powers and no secretariat and drew on the resources and goodwill of leading IRAs. Initially, IRAs from some member states refused to participate, such as the UK, while others appeared ineligible as they were not sectoral energy regulators, notably the German general competition authority, which had taken the lead at the Florence and Madrid forums (see Böllhoff 2005; Coen 2005). But over time IRAs from all member joined the NIRAs.

Phase 3: European Networks of Regulators (ERNs)

Between the late 1990s and 2002, restructuring European regulatory space again became the subject of significant discussion. One proposal was for federal European agencies (also termed 'Euro-regulators'), which would have involved considerable centralisation (*Financial Times* 3 July 1996, 19 December 1997, 16 September 2000, 8 June 2001). A second was for greater EU Commission control over IRAs. A third was for European networks of IRAs created through a 'double delegation' (see Coen and Thatcher 2008; also see Tarrant and Kelemen 2007) of functions and powers from the Commission and IRAs.

In most network industries, the third institutional option was taken through the creation of ERNs that were relatively weak in formal institutional terms (see Table 3). Their main functions were to advise the Commission on new legislation and sometimes to issue guidelines for implementation of EU legislation. They lacked powers to take decisions or impose them on their own members, and operated with only a small secretariat. The Commission had several controls, such as over budgets or attending meetings. Some changes were also made in line with the second option, as the Commission gained some limited powers (especially in telecommunications), to intervene in the decisions of IRAs,[16] but no European regulatory agencies or federal European Agencies were set up in the three sectors.

These institutional choices reflected battles among several groups of actors – the Commission, IRAs, national governments, the European Parliament and industry representatives.[17] In particular, the Commission feared inconsistent implementation, or even flouting of EU law. It sought greater centralisation of powers, preferably in its own hands, but also feared the development of federal European regulatory agencies that would be rivals to it. It wished to bring together national IRAs under its own aegis. For their part, IRAs opposed greater Commission control over their activities, but also needed to work with the Commission since they implemented EU legislation and could benefit from new EU legislation. National governments did not wish to lose power to the Commission, but were also concerned that uneven implementation of EU law might disadvantage their national suppliers, notably if other member states 'cheated' by blocking entry to their domestic markets by overseas European suppliers whilst also seeking access to those overseas markets for their own firms. Equally, governments and IRAs were concerned about their different national legal systems (Interview senior former British financial regulator). Suppliers, especially large firms, saw advantages in creating a single European market that allowed them to expand abroad and to face similar regulatory demands across countries, but were also worried by the creation of another level of regulation and loss of supportive national IRAs.[18]

Pressures for change arose from concerns about the slowness of 'classic' EU legislative decision-making, uneven implementation of EU law and the inappropriateness of making detailed EU rules through legislation in fast-moving markets. But the institutional choices were also influenced by problems in the previous phase of institutional development that resulted in

TABLE 3
EUROPEAN REGULATORY NETWORKS

Name	CESR Committee of European Securities Regulators	ERG European Regulators Group (for Telecommunications)	CEIOPS Committee of European Insurance and Occupational Pensions Supervisors	CEBS Committee of European Banking Supervisors	EPRA European Platform of Regulatory Authorities (broadcasting)	ERGEG European Regulators Group for Electricity and Gas
Creation	Created in June 2001 as a 'less bad option' than a European securities regulator, as part of the Lamfalussy process.	Created in July 2002 as a balance to the increased delegation of decision-making to NRAs, with a view to ensuring the implementation of the framework as close as possible to the market in the member states.	Created in late 2003 after the extension of the Lamfalussy process to banking and insurance.	Created in late 2003 after the extension of the Lamfalussy process to banking and insurance.	Created in April 2005 as a forum for discussion and exchange of opinions between regulatory authorities primarily in the field of broadcasting.	Created in November 2003 to advise and consult on the achievement of the single market in energy.
Role	To improve coordination among European Securities Regulators, act as an advisory group to assist the Commission and work to ensure better implementation of community legislation in the member states – includes a role in helping draft secondary legislation.	To improve coordination between NRAs in the field of electronic communications and to advise the Commission on related matters.	As with CESR except for insurance regulators.	As with CESR except for banking regulators.	To act as a forum for regulators mainly concerned with broadcasting. No binding powers.	Similar to ERG but for electricity and gas.

Source: Coen and Thatcher 2008.

pressures for greater centralisation. Thus the NIRAs and forums created earlier in the 1990s were criticised as inadequate, notably due to their lack of powers, reliance on consensus and slowness. Support for ERNs and sometimes detailed proposals came from existing NIRAs who sought the advantages of increasing resources for NIRA members without a powerful centralised regulator (an ERA, FERA or SER) that could take powers away from them. At the same time, the Commission saw ERNs as a way of creating closer links to IRAs and hence avoiding NIRAs developing greater autonomy from it. Moreover, the ERNs were often created either through absorption of NIRAs (e.g. in securities trading and other financial services) or in a process of close layering, as in telecommunications and energy, where they have the same membership and secretariat, and indeed often meet on the same day (the main difference being Commission attendance of ERN meetings, but not ones held by the networks of independent regulatory agencies such as the Independent Regulators Group in telecommunications). Hence they were built on NIRAs, satisfying both IRAs and the Commission.

The institutional debates and choices can be illustrated across several sectors. In securities, national governments, the Commission, IRAs, large firms and industry associations were worried that EU legislation moved too slowly with respect to rapidly changing financial markets (*Financial Times* 20 March 2001; Lamfalussy 2000, 2001). There were problems of lack of harmonisation, inadequate implementation of EU law, and too little cooperation among financial regulators (Commission 1998; Moloney 2002). International firms, especially from the US, sought common rules and definitions across the EU (Interview, senior former British financial regulator). The 1999 Financial Services Action Plan approved by the Commission and Council led to a wave of legislation to obtain considerable liberalisation and re-regulation with the aim of opening up the enormous but largely nationally segmented financial market in Europe. But implementation was argued to require institutional change, both in terms of EU legislation and national authorities. To make progress, the European Council in 2000 set up a 'committee of wise men', chaired by Baron Lamfalussy, who had previously worked on European Monetary Union. The Committee found that no fewer than 45 per cent of respondents to its consultation believed that arrangements for cooperation between national supervisors were inadequate (Lamfalussy 2000: 34). They criticised differences in supervisory powers, duplication of supervision, inadequate channels of cooperation, high costs and lack of expertise. FESCO was attacked for weaknesses due to lack of official status, decisions having to be taken by consensus and not being binding (Lamfalussy 2000: 17; *Economist* 1 March 2001). At the same time, the European Commission lacked resources for implementation or even verifying correct implementation by NRAs – around 100 people worked on financial services in total (*Economist* 7 March 2002). Baron Lamfalussy described the system as 'a remarkable cocktail of Kafkaesque inefficiency that serves no one' (*Financial Times* 15 February 2001).

One response to the perceived deficiencies of regulatory arrangements was the idea of a European Securities and Exchange Commission, perhaps modelled on the European Central Bank, an idea put forward by some French policy-makers, such as then Finance Minister Laurent Fabius (*Economist* 1 March 2001; *Financial Times* 12 July 2000, 16 September 2000). But, British policy-makers and most national IRAs opposed it, fearing loss of power to the EU level, and justified their position by arguing that a European SEC would lack a legal basis, draw attention away from other issues and 'belongs to a very distant future' (quote, unnamed member of Lamfalussy committee, *Financial Times* 16 September 2000; *Economist* 1 March 2001). FESCO itself supported its transformation into a European regulatory network with its own powers, and drew up a new constitution for its replacement (Interview senior European financial regulator 1; *Financial Times* 20 June 2001).

Faced with diverse opinions, the Lamfalussy committee's report recommended a new committee structure and a new legislative procedure to speed up EU decision-making and improve coordination. Its recommendations led to changes. One element was a network of IRAs named CESR (Committee of European Securities Regulators) that was proposed by FESCO, the existing informal Network of Independent Regulatory Agencies, and then absorbed FESCO. EU regulation was to follow a four-level process.[19] Level 1 comprises classic EU legislation. But level 2 involves further legal measures to implement level 1 legislation. Here the Commission asks CESR to provide 'technical' advice, and in so doing to consult with market practitioners and consumers; but CESR's role is only advisory – the Commission makes proposals to the European Securities Committee which acts as a normal 'regulatory committee within the EU's comitology procedures. Level 3 sees non-legally binding guidelines, interpretation and recommendations on national implementation of legislation issued by CESR. They are designed to ensure consistent policy, financial supervision and enforcement throughout EU member states. But they do not have legal force. Finally, level 4 is enforcement of EU rules by the Commission, using its legal powers. Moreover, 'sunset clauses' in legislation delegating powers means that delegation is temporary and must be renewed.

In telecommunications, the Commission argued in the late 1990s that IRAs had insufficient powers, resources and independence from incumbent public telecommunications operators and that member states were failing to implement EU legislation; Martin Bangemann (DG XIII and DG III Commissioner) supported the creation of a European-level agency to ensure even and effective implementation of EC regulation.[20] Parts of the telecommunications industry also argued for greater centralisation to avoid inconsistent decisions by national regulators (*Financial Times* 6 February

2003; *European Voice* 6 December 2001). Despite these pressures, no European regulator was created and the Commission pulled back from seeking one (see Humphreys and Simpson 2005: 103; Tarrant and Kelemen 2007; cf. Commission 1999a). The main reason was opposition from member states, which were not ready to accept such a powerful authority (*Agence Europe* 25 February 1997; *Financial Times* 19 December 1997). In its June 2000 proposals, the Commission, under a new Commissioner, Liikanen, did not seek to revive ideas of a Euro telecoms regulator (Commission 1999b). Instead the Commission acted in 'partnership' with national governments and was not prepared or able to strike out on its own (Thatcher 2001). It initiated two changes. One was for it to have the right of veto on how national regulatory authorities applied regulatory frameworks (Humphreys and Simpson 2005: 103–106; *European Voice* 29 November 2001). With support from the European Parliament, the Commission ultimately succeeded in gaining veto powers on two important regulatory issues decided by IRAs.[21] This move represented a considerable strengthening of the Commission's direct powers over IRAs, avoiding the need to undertake a slow and costly enforcement action before the ECJ against member states.

The second alteration was the creation of a European Regulatory Network, namely the European Regulators Group (ERG), established in 2002 (European Commission 2002; for ERG see Nicolaides 2006). The membership of the ERG is based on representatives from 27 IRAs, and observers from accession states and EEA states, while the Commission has formal observer status. The day-to-day functions are run by a small secretariat staffed by three IRA officials and based in the European Commission offices. It followed arguments by many IRAs that the informal Network of Independent Regulatory Agencies in telecommunications, the IRG, should be given a formalised basis for coordination (*Financial Times* 8 June 2001; *Communications Week International* 4 June 2001). It also allowed the Commission to bring together national IRAs and seek to influence them (Humphreys and Simpson 2005: 111–113, 180–181). However, the ERG was also a response by IRAs to threats by the Commission to take further powers over IRAs, which the IRG and IRAs strongly opposed (*Communications Week International* 4 March 2002; *European Voice* 29 November 2001). It is noteworthy that the ERG coexists with the previous informal network of regulatory agencies, namely the IRG, so that IRAs have both their own body and one formally linked with the Commission.

In energy, the European Regulators Group for electricity and gas (ERGEG) was created in November 2003 to advise and consult on the completion of the internal market for gas and electricity (see EC/2003/54 Electricity directive; EC/2003/55 Gas directive; Commission Press release 12 November 2003). It arose from a Commission initiative after difficulties in implementing the expanding EU energy regulatory framework, and frustration that the energy forums were slow, failed to produce real policy learning, were based on consensus and unable to reach difficult decisions on strategic internal market issues of cross-border tariffs, interconnection, and access pricing due to the role of suppliers (Bulmer *et al.* 2007: 131; Eberlein 2003: 147–150; *Financial Times* 1 February 2000). Indeed, ERGEG's mandate was to propose consistent regulatory application of EU directives and establish best regulatory practice across IRAs (*Public Utilities Fortnightly* 1 February 2004; Cameron 2002: 285–301). Its membership consisted of the 27 IRAs, while EEA and accession candidates had observer status. The Commission is present at the plenary sessions of ERGEG and runs the secretariat. As in telecommunications, the previous informal network of regulatory agencies, the CEER, has continued to coexist alongside the ERG, so have the Florence and Madrid forums.

Thus the development of regulatory space in energy has seen considerable 'layering' and 'conversion'. New networks such as the ERG and ERGEG have been established alongside existing bodies such as the IRG and CEER. The only body to disappear, FESCO, was converted into CESR. Moreover, those existing bodies were able to limit and shape the new ones, conserving their own role, ensuring much power for their national IRA members and, in alliance with national governments, preventing strong EU-level agencies (ERAs, FERAs or SERs) being established.

Phase 4: Current Debates: Strengthened ERNs versus Federal European Regulatory Agencies (FERAs) or European Regulatory Agencies (ERAs)

In the mid-2000s, the European Commission and ERNs have led vigorous debates about reforming the institutions for coordinating implementation of EU regulation in financial services, energy and telecommunications. The Commission has argued that current arrangements for implementation are inadequate, resulting in a failure to fully introduce the single market. It has pointed to continuing uneven implementation of EU law, the maintenance of entry barriers to national markets, difficulties in cross-border trade due to diverse national standards (see e.g. European Commission 2007a; 2006). Equally, it has argued that ERNs lack powers and the ability to enforce opening of markets, being constrained to act according to the 'lowest common denominator' among their membership due to the need to obtain consensus.[22] For their part, ERNs have themselves initiated debates and/or requested more powers (e.g. CESR 2004; ERGEG 2006, 2007a,b).

Three major institutional options have been debated, but the first two have faced strong opposition from ERNs themselves. One has been the creation of 'Euro-regulators'. Although their exact institutional design has not always been clarified, the main ideas seem to be either European Regulatory Agencies or FERAs. Thus, for instance, the Information Commissioner Vivien Reding declared that 'for me, it is clear that the most effective and least bureaucratic way to achieve a real level playing field for telecom operators across the EU would ... be by an independent European telecom authority', perhaps modelled on the European Central Bank, to obtain more 'efficient' markets and reduce the 'patchwork' of regulation that it claimed was damaging companies and consumers (*European Voice* 12 November 2006; *Financial Times* 17 November 2006, 17 February 2007). In energy, the Commission suggested that one of the two acceptable options was a European agency entrusted to apply EU standards to individual decisions in order to make cross-border trade work in practice (European Commission 2007a: 8). In securities trading, the European Commission noted problems of inconsistent regulation and there was discussion of whether Europe needed a European SEC (see also CEPS 2005; Hertig and Lee 2003; Lee 2005).

But FERAs have faced fierce opposition from existing ERNs and national IRAs, as well as some member states. These existing bodies have argued that FERAs are unnecessary and have little support in the industry. They have opposed 'transferring powers to Brussels'. Thus, for instance, in telecommunications, the ERG argued that 'national markets will always be better regulated by national regulators' (*Financial Times* 17 February 2007; see also *European Voice* 16 November 2006, 22 February 2007), while the British communications IRA Ofcom claimed that 'a central regulator received little support during the creation of existing rules and we see no reason why it might be appropriate now' (*Financial Times* 17 November 2006). In securities trading, CESR questioned the need for a European FERA that would be the equivalent of the US SEC (CESR 2004; *Agence Europe* 16 November 2005).

A second possibility is greater Commission powers over the decisions of national IRAs in order to ensure greater consistency. Thus, for instance, in telecommunications, as part of a review of the 2002 regulatory framework, Commissioner Reding argued that 'Europe does not yet have a satisfactory level of consistency and harmonisation of practices between national regulators' and worried about 'serious distortions of competition that arise in the internal market if similar remedies are not applied in similar situations' (*Agence Europe* 14 February 2006; European Commission 2006). She proposed strengthening Commission powers over IRAs, especially for cross-border disputes, extending its powers to issues such as remedies, allowing it to establish common EU guidelines over IRA appeals and even being empowered to issue authorisations (i.e. licences) that would allow service providers to operate throughout the EU (European Commission 2006: 8–9; *Agence Europe* 19 February 2007). But some national IRAs and ERNs have been sceptical about additional Commission powers, especially in telecommunications.[23]

Instead, ERNs have pressed for the third option, namely enhancement of their powers. In securities trading, CESR has argued that leaving integration to case law would result in divergence, whereas 'the market' wanted regulatory convergence, especially given its 'transnational' nature, proposing instead a 'bottom up' approach of strengthening CESR (Interview,

Fabrice Demarigny, Secretary General CESR, *Financial Times* 16 November 2005; Interview van Leeuwen, chairman CESR and Dutch financial authority, *Financial Times* 22 March 2004, 5 December 2004). This could involve CESR having the power to take 'pan-European' decisions or lead a mediation system between different national IRAs (CESR 2004; *Financial Times* 6 December 2004; *Agence Europe* 16 November 2005). In energy, ERGEG has argued for an ERGEGplus as part of a 'European System of Energy Regulation' with powers to enforce decisions, especially concerning a European grid, for instance to approve standards, place financial penalties on new pan-European electricity and gas grid organisations, have an enhanced role in advising on legislation and gathering data, and enjoy additional resources (See ERGEG 2007a: 24–32, 43).

Debates about change remain ongoing and legislative proposals are being made for telecommunications and energy in 2007–8. However, opposition by the ERNs as well as by member states appears to be contributing to blockage of FERAs. Instead, ERNs and the Commission appear to be bargaining and creating a mutually beneficial alliance to build on existing institutions. On the one hand, they support or accept an increased Commission role and powers. Thus, in energy, the Commission has allowed the possibility of an enhanced ERGEG enjoying powers to take decisions binding on IRAs on cross-border matters, albeit with 'the appropriate involvement of the Commission, where necessary, to ensure that due account was taken of the Community interest' (European Commission 2007a: 8). In response, ERGEG has proposed that it should become a new Regulators Council, led by an Administrative Board composed of equal numbers of national representatives and of the Commission. It would be a form of European Agency with extensive powers over implementation (ERGEG 2007b). Equally, it has proposed creating duties on national IRAs to implement EU law, which would potentially greatly increase the Commission's power over IRAs and indeed make it one of their principals (ERGEG 2007c). The new body would continue alongside the existing CEER, bringing together national IRAs in an informal Network of Independent Regulatory Agencies.

The Commission proposals in September 2007 largely followed ERGEG's ideas. It put forward an Agency for the Cooperation of Energy Regulators. Its functions would be to aid cooperation between national IRAs, advise the Commission and take technical decisions when asked by the Commission on cross-border issues concerned transmission. Although set up as a European agency, national regulators would keep many powers over it. The Agency would have both an Administrative Board, half of whom would be appointed by the Council and the other half by the Commission, and a Board of Regulators composed of one representative of each national energy IRA. Interestingly, the Commission explicitly acknowledges that a powerful body modelled on the ECB was not being proposed because it would require Treaty amendment (European Commission 2007d: 10).

The European Commission's legislative package also contains proposals to strengthen national IRAs. It would require that energy IRAs be legally and functionally independent not only of suppliers but also of public bodies, i.e. enjoy independence from governments. They should have 'legal personality, budgetary autonomy, appropriate human and financial resources and independent management' (European Commission 2007d: 9). Equally, they would have new market regulation powers.

Thus the Commission's proposals further centralise and formalise the network of national IRAs but also allow the latter a partnership in that network. Equally, they offer IRAs new resources to be independent of their national governments and to be more powerful. The package illustrates clearly the mutually beneficial relationship between the Commission and national agencies. Unsurprisingly, ERGEG, representing the national IRAs, welcomed the Commission's proposals.

In telecommunications, the EU Commissioner Vivian Reding began by suggesting greater European Commission powers over the decisions of IRAs or a European Telecommunications Agency (see European Commission 2006). But by January 2007 she was proposing that the ERG could be greatly strengthened, either becoming a classic European Agency, which would advise the Commission (notably on Article 7 enforcement decisions), or a FERA, with its own powers to making binding decisions concerning IRAs and market players, as well as legal personality and being open to challenge before the ECJ (European Commission 2006, 2007c). The latter option would mark a strong centralisation of powers and also independence from the Commission. In response, the ERG urged much greater cooperation between itself and the Commission over Article 7 actions, and accepted that, if it were given greater powers, its governance structures should be altered (ERG 2007). Although discussions are continuing, there seems strong opposition to a FERA (see *Financial Times* 24 September 2007 on divisions within the Commission; article by Ofcom's chief executive, *Financial Times* 31 October 2007). In securities trading, CESR's 2004 'Himalaya' document envisaged strengthening its powers, while the Commission's 2005-10 Action Plan suggested an increased Commission role in monitoring financial services, but neither proposed a European SEC (CESR 2004; European Commission 2005).

Thus current debates about regulatory arrangements seem to involve a further centralisation of powers, but building on existing organisations. In particular, regulatory space seems to involve continuation of roles for the Commission and EU bodies, bringing together national IRAs (both ERNs and informal Networks of Independent Regulatory Agencies). Evolution not revolution seems possible, with comprehensive restructuring or administrative simplicity being very difficult. Hence reforms involve building on existing organisations of the ERNs such as CESR and ERGEG and obtaining support for change, so that new institutions maintain their role and that of their members, namely national IRAs.

Conclusion

The institutions for implementing EU regulation have been reformed in an evolutionary manner since the late 1980s. Analysis of three key sectors – financial services, telecommunications and energy – has revealed how each stage has influenced later ones. New organisational forms have arisen from old ones, offering examples of institutional 'conversion'. In securities regulation, the new European Regulatory Network CESR grew out of the network of national independent regulatory authorities FESCO, while in energy and telecommunications, current proposals are to strengthen and convert existing European Regulatory Networks. Often institutional 'layering' has also taken place, as new organisations are added to existing ones, which survive reforms. For instance, European Regulatory Networks in telecommunications and energy have been grafted onto a regime with informal Networks of IRAs and forums. Institutional 'layering' and 'conversion' have meant that instead of streamlining, reforms have resulted in a cluttered European regulatory space filled with several types of bodies – Commission, forums, informal Networks of Independent Regulatory Agencies, European Regulatory Networks, European Regulatory Agencies – all with responsibilities for implementation of EU legislation.

Several reasons for this evolutionary development are revealed by process tracing of specific sectors. On the one hand, there are continuing pressures for change that are endogenous to previous reforms. Each stage of reform has been followed by criticisms and hence debates about further reforms, offering examples of processes of disappointment and learning, as policy-makers have accepted or desired further centralisation of powers. Existing organisations often make proposals, which usually involve their development and enhancement. On the other hand, existing bodies resist loss of powers or the creation of powerful rivals. Existing bodies are often well placed in struggles over institutional restructuring: they (or their members) have great expertise, whereas the Commission is small and has limited personnel; existing bodies have links to other actors such as national governments and industry. Thus, although proposals for federal European regulatory agencies have regularly returned to the table, suggesting both demand for radical change and inadequacies of alternatives, they have not been introduced. Once in place, a regulatory organisation limits radical changes and provides incentives to build on existing institutions.

However, evolutionary change has not prevented important transformations of European regulatory space. On the contrary, new forms of governance have been attempted. There has been a gradual strengthening of networks of national regulators, with increasing centralisation of powers; as EU-wide bodies have been created, their status has become more formalised and their powers enhanced (compare for instance, the largely informal and powerless forums and informal Networks of Independent Regulatory Agencies with current discussions of enhanced European Regulatory Networks).

Building networks of regulators allows the Commission and national policy-makers to cooperate and engage in exchanges. It is compatible with important features of the EU such as limited Commission resources and reluctance to pass major Treaty changes to transfer new powers to EU organisations. Hence evolutionary change has resulted in centralisation and institutionalisation of the EU's regulatory pace, but through strengthening of networks of existing actors rather than comprehensive reforms or replacement of existing bodies with very different new ones.

What does the analysis suggest for the wider understanding of the development of the EU? Two conclusions emerge from the cases. First, evolutionary analysis seems highly appropriate to the EU. Comprehensive reforms have not been introduced even in a domain such as regulation, which involves rules rather than spending and which therefore should be easier to modify than, for instance, welfare states or government bureaucracies, and despite several debates about major changes. The article puts forward mechanisms and reasons for evolutionary change taking place. Hence historical institutionalist approaches would seem to be valuable in explaining European integration, pointing to the role of existing organisations and institutions in limiting and shaping change.

A second linked conclusion concerns the process of European integration. A strong case has been made that European integration and institutionalisation are driven by functional demands, notably by large cross-border firms in alliance with EU-level organisations (see Sandholtz and Stone Sweet 1998; Stone Sweet *et al.* 2001). This 'demand' side for change has not been the focus of this article. Rather, we have focused on the 'supply side' of European institutions and endogenous forces for change as one set of organisations are put in place and leads to pressures for further changes. But our analysis does suggest that even if there are strong demand-side pressures for centralisation of regulation, existing institutional arrangements and organisations limit and shape the supply of new institutions. The outcome is that strong tensions persist between pressures to achieve a single European market and the institutions to implement EU regulation, and hence debates about radical change coexist with a fragmented, cluttered and complex European regulatory space.

Acknowledgements

The authors wish to thank ARENA for hospitality at the ARENA conference in Oslo of March 2007; they also thank Kenneth Armstrong, Dan Kelemen, Morten Egeberg and Colin Scott for comments; an initial version this paper was presented at the conference on Policy Instruments, CEVIPOF, Paris, June 2007; the work arises out of the NewGov project CIT1-CT-2004-506392. Over the course of the project the authors are alternating name order for different publications. This does not reflect input which is equal for both authors.

Notes

1. Given general usage, we refer here to the EU, but most regulation takes place under the European Community pillar of the EU.
2. Borzel (2002), Treib (2007) and Mastenroek (2003) illustrated that 60 per cent of directives are transposed late, while Steunenberg (2006) demonstrated empirically that while high-level players decide on policy, the lower level players have wide discretion in shaping and transposing the policy.
3. Among the vast literature, see for instance Sandholtz and Stone Sweet (1998) and Moravscik (1999); for recent principal–agent analysis see Pollack (2003).
4. For approaches focusing on rational comprehensive analyses and grand bargains, see for instance Moravscik (1998) on Treaty bargaining.
5. For discussions of 'regulatory space', see Hancher and Moran (1989) and Scott (2001); for 'administrative space', see Olsen (2003), although he is mostly concerned with convergence, whereas here we focus on the institutions of such space; we omit self-regulation since this is not formally a mode of implementing EU law, although it may be a mode of regulation. For a recent discussion, see Cafaggi (2006); for a comprehensive analysis of different modes of regulation in the EU, see Scott (2005).
6. For analyses of advantages and disadvantages of different models, see Coen and Doyle (2000).
7. Indeed, we can conceive of a situation in which greater centralisation of formal powers actually led to less power for the central EU body or indeed less effective implementation.
8. For a full discussion of the role of the European Commission in coordinating infringement proceedings and ECJ oversight procedure see Borzel (2002) and Falkner et al. (2005).
9. In terms of EU governance debates Sabel and Zeitlin (2007) would argue that these new networks are an experimentalist form of governance, whereas Héritier and Knill (2008) would argue that that these networks operate under a shadow of hierarchy that constrains development.
10. Similar forces were also seen to be at work in the modernisation of European Competition Policy (see Wilks 2005).
11. Information gathering agencies, such as the European Agency for Safety at Work are excluded, see Kelemen (2002) for the division between these and regulatory agencies.
12. Majone (1997, 2005) has been a strong proponent of the single regulatory model on the grounds of political and economic efficiency.
13. See Eising and Jabko (2000) for a detailed discussion of member state bargaining and Commission compromises in the creation of the energy liberalisation directives.
14. Although degree of detail must be distinguished from coercion, EU directives remained legally binding and if anything, became more coercive as their scope was extended into new sectors such as the utilities (see Kelemen 2004).
15. For a discussion how member states played the patchwork regulation see Héritier et al. (2001), and for how NRAs and Business managed the multilevel regulatory environment see Coen and Héritier (2001).
16. In particular, the Commission was empowered to veto two types of decisions by IRAs concerning competition (definitions of relevant markets and significant market power) that affected inter-member state trade, under Article 7 of the Framework Directive (European Parliament and Council 2002).
17. For a parallel discussion in relation to ERAs, see Kelemen (2002).
18. For instance, in telecommunications, a BT official noted 'opposition in the industry to creating a new layer of bureaucracy at a time when firms were actually calling for less regulation' (Financial Times 16 September 2000; cf. Coen and Doyle 2000).
19. For a principal-agent analysis of the new system, see Visscher et al. (2008).
20. Bangemann pressed over a considerable period for the creation of a EU telecommunications industry watchdog (Financial Times 3 July 1996, 19 December 1997, 11 March 1999; European Voice 11 March 1999).

21. The definitions of relevant market and of significant market definition and SMP definition Article 7 of EC/2002/21; Interviews with Commission and Telecommunication Regulator 2.
22. See for instance criticisms of the ERG for being based on the 'lowest common denominator' by the Information Commissioner (European Voice 22 February 2007) and criticism on energy (Commission 2007a: 8–9).
23. For instance, Ofcom in telecommunications argued that 'the balance of powers between the Commission and national regulators is broadly right' (Financial Times 17 November 2006); the ERG opposed 'uniformity' in the application of remedies (see ERG 2006a,b).

References

Armstrong, K., and S. Bulmer (1998). *Governance of the Single Market*. Manchester, Manchester University Press.

Bergman, L., G. Brunekreeft, C. Doyle, N. Von der Fehr, D. Newbury, M. Pollitt and P. Regibeau (1999). *A European Market for Electricity*. London: CEPR press.

Böllhoff, D. (2005). 'Developments in Regulatory Regimes: A Comparison of Telecommunications, Energy and Rail', in David Coen and Adrienne Héritier (eds.), *Redefining Regulatory Regimes: Utilities in Europe*. Cheltenham: Edward Elgar.

Börzel, T. (2001). 'Non-compliance in the European Union: Pathology or Statistical Artefact?', *Journal of European Public Policy*, 8:5, 803–24.

Bulmer, S. (1994). 'The Governance of the European Union: A New Institutionalist Approach', *Journal of Public Policy*, 13:4, 351–72.

Bulmer, S., and S. Padgett (2005). 'Policy Transfer in the European Union: An Institutionalist Perspective', *British Journal of Political Science*, 35, 103–26.

Bulmer, S., D. Dolowitz, P. Humphreys and S. Padgett (2007). *Policy Transfer in the European Union. Regulating the Utilities*. London: Routledge.

Cafaggi, Fabrizio, ed. (2006). *Reframing Self-Regulation in European Private Law*. The Netherlands: Kluwer Law International.

Cameron, P. (2002). *Competition in Energy Markets*. Oxford: Oxford University Press.

Capoccia, Giovanni, and R. Daniel Kelemen (2007). 'The Study of Critical Junctures', *World Politics*, 59:3, 341–69.

CEPS (Centre for European Policy Studies) (2005). *EU Financial Regulation and Supervision Beyond*. Brussels: CEPS.

CESR (2004). *Which Supervisory Tools for the EU Securities Markets? Preliminary Progress Report* ('Himalaya Report'). Paris: CESR.

Coen, David (2005). 'Changing Business–Regulator Relations in German and UK Telecommunication and Energy Sectors', in David Coen and Héritier Adrienne (eds.), *Redefining Regulatory Regimes: Utilities in Europe*. Cheltenham: Edward Elgar.

Coen, David, and Chris Doyle (2000). 'Designing Economic Regulatory Institutions for the European Network Industries', *Current Politics and Economics of Europe*, 9:4, 455–76.

Coen, David, and Adrienne Héritier, eds. (2005). *Redefining Regulatory Regimes: Utilities in Europe*. Cheltenham: Edward Elgar.

Coen, D., and M. Thatcher, eds. (2001). *Utilities Reform in Europe*. New York: Nova.

Coen, D., and M. Thatcher (2005). 'The New Governance of Markets and Non-majoritarian Regulators', *Governance*, 18:3, 329–46.

Coen, D., and M. Thatcher (2008). 'Network Governance and Multi-level Delegation. European Networks of Regulatory Agencies', *Journal of Public Policy*, 28:1, 49–71.

Commission of the European Communities (1992). *1992 Review of the Situation in the Telecommunications Services Sector*, SEC(92) 1048 Final. Brussels: Commission, 21 October 1992.

Commission of the European Communities (2001). *European Governance: A White Paper*, COM(2001) 428. Brussels: Commission of the European Communities.

Dehousse, R. (2002). *Misfits: EU Law and the Transformation of European Governance*. New York: NYU School of Law Jean Monnet Center.

Eberlein, Burkard (2003). 'Formal and Informal Governance in Single Market Regulation', in Tomas Christiansen and Simona Piattoni (eds.), *Informal Governance in the EU*. Cheltenham: Edward Elgar.

Eberlein, B., and E. Grande (2004). 'Beyond Delegation: Transnational Regulatory Regimes and the EU Regulatory State', *Journal of European Public Policy*, 12:1, 89–112.

Egeberg, M., ed. (2006). *Multilevel Union Administration. The Transformation of Executive Politics in Europe*. Basingstoke: Palgrave Macmillan.

Eising, R., and N. Jabko (2001). 'Moving Targets: National Interests and Electricity Liberalization in the European Union', *Comparative Political Studies*, 34:7, 742–67.

ERG (2006a). 'Effective Harmonisation within the European Electronic Communications Sector', *A Consultation by ERG 2006*, Brussels.

ERG (2006b). *Explanatory Memorandum Outlining Changes to the Revised ERG Common Position on Remedies*, ERG (06) 19, http://ec.europa.eu/information_society/policy/ecomm/info_centre/documentation/com_erg_discussion/index_en.htm.

ERG (2007). Letter to Viviane Reding, 27 February, http://ec.europa.eu/information_society/policy/ecomm/info_centre/documentation/com_erg_discussion/index_en.htm.

ERGEG (2006). *Compatibility of National Legal Conditions Concerning Regulatory Competences*. Brussels: ERGEG.

ERGEG (2007a). *ERGEG's response to the European Commission's Communication 'An Energy Policy for Europe' Ref.C06-BM-09-05*, 6 February, Brussels.

ERGEG (2007b). Paper 2: *Legal and Regulatory Framework for a European System of Energy Regulation*. Ref: C07-SER-13-06-02-PD, 5 June.

ERGEG (2007c). Paper 5: *Powers and Independence of National Regulators*. Ref. C07-SER-13-06-5-PD.

European Commission (1998). *Communication: Financial Services: Building a Framework for Action*. Brussels: European Commission, 28 October 1998.

European Commission (1999a). *Commission Communication on Implementing the Framework for Financial Markets: Action Plan*, COM 232. Brussels: Commission of the European Communities.

European Commission (1999b). *The 1999 Communications Review. Towards a New Framework for Electronic Communications Infrastructure and Associated Services*, COM (1999) 539. Brussels: European Commission.

European Commission (2002). Decision 627/20002/EC establishing the European Regulators Group for Electronic Communication Networks and Services, 30 July, OJ L200.

European Commission (2005). *White Paper on Financial Services Policy (2005–10)*. Brussels: EU Commission.

European Commission (2006). Letter Viviane Reding to ERG, 30 November, http://ec.europa.eu/information_society/policy/ecomm/info_centre/documentation/com_erg_discussion/index_en.htm.

European Commission (2007a). *Communication from the Commission to the European Council and the European Parliament An Energy Policy for Europe* {SEC(2007) 12}, Brussels, 10 January.

European Commission (2007b). *Communication from the Commission to the Council, the European Parliament, the European Economic and Social Committee and the Committee of the Regions on the Review of the EU Regulatory Framework for Electronic Communications Networks and Services* {SEC(2006) 816}{SEC(2006) 817}, Brussels, 28 June, COM(2006) 334 final.

European Commission (2007c). Letter from Fabio Colasanti [Director General DG Information Society] to ERG, 30 January, http://ec.europa.eu/information_society/policy/ecomm/info_centre/documentation/com_erg_discussion/index_en.htm.

European Commission (2007d). *Proposal for a Regulation of the European Parliament and of the Council Establishing an Agency for the Cooperation of Energy Regulators*, Brussels, 19 September, COM(2007) 530 final 2007/0197 (COD).

European Parliament and Council (2002). *Directive 2002/21/EC of the European Parliament and of the Council of 7 March 2002 on a Common Regulatory Framework for Electronic Communications Networks and Services (Framework Directive)*, OJ L108/33, 24 April.

Falkner, Gerda, Miriam Hartlapp, Simone Leiber and Oliver Treib (2005). *Complying with Europe: EU Harmonisation and Soft Law in the Member States.* Cambridge: Cambridge University Press.

Gatsios, Konstantine, and Paul Seabright (1989). 'Regulation in the European Community', *Oxford Review of Economic Policy*, 5, 37–60.

Gehring, T., and S. Krapohl (2007). 'Supranational Regulatory Agencies between Independence and Control: The EMEA and the Authorization of Pharmaceuticals in the European Single Market', *Journal of European Public Policy*, 14:2, 208–26.

Gilardi, Fabrizio (2005). 'The Institutional Foundations of Regulatory Capitalism: The Diffusion of Independent Regulatory Agencies in Western Europe', *Annals of the American Academy of Political and Social Science*, 598, 84–101.

Hancher, Leigh, and Michael Moran, eds. (1989). *Capitalism, Culture and Economic Regulation.* Oxford: Clarendon Press.

Héritier, Adrienne (2005). 'Managing Regulatory Developments in Rail', in David Coen and Adrienne Héritier (eds.), *Redefining Regulatory Regimes: Utilities in Europe.* Cheltenham: Edward Elgar.

Héritier, Adrienne (2007). *Explaining Institutional Change in Europe.* Oxford: Oxford University Press.

Héritier, Adrienne, and C. Knill (2008). 'The Shadow of Hierarchy and New Modes of Governance', *Journal of Public Policy*, 28:1, 1–17.

Héritier, A., D. Kerwer, C. Knill, D. Lehmkuhl, M. Teutsch and A.-C. Douillet (2001). *Differential Europe: The European Union Impact on National Policymaking.* Lanham: Rowman & Littlefield.

Hertig, G., and R. Lee (2003). 'Four Predictions About the Future of EU Securities Regulation', *Journal of Comparative Law Studies*, 3:2, 359–77.

Humphreys, P., and S. Simpson (2005). *Globalisation, Convergence and European Telecommunications Regulation.* Cheltenham: Edward Elgar.

Kelemen, D. (2002). 'The Politics of "Eurocratic" Structure and the New European Agencies', *West European Politics*, 25:4, 93–118.

Kelemen, D. (2005). 'The Politics of Eurocracy: Building a New European State?', in N. Jabko and C. Parson (eds.), *The State of the European Union*, 7. Oxford: Oxford University Press.

Keleman, R.D. (2004). *The Rules of Federalism.* Cambridge, MA: Harvard University Press.

Kohler Kock, B., and R. Eising (1999). *The Transformation of Governance in the European Union.* London: Routledge.

Lamfalussy, A. (2000). *Initial Report of the Committee of Wise Men on the Regulation of European Securities Markets.* Brussels: European Commission, 7 November.

Lamfalussy, A. (2001). *Final Report of the Committee of Wise Men on the Regulation of European Securities Markets.* Brussels: European Commission, 15 February.

Lee, R. (2005). *Politics and the Creation of a European SEC*, GEM. Paris: Sciences Po.

Levi-Faur, D. (2001). 'The Rise of the Competition State', in D. Coen and M. Thatcher (eds.), *Utilities Reform in Europe.* New York: Nova.

Levi-Faur, D. (2005). 'The Global Diffusion of Regulatory Capitalism', *The Annals of the American Academy of Political and Social Science*, 598:1, 12–32.

Mahoney, J. (2000). 'Path Dependence in Historical Sociology', *Theory and Society*, 29:4, 507–48.

Majone, G. (1996). *Regulating Europe.* London: Routledge.

Majone, Giandomenico (1997). 'The New European Agencies: regulation by information', *Journal of European Public Policy*, 4:2.

Majone, G. (2005). *Dilemmas of European Integration: The Ambiguities and Pitfalls of Integration by Stealth*. Oxford: Oxford University Press.

Moloney, Niamh (2002). *EC Securities Regulation*. Oxford: Oxford University Press.

Moravcsik, A. (1998). *The Choice for Europe: Social Purpose and State Power from Messina to Maastricht*. Ithaca, NY: Cornell University Press.

Nicolaides, P. (2006). *Regulatory Integration and Cooperation: The Case of the European Regulators Group on Electronic Communications*. Maastricht: EIPA.

Olsen, J.P. (2003). 'Towards a European Administrative Space', *Journal of European Public Policy*, 10:4, 506–31.

Pelkmans, J. (1987). 'The New Approach to Technical Harmonization and Standardization', *Journal of Common Market Studies*, 25, 249–69.

Pierson, Paul (2000). 'Increasing Returns, Path Dependence, and the Study of Politics', *American Political Science Review*, 94:2, 251–67.

Sabel, C., and J. Zeitlin (2007). *Learning from Difference: The New Architecture of Experimentalist Governance in the European Union*. Connex working paper, *European Governance Papers (EUROGOV)* No. C-07-02, available at http://www.connex-network.org/eurogov/pdf//egp-connex-C-07-02.pd.

Sandholtz, Wayne, and Alec Stone Sweet, eds. (1998). *European Integration and Supranational Governance*. Oxford: Oxford University Press.

Schmidt, V. (2002). *The Futures of European Capitalisms*. Oxford: Oxford University Press.

Schneider, V., and Werle, R. (1990). 'International Regime or Corporate Actor? The European Community in Telecommunications Policy', in K. Dyson and P. Humphreys (eds.), *The Political Economy of Telecommunications*. London and New York: Routledge.

Scott, C. (2001). 'Analysing Regulatory Space: Fragmented Resources and Institutional Design', *Public Law*, Summer, 329–53.

Scott, Colin (2005). 'Agencies for European Regulatory Governance', in Damien Geradin, Rodolphe Munoz and Nicolas Petit (eds.), *Regulation through Agencies in the EU*. Cheltenham: Edward Elgar.

Stone Sweet, A., W. Sandholtz and N. Fligstein (2001). *The Institutionalization of Europe*. Oxford: Oxford University Press.

Streeck, W., and K.A. Thelen (2005). *Beyond Continuity: Institutional Change in Advanced Political Economies*. Oxford, Oxford University Press.

Tarrant, Andy, and R. Daniel Kelemen (2007). 'Building the Eurocracy. The Politics of Networks and Agencies'. Paper prepared to the European Studies Association Conference Montreal, May.

Thatcher, M. (2001). 'The Commission and National Governments as Partners: EC Regulatory Expansion in Telecommunications 1979–2000', *Journal of European Public Policy*, 8:4, 558–84.

Thatcher, Mark (2002a). 'Analysing Regulatory Reform in Europe', *Journal of European Public Policy*, 8:5.

Thatcher, Mark (2002b). 'Delegation to Independent Regulatory Agencies', *West European Politics*, 25:1, 125–45.

Thatcher, Mark (2005). The Third Force? Independent Regulatory Agencies and Elected Politicians in Europe', *Governance*, 18:3, 347–74.

Thatcher, Mark (2007). *Internationalisation and Economic Institutions: Comparing European Experiences*. Oxford: Oxford University Press.

Thelen, K. (2004). *How Institutions Evolve: The Political Economy of Skills in Germany, Britain, the United States and Japan*. Cambridge: Cambridge University Press.

Varone, Fréderic et al. (2008). 'Financial Regulators', *Journal of Public Policy*, January.

Visscher, C. de, O. Maiscocq and F. Varone (2008). 'The Lamfalussy Reform in the EU Securities Market', *Journal of Public Policy*, 28:1, 19–47.

Vogel, S. (1996). *Freer Markets, More Rules*. Ithaca, NY: Cornell University Press.

Vos, E. (2000). *Agencies and the European Union*. Florence: EUI, Robert Schuman Centre, paper 2000/51.

Wilks, S. (2005). 'Agency Escape: Decentralization or Dominance of the European Commission in the Modernization of Competition Policy?', *Governance*, 18:3, 431–52.

Young, A.R. (2005). 'The Single European Market: A New Approach to Policy', in H. Wallace, W. Wallace and M.A. Pollack (eds.), *Policy-Making in the European Union*. 5th edn. Oxford: Oxford University Press, 93–112.

Halfway House: The 2006 Comitology Reforms and the European Parliament

KIERAN ST CLAIR BRADLEY

The 2006 comitology reforms were designed to give the European Parliament, for the first time, a significant role in the supervision of the content of implementing legislation. For most of the previous 45 years, Parliament's predominant goal had been to eliminate comitology, or at least the procedures of which it disapproved most strongly. In that respect, it was singularly unsuccessful, though this merely reflects its lack of real influence on certain aspects of institutional reform, and the member states' attachment to this form of decision-making. Even when the introduction of the co-decision procedure in 1993 provided Parliament with the means of enforcing its views on the content of primary legislation, it implicitly accepted comitology, by agreeing in the so-called *modus vivendi* not to block implementing arrangements in such legislation in return for a minimal degree of transparency in the workings of the comitology committees, but no real supervisory powers (Bradley 1999: 71–76). The failure of

---

The views expressed are personal and may not be attributed to the service or institution with which the author is associated.

Parliament's efforts to abolish or even stem the spread of comitology led the present author to wonder in 1996 if the Parliament were not 'On the road to nowhere' in this regard (Bradley 1997).

The situation would have been completely reversed by the Constitution for Europe signed by the member states in October 2004. The Constitution would have provided Parliament and the Council with a choice of effective supervisory powers over 'delegated European regulations', while the procedures for adopting lower-level implementing acts would have been adopted under a co-decision procedure. The relevant constitutional provisions were intended to be, as it were, the end of the road.[1]

In the meantime, as we shall see, the 2006 reforms could be said to have produced a sort of halfway house. The story of their negotiation is a case study in relations between the institutions in an area where, exceptionally, the institutions themselves can reform a decision-making procedure. As the comitology decision is based on a Treaty provision which may not itself be amended in the process, the reform power is subject to significant legal constraints, which weigh heavily on the institutions' room for manoeuvre. Moreover, in the present case, though the reforms were instigated essentially at the behest of the European Parliament, this institution only enjoys a minimal formal role in the procedure for adopting the comitology arrangements. Conversely, the Council, with the final power of decision, long took the view that it had no interest in such reform. The story is therefore one of politics in practice, rather than political science, which tells of how Parliament was obliged to use its formal powers to promote institutional reform, how it was able to influence, though not determine, the outcome, and how and why the other institutions agreed to negotiate such a deal.

This article will start with a brief presentation of the legal constraints on comitology reform, of the political background, and of how each influenced the result. Next the amended comitology arrangements are analysed, and some closing comments are proffered.

The Political Impact of Legal Ambiguity

As noted above, the comitology reform process takes place within the confines of the EC Treaty, as interpreted by the Court of Justice. In the present case, however, the limits of the legal possibilities are far from clear, and each of the parties to the negotiations tended to interpret the relevant provisions to its own advantage. In particular, an unpublished opinion of its own legal service of 2 February 2006 appears to have been treated by the Council as laying down red lines (Schusterschitz and Kotz 2007: 78–79; Szapiro 2006: 567–568),[2] though some of the basic premises on which its analysis was based could not be said to be generally accepted outside the confines of the Council's Justus Lipsius complex in Brussels. As these provided the immutable background to the reform, some examination of the legal issues is unavoidable.

Any legal analysis of the comitology system starts with two ambiguities. The Treaty foundation for such arrangements, Article 202, third indent, EC, uses the term 'the Council' throughout. However, it is clear that in some circumstances this term refers in fact to 'the legislature', meaning either 'Parliament and the Council' or 'the Council acting alone', depending on the legislative procedure applied for adopting the basic legislation (ECJ 1997). Thus, for the first and second sentences of this indent, which concern respectively the conferral of implementing powers on the Commission and the possibility of imposing 'certain requirements' on the exercise of such powers (the euphemism for the comitology system), 'the legislature' is intended. On the other hand, the 'Council' referred to in the last sentence of this provision is equally evidently the Council acting alone, given the explicit reference to the consultation of Parliament.

The only real possible ambiguity arises in relation to the third sentence of this indent, according to which 'the Council may...reserve the right, in specific cases, to exercise directly implementing powers itself'. If 'the Council' is here taken to refer to 'the legislature', then, acting jointly with the Council, Parliament could exercise such implementing powers directly. Alternatively, if 'the Council' were interpreted as meaning 'the Council acting alone', then Parliament would be excluded from exercising any such powers, which is the view traditionally ascribed to the Council (Schusterschitz and Kotz 2007: 77–79). As the reservation of powers must be effected in the legislative act itself, one could argue that the former view is more plausible, on the grounds that the person reserving the powers and the person exercising these should in principle be one and the same. However, until the latest round of comitology reforms, Parliament was excluded not only from the exercise of implementing powers, but even from passing judgement on the measures being proposed other than as regards their legality.

The second ambiguity arises in respect of the term 'implementing powers', which the EC Treaty does not define, even in outline, at any point. It appears from the case law of the Court of Justice that the legislature must define the essential elements of the matter to be dealt with and may not therefore delegate a power to make policy choices (ECJ 1970: para. 6; ECJ 1992: para. 37). Outside this core area, the legislature may delegate wide powers to the Commission. In practice, these come in three categories: decisions *applying rules* to specific cases, *rules implementing* the essential elements of the basic act, and *measures modifying* the non-essential[3] elements of the basic act. While the first two categories may be considered the standard fare of implementation in Community law (ECJ 1989: para. 11), the third is nonetheless a technique which has long been used in certain areas, particularly where the Commission is charged with adapting annexes of a basic act to scientific and technical progress, and on which Parliament had expressed certain reservations as far back as 1984 (EP 1984). The 1999 comitology decision (EU Council 1999) thus identified this category of implementing measures as one to which the regulatory procedure should be applied (EU Council 1999: Article 2(1)(b), second indent).

These ambiguities were each exploited for political ends in the debate on the proper role of the European Parliament in the comitology system. In the run-up to the adoption of the 1999 comitology decision, the use of the term 'the Council' in Article 202, third indent, EC, was relied upon to support the view (Kortenberg 1998) that implementing powers should in principle be exercised by the member states, and only exceptionally by the Commission; by this token, the Council acts as a conference of the member state governments in this context, and Parliament's intervention should be limited to the supervision of legality of implementing measures, in order to preserve its prerogatives in the adoption of the basic legislation. This view has been comprehensively criticised (Lenaerts and Verhoven 2000; Bradley 2007); although the Council modified somewhat its initial stance on the matter, traces of this analysis still encumber the final text of the 2006 comitology decision.

The absence of any clear definition of implementing powers was used first as an argument to exclude Parliament from any role in their supervision, on the grounds that the legislature could not, and should not, interfere with the activities of the executive. Subsequently, the distinction between implementing measures which amend the basic act and other implementing measures provided the opening which both allowed Parliament some supervisory role beyond that of the merely controlling the *vires* of proposed measures, and marked out the material limits of that role.

Run-up to the 2006 Reforms

The 1999 Comitology Decision and the European Parliament

Notwithstanding the inter-institutional tensions which preceded its adoption (Bradley 1997; Lenaerts and Verhoven 2000), the 1999 comitology decision did not seek to give Parliament any meaningful role in the political supervision of implementing legislation. This is true even as regards measures implementing primary legislation adopted jointly by Parliament and the Council under the co-decision procedure. The view that Parliament won equality with the Council in 1999, 'its most important victory' (Bergström 2005: 270), is not widely shared, while others consider that the 1999 decision did operate a shift in the institutional balance, but in favour of the Commission rather than Parliament (Schusterschitz and Kotz 2007: 72).

In any case, the claim in the preamble that the decision seeks 'to improve the involvement of the European Parliament' is belied by the minimalist character of such improvements, as is evident from a cursory examination of its material provisions. In respect of all draft measures subject to comitology, Parliament enjoyed a 'right to information' embracing the agendas, meetings, voting records and summary records of the committee meetings, as well as the lists of the authorities and organisations to which the committee members belong. For measures which implemented acts adopted under co-decision, Parliament was entitled to receive the text of the Commission's draft, and to adopt a resolution indicating that the measure would exceed the implementing powers provided in the basic act, the so-called 'right of scrutiny'. In this case, the Commission was obliged to inform Parliament of the action it intended to take and of its reasons for so doing, but was not obliged to take account of, still less follow, Parliament's opinion. Where the Commission submitted a proposal to the Council under the regulatory procedure, Parliament was entitled to inform the Council that, in its view, the proposal exceeded the implementing powers provided in the basic act. The Council was not obliged to follow such an opinion either.

In February 2000, Parliament concluded a complementary agreement with the Commission (but not the Council) on the application of the 1999 decision. This provides, for example, that Parliament receive the necessary comitology documents 'at the same time and on the same terms' as members of the committees themselves, and that it may on request have access to 'specific draft measures' other than those which implement co-decisional acts. Rather remarkably, in view of the constraints on its working methods, Parliament agreed that it would have just one month in which to prepare and adopt resolutions objecting to draft measures on grounds of *ultra vires*. As plenary sessions are usually only held once every four weeks, a draft measure tabled by the Commission in the week before one plenary session could only be examined by the committee two weeks later, and any resolution would be adopted after the expiry of the deadline. While it is true that some comitology measures are urgent, this is not normally so of those covered by the right of scrutiny. It is not entirely clear why Parliament accepted such an unfavourable regime; perhaps the majority felt that some progress is better than none, though there were dissenting voices (Bergström 2005: 283–284).

The 'Lamfalussy' Arrangements

In response to the special pleading of securities operators for speedier market regulation, the institutions agreed, following the Lamfalussy report of February 2001 (Vaccari 2005), that primary legislation in this area should be limited to the basic principles, while the adoption of the necessary implementing measures would be left to the Commission, assisted by various groups of national officials and experts. Such implementing measures, it was argued, could be adopted much more swiftly to take account of developments in the market than the co-decision procedure would allow. To compensate for Parliament's loss of legislative input, the Commission offered it various concessions going well beyond the 2000 Agreement. These included a more comprehensive supply to the relevant parliamentary committee of draft texts and other documents, regular (if informal) meetings between the Commission and the parliamentary committees, and an extension from one to three months of the deadline within which Parliament was entitled to react to draft implementing measures. This latter concession from the Commission shows that the original one-month deadline, which still applies outside the new procedure, is not, or not always, justified.

Most significantly, perhaps, Parliament decided, with the agreement of the Commission and the Council, systematically to introduce into each of the relevant basic legislative acts a 'sunset clause', whereby the delegation of implementing powers would lapse after a specified period (in practice four years) unless renewed by amending legislation adopted in accordance with co-decision. This procedural mechanism was to provide the principal incentive for the Council to reconsider comitology reform in late 2005, while the imminence of the expiry of the first such clause in April 2007 (Parliament and EU Council 2003: Article 17(4)) in effect set the timetable for its accomplishment.

Formal Proposals for Reform

The procedure to amend the comitology decision was formally launched by the presentation of the first Commission proposal in December 2002 (EC Commission 2002). Intended somewhat optimistically as a temporary measure pending the entry into force of the Constitutional Treaty the European Convention was then in the process of drafting, the proposal sought to put Parliament and Council on an equal footing as regards the supervision of measures implementing acts adopted in co-decision. A special regulatory procedure would apply for measures which 'widely implement [*sic*] the essential aspects of the basic instrument or adapt certain other aspects of it'. The procedure would have an 'executive phase', during which the draft measures would be examined by a regulatory committee, and a 'supervisory phase'. During this latter phase, Parliament and the Council would each have a month in which to oppose the final draft measure, though the Commission would still be able to adopt the measure 'possibly amending its draft to take account of the objections'. As different commentators have noted, the Commission's approach throughout has been 'tactical' (Bergström 2005: 318–319; Jacqué 1999: 68), not to say self-seeking.

Following intensive talks with the Commission on a first set of draft amendments in mid-2003, Parliament adopted its position officially on 2 September 2003. It accepted that the Commission would be able to continue with its proposed comitology measure in the teeth of Parliamentary or Council opposition, contenting itself with obliging the Commission to 'take account' of the respective positions of Parliament and the Council. An amended version of the Commission's proposal, incorporating most of Parliament's September amendments, followed some months later (EC Commission 2004). The Council did not adopt this, inter alia precisely because it would have allowed the Commission to override the Council's firm objections, albeit in limited circumstances (Schusterschitz and Kotz 2007: 73).

The distinction between 'implementation which amends' basic legislation and 'ordinary' implementation is also reflected in the text of the Constitution for Europe adopted by the member states in October 2004. Article I-36 would allow the Commission to adopt 'delegated European regulations to supplement or amend certain non-essentials of the law or framework law' in accordance with a precisely circumscribed delegation set out in the primary legislation. The legislator would be able to supervise the exercise of such powers either by 'call back' (a revocation of the delegation by either Parliament or the Council) and/or[4] by objecting to a proposed individual delegated regulation. Article I-37 allows for a conferral of implementing powers on the Commission, the exercise of which would be subject to member state control, though under arrangements adopted jointly by Parliament and the Council.

Operation of the Comitology Arrangements in Practice

While a certain parliamentary discontent with the operation of the comitology arrangements has long been a feature of the Community's institutional landscape (Bradley 1997), a number of incidents, particularly in the area of environmental policy, gave this additional prominence. In early February 2005, Parliament's environment committee discovered, on consulting the *Official Journal*, that the Commission had adopted a decision amending the end-of-life vehicles directive under a regulatory procedure (EC Commission 2005a), without ever informing Parliament of this initiative, in clear violation of the comitology decision. Annulment proceedings were avoided when the Commission undertook to withdraw the offending decision, which it did (EC Commission 2005b).

The same committee meeting also examined a proposed amendment to the 2003 directive prohibiting of the use of certain hazardous substances in electrical and electronic equipment, the so-called 'RoHS' Directive (Parliament and EU Council 2002), which the Commission had equally omitted to refer to Parliament. On this occasion, the Commission agreed to resubmit the draft measures in order to enable Parliament to adopt a resolution under Article 8 of the comitology decision.

The resolution which was adopted on 12 April 2005[5] was not confined to expressing Parliament's disagreement with the Commission's interpretation of its powers under the RoHS directive. Parliament raised several other apparent legal problems with the proposed amendment, and noted that 'on the basis of the limited information available' the Commission's non-compliance with the comitology decision in this instance 'is not an isolated case'. The resolution requested the Commission to make 'a detailed assessment of all cases of non-compliance' within three months.

The Commission's reply of 24 August 2005 makes interesting reading. It identified some 50 occasions on which the Commission had failed to respect Parliament's rights under the comitology decision between December 2003 and February 2005. Most of these occurred in three areas of Commission activity (environment, health and consumer protection, and humanitarian aid), which, perhaps by unhappy chance, are all matters of direct concern to individuals. While, according to the Commission, the 50 omissions only represent 2.5 per cent of some 2,000 or so measures subject to Parliament's right of scrutiny within the reference period, the 37 omissions in the areas of public health and the environment alone add up to 40 per cent of the draft implementing measures within the competence of Parliament's environment committee. The Commission's reply was widely seen as providing concrete proof that the 1999/2000 comitology arrangements were not working (Szapiro 2006: 560–561), and gave added impetus for political action on a grander scale.

A further Commission amendment of the RoHS directive generated a parliamentary resolution on 6 July 2005, in which Parliament again took the view that the Commission had exceeded its implementing powers. The Commission ignored Parliament's resolution, and although neither the regulatory committee nor the Council approved the proposed decision, the Commission adopted it on 13 October 2005 (EC Commission 2005c). The legality of the decision was successfully challenged by Parliament and several member states (ECJ 2008).

At the same time, Parliament and the Council had agreed to extend the use of sunset clauses to legislation outside the area of financial services, to resort to co-decision rather than comitology for the modification of certain basic legislation, and to shorten the validity of the sunset period to a mere two years in a handful of legislative acts. In giving its first reading opinion on the capital adequacy directive in September 2005, Parliament inserted (with the Council's agreement) a recital in the preamble to the effect that it considered that the Commission's proposal to amend the 1999 Comitology decision 'does not preserve [Parliament's] legislative prerogatives' (Parliament and EU Council 2006a: Recital 37). This was one of two directives whose adoption Parliament delayed in order to put pressure on the Council (Schusterschitz and Kotz 2007: 76).

The momentum for reform gathered pace after the summer break when members of Parliament had digested the Commission's confessions of 24 August 2005. In commenting on the Commission draft work programme for 2006 on 6 September 2005, the college of committee chairmen called on the Commission to propose a new agreement along the same lines as the Constitution for Europe for the supervision of measures implementing co-decision acts.

In these circumstances, the United Kingdom Presidency of the Council created a group of 'Friends of the Presidency' in October 2005 to reconsider the stalled Commission proposal to amend the 1999 Decision. Conscious of the dangers of fragmentation and contradiction, that same month Parliament appointed a two-man team, comprising Joseph Daul, chairman of the college of committee chairmen, and Richard Corbett, *rapporteur général* on comitology, to carry out 'exploratory talks' with the other institutions regarding comitology reform. On the basis of the deliberations of the Friends of the Presidency, the talks between the Austrian Council Presidency and Parliament's negotiators started in earnest in March 2006, and carried on until the middle of June, when agreement was reached on the amendment of the comitology decision and on various accompanying texts (Schusterschitz and Kotz 2007: 79–88).

The 2006 Comitology Reforms

Decision 2006/512/EC of 17 July 2006

In order not to open a debate on the other comitology procedures, Council Decision 2006/512/EC amends, but does not replace, the 1999 comitology decision. It adds a new procedure, partly inspired by the previous reform proposals of the Commission and the European Convention, the 'regulatory procedure with scrutiny' (RPS), and defines the conditions under which it must be applied. The decision was formally adopted on 17 July 2006 and entered into force, without the benefit of any transitional provisions, on 23 July 2006 (EU Council 2006a, 2006b).

There are four aspects of the new procedure which deserve special attention: its compulsory character, its material scope of application, the grounds for opposition, and the deadline for the two branches of the legislature to react. A number of ancillary declarations were adopted along with Decision 2006/512.

Compulsory character. The most striking feature of the RPS procedure is its compulsory character. Whereas the criteria of Article 2(1) are guidelines 'of a non-binding nature' according to recital 5 in the preamble,[6] this is not so of recourse to RPS; where the relevant legal conditions are fulfilled, '[it] is necessary to follow' this procedure, according to recital 7. This is also reflected in the use in Article 2(2) of the imperative 'shall be adopted', as opposed to 'should be adopted', which is the formulation of the guideline for the choice of the other committee procedures in Article 2(1).[7]

The failure to provide in a co-decisional act for this procedure, where the conditions for its application are fulfilled, would therefore constitute prima facie grounds for the (at least partial) annulment of any such act. The legal question of whether RPS could be applied voluntarily, where the relevant conditions are not fulfilled, remains open.

Scope of application. The revised comitology decision is far from giving Parliament a general right to supervise the Commission's exercise of implementing powers. Article 2(2) of the decision restricts RPS to:

- the implementation of acts adopted under co-decision;
- the adoption of measures of general scope;

- where those measures are 'designed to amend non-essential elements of [the basic act], inter alia, by deleting some of those elements or by supplementing the [basic act] by the addition of new non-essential elements'.

The first criterion should give rise to few real problems in practice. It appears to have increased the temptation for certain parliamentary committees faced with a proposal under the consultation procedure to push for legal bases which provide for co-decision, where significant implementing powers are to be delegated to the Commission. The change of legal basis in such circumstances is, however, subject to a number of procedural and political hurdles within and outside Parliament.

The exclusion of individual decisions taken under comitology, while consistent with the Council's views on the proper scope of parliamentary supervision, was a bitter pill for certain groups and members of the European Parliament to swallow. In particular, the high-handed behaviour of the Commission, which in 1997 authorized certain strains of genetically modified maize notwithstanding the vehement opposition of Parliament and all but one member state government, has not been forgotten (Bradley 1998; and, less critically, Toeller and Hofmann 2000). No doubt imaginative proposals to get around this restriction will not be lacking. It was suggested, for example, that certain authorisations under the 2006 regulation on the registration of chemicals should be considered within the new procedure, though this view was not accepted (Parliament and EU Council 2006b: recital 124).

The use of the familiar term 'measures of general scope' will allow the institutions' lawyers to take refuge in the (relatively) safe haven of the established case law of the Court on what is now Article 230, fourth indent, EC. Measures of general scope are usually defined in contradistinction to individual measures which affect 'natural and legal persons...by reason of certain attributes peculiar to them, or by reason of a factual situation which differentiates them from all other persons and distinguishes them individually in the same way as an addressee' (ECJ 2004: para. 45).

This is not to say that disputes between the institutions will not arise in this regard. Already there are indications that some within the Commission may seek to avoid RPS for certain implementing measures on the grounds that these are closely linked to measures of individual application. This argument is based on the Court's judgment in the 'Forest Focus' case (ECJ 2006b: para. 41), though there the Court was distinguishing between the scope of application of the management and regulatory procedures, which is rather different matter. Such an approach is inconsistent with the compulsory character of RPS, and is legally untenable. It illustrates, however, the continuing impact of legal considerations, this time in the application of the comitology decision.

Opposition by the legislature to a draft implementing measure. Whether the RPS committee has approved a draft implementing measure or not, Parliament may oppose its adoption under the same conditions in each case, that is 'by indicating that the draft measures proposed...exceed the implementing powers provided for in the basic instrument or that the draft is not compatible with the aim or the content of the basic instrument or does not respect the principles of subsidiarity or proportionality'. This ungainly clatter of reasons for blocking a draft measure is the result of the irresistible force of Parliament's demands for substantive political supervision of such measures meeting the immovable object of Council's refusal to cede Parliament parity of position in fact, even here where it had ceded this in principle.

The drafting of this provision reflects a hard-won compromise, and illustrates the somewhat tortuous character of the negotiations between the institutions. By mid-March 2006, the Presidency of the Council had proposed that Parliament be entitled to oppose a draft measure on the grounds that it was *ultra vires* the basic act or incompatible with it. This Parliament rejected as comprising an essentially legal criterion, little different from the then existing situation; in any case, respect for both the *vires* and the material provisions of the basic act are primarily a matter within the jurisdiction of the Court of Justice, which Parliament is perfectly able, and willing, to invoke if need be (e.g. ECJ 1996). Subsequent negotiations added incompatibility with 'the aim and content' of the basic act, rather than merely with its material provisions, and with the principles of subsidiarity or proportionality as further possible reasons for opposition. To get away further still from (the appearance of) review on legal grounds, the Presidency proposed that the simple indication by Parliament (or, where the committee's opinion has been positive, the Council) would be enough to prevent the adoption of the unwanted measures. It was argued that the rule in Article 5a (3)(c) and (4)(1) of the decision, whereby 'if...Parliament opposes the proposed measures, the latter shall not be adopted',[8] combined with the broad sweep of the possible reasons for opposing the Commission's draft, granted Parliament the possibility of exercising something equivalent to political supervision over the content of such measures (Szapiro 2006: 57; cf. Schusterschitz and Kotz 2007: 84).

Deadlines. For RPS, Parliament will have a period of three months, rather than one month, starting from the date of referral in which to oppose draft measures approved by the committee, and four months from referral where the comitology committee has not approved the Commission draft. In the latter case, the Council is in effect given two months to deliberate first, and then Parliament a further two months to act in the light of the Council's position.

Various derogations are provided for, though, in line with the Council's marked proclivity for imposing criteria of greater or lesser utility, in each case recourse to these is circumscribed rather than being left to the discretion of the legislature, at least in theory. Hence the general time limits for Parliament and the Council may be extended by a month 'when justified by the complexity of the measures', or curtailed by an unspecified amount 'where justified on the grounds of efficiency'. These vague criteria are a likely source of inter-institutional friction; it would have been much more sensible to provide a procedure for deciding jointly on any variation in the normal deadlines in each case.

More obviously necessary are the limitations on recourse to the urgent procedure of Article 5a (6), which allows for significant derogations from the normal procedure. The procedure may only be applied where the normal time limits cannot be complied with 'on imperative grounds of urgency', a criterion with certain objective elements the existence of which the institutions, including the Court, will be able to verify should the case arise. Here opposition by Parliament or the Council would lead to the repeal of measures already in force; whether or not these have created legitimate expectations in the legal sense of the term, it is clearly a situation which could give rise to legal and practical difficulties. Notwithstanding this risk, the right of the Commission provisionally to maintain the measures in force is limited to health protection, safety and environmental grounds.

By far the most difficult criterion for recourse to RPS is that which requires that the implementing measure be 'designed to amend non-essential elements' of the basic act. Clearly where the implementing measure formally amends the basic act, for example by adding new provisions or deleting existing provisions of the act or its annexes, the obligation to employ RPS is clear-cut. The problem arises where the implementing measure supplement the basic act 'by the addition of new non-essential elements'. This is of course the Lamfalussy paradigm which the 2006 decision seeks to generalise; however, in this paradigm by prior agreement the basic act contains little more than the essential elements of the matter regulated and the relevant comitology provision. This is not normally the case in other areas of regulation, where the basic act may itself contain many of the non-essential elements required for proper regulation, and where the Commission may be empowered to adopt individual decisions and non-amending rules, as well as provisions amending the non-essential elements.

The Accompanying Declarations

The formal modification of the comitology decision was accompanied by the usual raft of uni-, bi-, or multilateral declarations, some adopted with great pomp and ceremony and duly published in the *Official Journal* in all the working languages, others concocted hugger-mugger like a secret oath, and not published in any easily accessible source. Of the former, by far the most important is the (undated) 'Statement by the European Parliament, the Council and the Commission' on Decision 2006/512/EC (Parliament, EU

Council and EC Commission 2006). In many respects, this text was more difficult to negotiate than the formal decision itself.[9] Parliament saw this as its only bargaining chip, given that the Council alone takes responsibility for the comitology decision; for the Council, this was the *quid pro quo* for what it saw as the widespread concessions it had made to Parliament in amending the comitology decision. This difference of perspectives is reflected revealingly, if trivially, on the failure to agree on a short title for the statement. For the Council, it is a 'peace settlement', for Parliament a 'ceasefire declaration', the nuance being that Parliament would be prepared to take up arms again if need be.

The Council's main objective in agreeing on such a statement was that Parliament would stop blocking funds for the practical operation of comitology committees and refrain from imposing sunset clauses on the delegation of implementing powers. Parliament was willing to go along with the former by acknowledging the new decision as 'a horizontal and satisfactory solution to [its] wish to scrutinise the implementation of instruments adopted under the codecision procedure'. Mindful of the possibility of the entry into force of the Constitution, or of some intermediate Treaty reform, Parliament nonetheless insisted that its satisfaction could only be assumed 'in the context of the existing Treaty'.

The real sticking point concerned sunset clauses; for some within Parliament, and particularly members of its economic and monetary community who had grown accustomed to such clauses, the legislature neither could nor should, as a matter of principle, limit its freedom of legislative action for the future. For the Council, this was a red line; no renunciation of sunset clauses, no deal. The solution reflected in paragraph 3 is that Parliament and the Council in effect agree not to resort to sunset clauses as a matter of practice, while maintaining this possibility as a matter of principle; the institutions therefore recognise that the delegation of implementing powers to the Commission should be 'without time limit' in accordance with something known as 'the principles of good legislation'. This solution is '[without] prejudice to the rights of the legislative authorities', presumably to set such principles aside as the occasion demands. Instead of sunset clauses, the legislator may insert a revision clause 'where an adaptation is necessary within a specified period' to limit or abrogate the provision delegating implementing powers to the Commission. As this clause would require a Commission proposal to become operational, it would in effect depend on the Commission's criticising the exercise of its own implementing powers.

The other essential element of the agreement is a list of existing co-decision acts to which RPS would be applied retroactively and 'as a matter of urgency' set out in paragraph 5 of the statement. Within the Council some delegations apparently wished to restrict the list to the handful of Lamfalussy and other acts which actually contained sunset clauses, some of which would come into operation as early as the first half of 2007, and which would be rapidly replaced by RPS. Wiser counsel prevailed; Parliament's representatives argued that pandering to a single committee in this respect would be the surest way of stirring hostility from all the other committees and stymieing the entire deal. A list of 25 priority measures was agreed on, being somewhere between the (minimum) list of the instruments currently including sunset clauses and the 80-plus acts identified by the parliamentary committees as deserving of priority treatment. Again, mindful of their legislative prerogatives, Parliament and the Council would not undertake to adopt the relevant Commission proposals on first reading as the Commission had suggested, but only 'as rapidly as possible'. In accordance with an unpublished Commission declaration, this exercise was to be complemented before the end of 2007 by a more general screening of all existing co-decision acts with a view to the possible inclusion of RPS.

Some Comments

For the first time, the Council has recognised in its decision of 17 July 2006 the legitimacy of Parliament's playing an active role in the supervision of the exercise of implementing powers, beyond the rather technical issue of *vires*. In contrast to the 1999 decision, this represents more than merely cosmetic progress. One might regret that, more than a dozen years after the co-decision procedure came into operation, Parliament had to use the full panoply of its institutional prerogatives, legislative, budgetary, and jurisdictional, to achieve such a modest objective. These are for the most part weapons of mass obstruction, in principle ill-suited for encouraging inter-institutional dialogue on the reform of decision-making procedures. Yet the fact is that, without recourse to such tactics, it seems unlikely that the 2006 reforms would ever have got off the ground.

It is clear in particular that Parliament's insistence on sunset clauses, for perfectly valid reasons, in Lamfalussy and latterly other legislation, played a major role in paving the way for the 2006 agreement. In inter-institutional relationships, a little stubbornness can sometimes pay handsome dividends. Nor was the settlement such a leonine agreement as some within the Council appeared to think; calling in delegated powers is in principle both effective and legitimate as a technique for supervising the exercise – at least the authors of the Constitution for Europe thought so – and indeed, the sunset clause is based on roughly the same idea as that which underlies parliamentary democracies with fixed-term mandates, and its use was accepted by both the Council and the Commission. There was therefore no particular reason the legislature should not have employed this technique across the board, until and unless it had a superior technique at its disposal.

Given the unpropitious political background, including the 'strong resistance among a substantial number of member states, who regarded any participation of Parliament [as] either not possible or not desirable (or both)' (Schusterschitz and Kotz 2007: 79–80), the conclusion of any such agreement was in itself a considerable achievement. Moreover, some of the criticism directed at the content of the agreement seems to be so much carping. Thus, for example, the suggestion that the 2006 decision 'significantly increased the complexity of the comitology system' by adding a further procedure, and one which may lengthen the time to adopt implementing legislation to boot (Christiansen and Vaccari 2006: 15), appears to overlook that fact that RPS in effect replaces decision-making by co-decision by a procedure which adds a maximum of four months to the normal regulatory procedure, and that recourse to this procedure, unlike the choice between the other three procedures, is guided by binding legal rules agreed between the institutions. The suggestion that Parliament and the Council may be unable to establish the necessary infrastructure (Christiansen and Vaccari 2006: 15) also seems a little gratuitous, for two institutions which have taken successive versions of the co-decision and budgetary procedures in their stride.

Moreover, the agreement contains some positive elements for each of the interested parties, as well as Parliament. While the member states will not all welcome parliamentary supervision, those who find themselves outvoted in the committee or in the Council on a particular decision may have the opportunity to overturn this in Parliament. The Council too will be able to exercise a more systematic control over the Commission, and the national officials who sit in comitology committees, in respect of the measures subject to RPS. The Commission did not obtain the possibility to override the objections of the legislature it had sought, though, given that the measures to which RPS applies fall in principle within the competence of Parliament and the Council, such a claim might be considered somewhat exorbitant. In the short run, the Commission might see more of its draft measures flounder, because of Parliament or Council opposition; however, in the long run the new procedure should encourage the legislature to delegate more freely the power to adopt measures of general scope to the Commission.

Also on the positive side is the constructive attitude displayed by both sides in adopting and operating a negotiation procedure, once the Council had acknowledged that agreement with Parliament was necessary. One of Parliament's major gripes at the time of the first comitology decision was that the Council neither took any account of its opinion nor re-consulted it on the decision the Council intended to adopt. In this case, notwithstanding the procedure provided for in Article 202, third indent, EC, the institutions applied a procedure in some respects akin to co-decision (Christiansen and Vaccari 2006: 13), in which, coincidentally, Parliament had three readings of the text before it was adopted in a form both institutions could approve of. Much of the credit for this must go to the United Kingdom Council Presidency, which started the ball rolling again 18 months after the submission of the second Commission proposal, and perhaps even more so to the representatives of the Austrian Presidency who, along with Parliament's negotiators, showed remarkable diplomatic skills and frequently great inventiveness in achieving the end result.

On the negative side, the 2006 decision only partly satisfies Parliament's long-standing claims for a genuine supervisory role over implementing acts. For measures which implement acts adopted under co-decision, its claim was based on the parity between the two branches of the legislature which is the fundamental characteristic of this procedure (ECJ 2006a: paras. 64 and 77), and, indirectly, the *raison d'être* of this decision. Such inequality takes a number of forms. In the first place, where under RPS the committee has not approved the Commission's draft measures, the Council may oppose these without restriction, whereas Parliament must indicate one of the three reasons listed in Article 5a(4)(e) of the comitology decision. Moreover, the imposition of such a requirement was clearly intended to preclude parliamentary opposition on grounds of political opportunity, however these criteria are applied in practice. Secondly, in these circumstances, the Council may adopt implementing measures, unless Parliament opposes them for cause, whereas there are no circumstances in which Parliament exercises such a power, even jointly with the Council.

Beyond parity, Parliament is really seeking some form of democratic supervision over measures which are not subject to parliamentary supervision at the national level. For all other measures which implement co-decisional acts and which do not fall under RPS, as well as measures implementing acts adopted by other procedures, Parliament's role remains limited to that defined in the 1999/2000 arrangements adumbrated above.

Despite their restricted character, the 2006 reforms are clearly intended to take comitology off the political agenda for some time to come, as is evident in particular from the joint Statement of Parliament, the Council and the Commission. This is obviously a laudable objective; a war of attrition is hardly a sensible means of running inter-institutional relations on a day-to-day basis. As a result, however, the deeper problems of comitology, what has been termed the 'attempt to recruit technocratic legitimacy for government regulation as a substitute for democratic legitimacy' (Shapiro 2004: 5), remain, if not untouched, at least not properly resolved. In this sense too, the 2006 reforms are only a halfway house.

Notes

1. The Treaty of Lisbon, which Member States signed on 13 December 2007, would reach the same destination.
2. While writing in a personal capacity, the authors are officials respectively of the Austrian Ministry for Foreign Affairs and the Secretariat General of the Commission.
3. 'Non essential', as the essential elements may only be amended by the legislature using the Treaty-designated procedure (ECJ 1970). While the matter might be obvious for the lawyer, the wording of this provision has caused some uncertainty in applying the decision.

4. The text of Article I-36(2) does not preclude the use of both techniques for a single delegation.
5. The draft decision was transmitted to Parliament on 25 February 2005, a few working days before the next plenary session was due to start; in the circumstances, the Commission does not appear to have objected to this minor infraction of the one-month deadline.
6. The Court of Justice has held, somewhat bizarrely, that the legislature must provide reasons for not following the non-binding criteria (ECJ 2003).
7. The French version of Article 2(1)(b), 2nd indent, uses the term 'sont arrêtées'; while this is out of step with other language versions, it was not corrected in the unofficial consolidated version.
8. The same criterion applies in the framework of the urgent procedure of Article 5a(6)(b), though this has been incorrectly rendered in English as Parliament 'may oppose...*on the grounds* that...'.
9. The only occasion on which negotiations between Presidency and Parliament representatives actually broke was during the discussion of the wording of paragraph 3; thanks to a little legal finessing, talks were shortly resumed, and completed in time for the start of that evening's World Cup encounter.

References

Bergström, Fredrik (2005). *Comitology – Delegation of Powers in the European Union and the Committee System*. Oxford: Oxford University Press.
Bradley, Kieran St. C. (1998). 'Alien Corn, or the Transgenic Procedural Maze', in Rinus van Schendelen (ed.), *EU Committees as Influential Policymakers*. Dartmouth: Ashgate, 207–22.
Bradley, Kieran St. C. (1999). 'Institutional Aspects of Comitology: Scenes from the Cutting Room Floor', in Christian Joerges and Ellen Vos (eds.), *EU Committees: Social Regulation, Law and Politics*. Oxford: Hart Publishing, 71–93.
Bradley, Kieran St. C. (1997). 'The European Parliament and Comitology: "On the Road to Nowhere?"', *European Law Journal* 3/3, 230–54.
Bradley, Kieran St Clair (2007). 'Delegated Legislation and Parliamentary Supervision in the European Community', in Astrid Epiney, Marcel Haag and Andreas Heinemann (eds.), *Challenging Boundaries*. Baden-Baden: Nomos Verlag and St. Gallen: Dike Verlag Zürich, 286–301.
Christiansen, Thomas, and Beatrice Vaccari (2006). 'The 2006 Reform of Comitology', *EIPAScope* 2006/3, 9–17.
EC Commission (2002). COM (2002)719 final, 11 December.
EC Commission (2004). COM (2004)324 final, 22 April.
EC Commission (2005a). Decision 2005/63/EC, OJ L 25/73.
EC Commission (2005b). Decision 2005/438/EC, OJ L 152/19.
EC Commission (2005c). Decision 2005/717/EC, OJ L 271/48.
ECJ (1970). Case 25/70, *Köster* [1970] ECR 1161.
ECJ (1989). Case 16/88 *Commission* v *Council* [1989] ECR 3457.
ECJ (1992). Case C-240/90, *Germany* v *Commission* [1992] ECR I-5383.
ECJ (1996). Case C-303/94, *Parliament* v *Council* [1996] ECR I-2943.
ECJ (1997). Case C-259/95, *Parliament* v *Council* [1997] ECR I-5322.
ECJ (2003). Case C-378/00, *Commission* v *Parliament and Council* [2003] ECR I-937.
ECJ (2004). Case C-263/02 P, *Commission* v *Jégo-Quéré* [2004] ECR I-3425.
ECJ (2006a). Case C-344/04 *IATA* [2006] ECR 403, Opinion of Advocate General Geelhoed.
ECJ (2006b). Case C-122/04, *Commission* v *Parliament and the Council* [2006] ECR I-2001.
ECJ (2008). Joined Cases C-14/06 *Parliament v Commission*, and C-295/06 *Denmark v Commission*, judgment of 1 April 2008, not yet reported.
EP (1984) Parliament, Resolution of 21 May 1984 on committees for the adaptation of legislation to scientific and technical progress.

EU Council (1999). Decision 1999/468/EC, OJ L 184/23.
EU Council (2006a). Decision 512/2006, OJ L 200, 11.
EU Council (2006b). Decision 1999/468/EC as amended, OJ C 255, 4.
Jacqué, Jean-Paul (1999). 'Implementing Powers and Comitology', in Christian Joerges and Ellen Vos (eds.), *EU Committees: Social Regulation, Law and Politics*. Oxford: Hart, 59–70.
Kortenberg, Helmut (1998). 'Comitologie: le retour', *Revue trimestrielle du droit européen*, 34, 317–27.
Lenaerts, Koen, and Amaryllis Verhoeven (2000). 'Towards a Legal Framework for Executive Role-Making in the EU? The Contribution of the New Comitology Decision', *Common Market Law Review*, 37:3, 645–86.
Parliament and EU Council (2002). Directive 2002/95, OJ 2003 L 37/19.
Parliament and EU Council (2003). Directive 2003/6, OJ 2003 L 96/16.
Parliament and EU Council (2006a). Directive 2006/49/EC, OJ 2006 L 177/201.
Parliament and EU Council (2006b). Regulation (EC) No 1907/2006, OJ 2006 L 396/1, 38.
Parliament, EU Council and EC Commission (2006). OJ 2006 C 255, 1.
Schusterschitz, Gregor, and Sabine Kotz (2007). 'The Comitology Reform of 2006. Increasing the Powers of the European Parliament Without Changing the Treaties', *European Constitutional Law Review*, 3, 68–90.
Shapiro, Martin (2004). '"Deliberative", "Independent" Technocracy v. Democratic Politics: Will the Globe Echo the E.U.?', IIJL Working Paper 2004/5, http://www.iilj.org/papers/2004/documents/10120511_Shapiro.pdf.
Szapiro, Manuel (2006). 'Comitologie: rétrospective et prospective après la réforme de 2006', *Revue du droit de l'Union européenne*, No.3, 545–86, 567–8.
Toeller, Annette, and Herwig Hofmann (2000). 'Democracy and the Reform of Comitology', in Mads Andenas and Alexander Türk (eds.), *Delegated Legislation and the Role of Committees in the EC*. The Hague: Kluwer Law International, 25–50.
Vaccari, Beatrice (2005). 'Le processus Lamfalussy: une réussite pour la comitologie et un exemple de "bonne gouvernance européenne"', *Revue du droit de l'Union européenne*, 4, 803–22.

Index

Page numbers in *Italics* represent Tables

accountability: and accountability forums 16; definition 15-16; and executive order 13-17; legitimacy problems 16-17
administrative space 24-38; agenda setting 28, 30; bureaucratic change 39-62; civil service politicisation 42-3, 46-7; closed civil service systems 41-2; comitology procedures 29; Commission recruitment and career system openness 44-6; development 25-30; European Agencies (EA) 137-40; functional adaptation 50-2; horizontal relation 26-7; implementation phase 29-30; institutional isomorphism 53-5; institutional path dependency 52-3; integrated administration 27-33; Lamfalussy procedures 29; negative integration 26; open civil service systems 41-2, 44, 46, 47-50; policy windows impact 55-6; polity-building 133-50; and regulation causes and consequences 30-2; shared sovereignty 32-3; subsidiarity 27-8; vertical relation 26
Agency for the Cooperation of Energy Regulators 189
Amsterdam Treaty (1997) 5
aquis communautaire 25
Area of Freedom: Security and Justice (AFSJ) 141-5, 147

Balint, T.: Bauer, M.W.; and Knill, C. 5, 39-62
Bangemann, M. 180, 185
Barroso, J.M. 94, 154
Bauer, M.W.: Balint, T.; and Knill, C. 5, 39-62
Beach, D. 9

Beyers, J.: and Dierickx, G. 68, 85
bilateral diplomacy 2, 3
Bovens, M. 15-16
Bradley, K.S.C. 199-216
Brass, D. 69
Broscheid, A.: and Coen, D. 92

Calmes, C. 118
Cassis de Dijon ruling 27
centralisation: fragmentation and polity-building 133-50
Centre for Development of Vocational Training (CEDEFOP) 137
Chiti, E. 138
Christiansen, T.: and Vanhoonacker, S. 113-32
Cini, M. 65
Claude, I.L. 2
closed civil service systems: European Commission 41-2, 45, 48
Coen, D.: and Broscheid, A. 92; and Thatcher, M. 13, 168-98
Cologne European Summit (1999) 121, 122
comitology committees 10, 29, 89, 95
comitology reforms (2006): and accompanying declarations 210-12, 214; comitology decision (1999) 201-3, 207; compulsory character 207; deadlines 209-10; Decision 2006/5/12/EC 207-12; and European Parliament (EP) 199-216; Forest Focus judgment 208; formal proposals 204-5; Friends of the Presidency group 207; Lamfalussy arrangements 203-4; legislature opposition to draft implementing

218 *Index*

measure 209; and political impact of legal ambiguity 200-2; pre-reform arrangements in practice 205-7; regulatory procedure with scrutiny (RPS) 207-14; RoHS Directive 205-6; scope of application 207-8
commisarial management 134, 135-6; consensus orchestration 136-7; guiding idea 136; independent administration 135-6
Committee of European Energy Regulators (CEER) 181, 187
Committee on European Postal Regulations (CEPT) 178
Committee of European Securities Regulators (CESR) 185, 187, 188-9, 190, 191
Committee of Permanent Representatives (COREPER) 29, 118, 119
Common Foreign and Security Policy (CFSP) 9, 121, 122, 123, 124
Community Plant Variety Office (CPVO) 137, 139, 160, 162
Concert of Europe 3
Congress of Vienna (1815) 3, 17
Consultative Committees of Appointment (CCA) 49
Corbett, R. 206
Costa v ENEL (1964) 26
Council of Ministers 1, 7, 10, 14, 15, 16, 17, 18, 30, 31, 68, 134, 142, 152, 153, 156, 162, 164-5; and comitology reforms 200-14
Council Secretariat 9-10, 15; administrative function expansion 119; Common Foreign and Security Policy (CFSP) 121, 122, 123, 124; and compromise formulation 119, 120; Council Rules of Procedure (RoP) 118, 122; dorsale unit 121; early function 118; empty chair crisis (1965-6) 119; enlargement impact 126-7; establishment and growth 117-24; and EU Military Staff 122-3, 129; and European Council creation (1974) 119-20; European External Action Service (EEAS) 129; and European Political Cooperation (EPC); secretariat 121; European Security and Defence Policy (ESDP) 121-2, 123, 128; executive function 123-4, 126; formal recognition 120; and High Representative role 122, 123, 129; historical institutionalist perspective 115-17; honest broker idea 117, 119; initial design and consequences 125-6; institutional cohesion 127; institutional development 113-32; institutional growth 119-22; institutional path dependency 116, 117-18, 124-8; institutionalisation 118; Intergovernmental Conferences (IGCs) 120, 126; internal dynamics 126; Justice and Home Affairs (JHA) 121; mission statement 127; Policy Unit 122, 123; seconded experts/diplomats integration 123-4; Situation Centre (SITCEN) 122-3, 124, 143-4
Cresson, E. 65-6
Cross, M.K.D. 3
Curtin, D.: and Egeberg, M. 1-23

Daul, J. 206
Dehousse, R. 151-67
delegation of powers: comparative politics perspective 153-5; composite principals 156; control channels and agency accountability 162-3; draft inter-institutional agreement (IIA) 154, 164-5; and EU politics of delegation 157-61; and EU Principal absence 156-7; intergovernmental model 154-5, 160; Meroni ruling 154, 161, 176; multiple agents 156; principal-agent models 153-6
Delors, J. 51, 52, 134
democratic accountability: European executive order 13-17
Dierickx, G.: and Beyers, J. 68, 85
DiMaggio, P.J.: and Powell, W.W. 53-4
Directorate-General for External Relations (DG E) 121, 122
Directorates-General: European Commission 6-7, 49, 50, 66, 89, 92-4, 96-108
Döring, H. 7

Index 219

double-hattedness: and multi-level executive governance 12-13, 18

Economy and Society (Weber) 135
Egeberg, M. 66, 80; and Curtin, D. 1-23
energy: Committee of European Energy Regulators (CEER) 181, 187; European Regulators Group for electricity and gas (ERGEG) 186-7, 188, 190; regulatory space 180-1, 186-7, 189, 190
Ersboll, N. 120
EU Plan of Action on Combating Terrorism 143-4
European Agencies (EA) 10, 133, 137-47; 1990s second wave 137; 2000s third wave 137-8; accountability 139, 140, 146, 162-3; autonomy 139; capacity argument 140; categorisation 138; cooperative agencies 138; criticisms 140; delegation of powers 151-67; democratic challenge 145-6; diversity 139; draft Interinstitutional Agreement (IIA) 154, 164-5; efficiency argument 140; epistemological argument 140; establishment 139; executive agencies 138; fragmentation argument 140; hollowing-out argument 140; implementation agencies 138; integration by stealth 146, 148; internal security 141-5; justifications 140; legal personality 139; network agencies 138; not-so-independent argument 140; observatory agencies 138; principal-agent models 153-6; separation argument 140; trust/isolation argument 140
European Agency for the Evaluation of Medicinal Products (EMEA) 137, 139, 155, 160, 161, 166, 176
European Agency for the Management of Operational Cooperation at the External Borders (FRONTEX) 138, 145, 146
European Agency for Reconstruction (EAR) 138, 152
European Aviation Safety Agency (EASA) 152, 160-1, 162, 163-4, 176
European Central Bank (ECB) 134

European Centre for Prevention and Control of Diseases (ECDC) 159
European Coal and Steel Community (ECSC) 26, 118; High Authority 4
European Commission 1-2, 29, 30; administrative change and bureaucracy 39-62; agency creation wave 155; assessment centre method 49; autonomy 5; career network 69, 80; civil service politicisation 42-3, 46-7; closed civil service systems 41, 45, 48; and commissioners 7-8; Consultative Committees of Appointment (CCA) 49; contact persons choice model 76-9; and delegation of powers 151-66; Directorates-General 6-7, 49, 50, 66, 89, 92-4, 96-108; and European Parliament (EP) 8, 14, 18, 95; European Regulatory Networks (ERNs) 182, 184; executive centre formation 4-9, 17; expert groups 87-112; functional adaptation 50-2; informal networks of independent regulatory agencies (NIRAs) 181; institutional isomorphism 53-5; institutional path dependency 52-3; Kinnock reform 55, 155; language issue 75-6; leisure network 69, 80; maximum recruitment age 47-8; national networks 71-3; nationality effect 65-7; network analysis 63-86; networks and organizational network theory 67-71; officials 5-7, 66-7; open civil service systems 41-2, 44, 46, 47-50; organizational network theory 67-71; policy windows impact 55-6; President 5; recruitment and career system openness 44-50; regulatory space 168-98; revised career system 48-50; task-related formal network 69; task-related informal network 69-70, 78
European Court of Justice (ECJ) 26, 145, 161, 170, 172
European Defence Agency (EDA) 138, 139
European Environment Agency (EEA) 137, 160
European executive order 1-23; and accountability 13-17; bilateral diplomacy

2, 3; comitology committees 10, 29, 89, 95; Concert of Europe 2; EU-level agencies 10; and executive centre formation 4-9; and executive satellite formation 9-10; inter-governmental organizations (IGOs) 2, 3-4, 10, 11, 17; multi-level executive governance 10-13
European External Action Service (EEAS) 129
European Food Safety Authority (EFSA) 159, 160, 176
European Foundation for the Improvement of Living and Working Conditions (EUROFUND) 137, 138
European Institute for Security Studies (ISS) 138, 151
European Judicial Cooperation Unit (EUROJUST) 138, 143, 144, 151
European Monitoring Centre for Drugs and Drug Addiction (EMCDDA) 160
European Parliament 186
European Parliament (EP) 8, 14, 15, 16, 18, 145, 146, 155, 163, 164, 165; co-decision procedure 199, 213; and comitology reforms (2006) 199-216; and delegation of powers 158-9; role reinforcement 120
European Personnel Selection Office (EPSO) 48
European Police College (CEPOL) 138, 144
European Police Office (EUROPOL) 138, 139, 141, 143, 144-5, 151
European Political Cooperation (EPC): secretariat 121
European Regulators Group for electricity and gas (ERGEG) 186-7, 188, 190
European Regulators Group (ERG): telecommunications 186, 190
European Regulatory Agencies (ERAs) 175-6; future debate 187-90
European Regulatory Networks (ERNs) 175-6, 181-7; strengthening debate 187-90
European Securities and Exchange Commission 185
European Security and Defence Policy (ESDP) 9, 121-2, 123, 128
European Training Foundation (ETF) 137, 160
European Union Satellite Centre (EUSC) 138
executive centre formation: European Commission 4-9
expert groups 87-112; administrative capability argument 93-4, 102-3, 107; design perspectives 90; distribution 95-7; and distributive policy areas 98, 107; formal/informal distinction 105; growth 95, 97; institutional perspectives 92-3; legal competence argument 93, 100-2; policy task argument 90-1, 98-9; public policy domains 96; register 94-5; and regulatory policy areas 99, 107; sectoral specialisation and horizontal coordination 103-7; and service budget share 91, 98; structure institutionalisation and stability 104-7; supply-side argument 91-2, 99-100; technical specialisation 98, 99; temporary/permanent distinction 105; theoretical approaches and expectations 89-94; uneven distribution 96-103

Federal European Regulatory Agencies (FERAs) 176-7, 187-90
Financial Services Action Plan (1999) 184
Florence Forum: electricity 180-1
Forum of European Securities Commissions (FESCO) 181, 184, 185, 187, 191
forums: network industries 179-81, 182; regulatory space 175, 191
fragmentation: centralisation and polity-building 133-50
functional adaptation: European Commission 50-2

Geradin, D.: and Petit, N. 138
Gornitzka, A.: and Sverdrup, U. 87-112

Haas, E.B. 135
Hallstein, W. 46
Harlow, C.: and Rawlings, R. 16
High Authority of the European Coal and Steel Community (ECSC) 4, 40

historical institutionalism: and Council Secretariat 115-17
Hofmann, H.C.H. 24-38
Hooghe, L. 6-7, 68, 80, 81, 85

Independent Regulators Group (IRG): telecommunications 181, 186
independent regulatory agencies (IRAs) 169, 171, 175, 176, 180, 182, 186, 188, 189, 190
indirect implementation: multi-level executive governance 12-13
informal networks of independent regulatory agencies (NIRAs): network industries 179-81, 182, 190, 191; and regulatory space 175
institutional isomorphism: European Commission 53-5
institutional path dependency: Council Secretariat 116, 117-18, 124-8; European Commission 52-3
integrated administration 11, 18, 27-30, 31-2, 33; and shared sovereignty 32-3
Integrated Border Management (IBM) 145
inter-governmental organizations (IGOs) 2, 3-4, 10, 11, 17, 18
internal security: polity-building and agencies 141-5
International Organization of Securities Commissions (IOSCO) 178

Joana, J.: and Smith, A. 80

Kelemen, R.D. 156
Keohane, R.O.: and Nye, J.S. 4
Kingdon, J.W. 50, 55, 57
Knill, C.: Balint, T.; and Bauer, M.W. 5, 39-62
Kohler-Koch, B. 92

Lamfalussy procedures 29, 184-5, 203-4
language issue: networks 75-6
Larsson, T.: and Trondal, J. 88
Liikanen, E. 186

Madrid Forum: gas 180-1
Majone, G. 145, 146, 161
March, J.G.: and Simon, H.A. 68

Meroni ruling: and delegation of powers 154, 161, 176
Michelmann, H.J. 6, 80
Mitrany, D. 140
Moe, T. 162-3
Mulgan, R. 13
multi-level executive governance 10-13; double-hatted national agencies 11-12, 18; indirect implementation 10-11, 12; integrated administration 11, 18, 27-30, 31-2, 33; networked implementation 12
multi-principals model: EU delegation of powers 151-67
mutual recognition principle: Cassis de Dijon ruling 27

national regulatory authorities (NRAs) 172, 175
nationality effect: European Commission 65-7, 68, 69, 70-3; large member states 72; North-South division 66, 68, 72-5, 79
network industries: Committee of European Energy Regulators (CEER) 181; Committee of European Securities Regulators (CESR) 185; EU-supervised national implementations 179; European Regulators Group for electricity and gas (ERGEG) 186-7; European Regulators Group (ERG) 186; European Regulatory Networks (ERNs) 181-7; Florence Forum 180-1; Forum of European Securities Commissions (FESCO) 181; Independent Regulators Group (IRG) 181; informal networks of independent regulators (NIRAs) 179-81; Madrid Forum 180-1; regulatory space 177-90
networked implementation: multi-level executive governance 12-13, 31
networks: career 69; Commission contact persons choice model 76-9; concept definition 68; European Commission 63-86; formal task-related 69; informal task-related 69-70; language issue 75-6; leisure 69; logistic regression 77-8; member state size 72, 77, 78, 80; multinational organisations and national networks 71-3; nationality effect 65-7,

68, 69, 70-3; North-South division 66, 68, 72-5, 79; and organizational network theory 67-71; and portfolio role 78-9, 80; and social capital 67
North-South division: nationality effect 66, 68, 72-5, 79
Nugent, N. 93
Nye, J.S.: and Keohane, R.O. 4

Office for Harmonisation in the Internal Market (OHIM) 155, 160, 162
Olsen, J.P. 88
open civil service systems: European Commission 41-2, 44, 46, 47-50
open method of coordination (OMC) 29, 30, 134
Organization for Economic Cooperation and Development (OECD) 3-4
organizational network theory: European Commission 67-71

Petit, N.: and Geradin, D. 138
policy windows: European Commission 55-6
politicisation: civil service 42-3, 46
polity-building: administrative techniques 135-7; Area of Freedom Security and Justice (AFSJ) 141-5; centralisation and fragmentation 133-50; commisarial management 134, 135-6; democratic challenge 145-6; European Agencies (EA) 133, 137-40; integration by stealth 146, 148; Prüm Group 144; Schengen process 141, 144; terrorism 143-4
Pollak, J.: and Puntscher Riekmann, S. 133-50
Powell, W.W.: and DiMaggio, P.J. 53-4
Prodi, R. 160
Prüm Group 144
Puntscher Riekmann, S.: and Pollak, J. 133-50

qualified majority voting (QMV) 7, 14-15, 18-19

Rapid Border Intervention Teams (RABIT) 138
Rawlings, R.: and Harlow, C. 16

Reding, V. 187, 190
regulatory space: acronyms *178*; Committee of European Energy Regulators (CEER) 181; energy 180-1, 186-7, 189, 190; EU monitoring and supervision 172, 175; Euro regulators 182, 187; European Regulators Group for electricity and gas (ERGEG) 186-7; European Regulatory Agencies (ERAs) 175-6, 187-90; European Regulatory Networks (ERNs) 175-6, 181-90; evolutionary analysis 168-98; Federal European Regulatory Agencies (FERAs) 176-7, 187-90; Forum of European Securities Commissions (FESCO) 181; forums 175, 179-81, 182, 191; and implementation importance 168-70; Independent Regulators Group (IRG) 181, 186; independent regulatory agencies (IRAs) 169, 171, 175, 176, 180, 181, 182, 186, 187, 189, 190; informal networks of independent regulatory agencies (NIRAs) 175, 179-81, 182, 190, 191; institutional model typology *173-4*; institutional models 172-7; national regulatory authorities (NRAs) 172, 175; network industries 177-90; securities trading 177, 181, 184-5, 188-9, 190; Single European Regulator (SER) 177; telecommunications 181, 184, 185-6, 189, 190

Santer, J. 65, 134
Schengen process 141, 144
Securities and Exchange Commission (SEC) 177
securities trading: regulatory space 177, 181, 184-5, 188-9, 190
shared sovereignty: European administrative space 32-3
Simon, H.A.: and March, J.G. 68
Single European Regulator (SER) 177
Situation Centre: Council Secretariat 122-3, 124, 143-4
Slaughter, A.-M. 4
Smith, A.: and Joana, J. 80
Södermann, J. 48

Solana, J. 9, 121, 122
Spierenburg report (1979) 45, 51-2
Stevens, A.: and Stevens, H. 65, 67
Stone Sweet, A.: and Thatcher, M. 155
subsidiarity 27-8
supranationality: and sovereignty 25
Suvarierol, S. 6, 63-86
Sverdrup, U.: and Gornitzka, A. 87-112

telecommunications: European Regulators Group (ERG) 186, 190; Independent Regulators Group (IRG) 181, 186; regulatory space 181, 184, 185-6, 189, 190
territoriality 26, 27
Thatcher, M.: and Coen, D. 13, 168-98; and Stone Sweet, A. 155

Thomson, R. 7
Treaty of Westphalia (1648) 2, 17
TREVI ministerial working group 141
Trondal, J. 85; and Larsson, T. 88

United Nations (UN) 63

Van Gend en Loos v Nederlandse Administratie der Belastingen (1963) 26
Vanhoonacker, S.: and Christiansen, T. 113-32

Weber, M. 135
White Paper on European Governance (2001) 152, 154, 158, 164
Wille, A. 8
Wonka, A. 7